Expanded Awareness

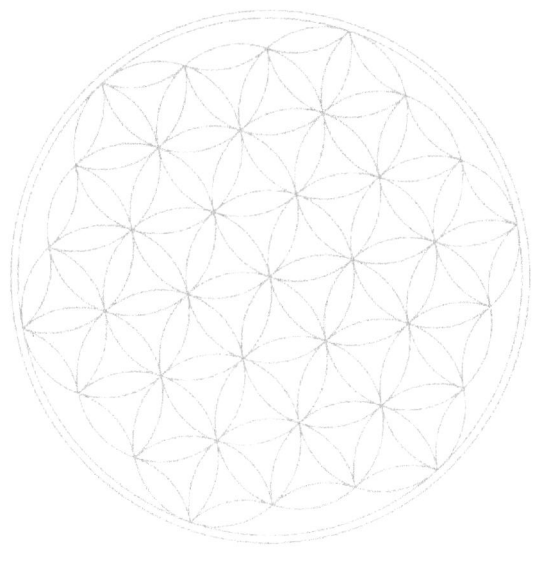

EXPANDED AWARENESS

A HEALTH PSYCHOLOGIST'S JOURNEY BEYOND THE MIND-BODY DUALITY

Sophie Guellati-Salcedo, Ph.D.

Published in the United States by SGS Quantum Press

ISBN: 978-1-968465-00-1

Printed in the United States of America

For information or permissions, visit:
www.sophieguellati.com

To Cirlethia,
my soul counterpart,
the one who held the blueprint,
before I could ever see the path.

This work is also dedicated to the unseen guides and intuitive forces that whispered through dreams, synchronicities, and channelers, reminding me that I had a message to share.

Your presence guided every step of this journey, especially when I reached my own edges in Chapter 8, where embodiment met complexity, and in Chapter 10, where consciousness met form.

You reminded me to keep following my inner compass.

PREFACE

I did not wake up one day with a blazing certainty that I had to write a book. There was no thunderbolt from the heavens, no contract from a publisher landing in my inbox. What I did have was a growing pile of conversations, notes, client stories, scribbled diagrams, and a persistent husband who kept saying, "You really should write a book."

I brushed it off, many times.
"It's all been said before."
"I'm not a writer, I'm a talker."
"Besides, who has the time?"

But the truth is, this book has been chasing me for years. It started as whispers, usually right after a particularly deep conversation about health or healing or the inexplicable weirdness of being human. Then came the synchronicities. Then came the clients who would say, "You need to share this with more people." And eventually, the resistance gave way. Not because I suddenly felt ready, but because I realized: this is not about me. It is about the message. It is about giving form to something that has lived in the margins of science and spirit for too long.

So here it is. My first book. Equal parts science, soul, and stubbornness.

Let me be honest with you. Some parts of this book may feel dense. There are sections with terms like *psychoneuroimmunology* and *quantum coherence* that might make you wish for a glass of wine (or three). I get it. I wrote it and *I* still needed snacks.

But stay with me.

Those sections are not there to impress; they're there to liberate. To give you the vocabulary and context that have been missing from most conversations about healing. If we want to reclaim our health and agency, we need to understand what we're made of, not just metaphorically, but energetically, biologically, and consciously.

I made every effort to explain complex ideas using language that feels both grounded and expansive, accessible to the mind and resonant with the heart. Along the way, you will find a glossary of terms and callout boxes that offer simplified frameworks for understanding. And where it felt aligned, I brought in personal stories and spiritual side quests—because healing is never just clinical; it is a multidimensional invitation.

If you're wondering what kind of psychologist ends up talking about scalar fields, morphic resonance, and the geometry of the soul... the short answer is: *the kind who does not like to conform, but was trained in institutions that do.*

My path into this work did not begin with New Age philosophy. It began with science. I earned a clinical post-master diploma at René Descartes University in Paris, followed by a research post-master at Nanterre Paris X University, and completed my doctorate at the University of Miami. My clinical internship took place at the Danielsen Institute at Boston University, a rare space where evidence-based therapy meets theology and where the psyche is explored through both psychological and spiritual lenses. This blend—rigor and reflection, science and soul—has shaped the way I see the world and approach healing.

I did not come to alternative healing because I was bored with science. I came because science, as it is often practiced, left too many important questions unanswered.

The first true crack in the foundation came through Dr. Brian Weiss—a conventionally trained, academically grounded psychiatrist and hypnotherapist. A graduate of Columbia and Yale, he became Chair of Psychiatry at Mount Sinai Medical Center in Miami and taught at the University of Miami. He was not seeking spiritual phenomena; he was seeking clinical solutions. But during a hypnosis session with a patient, he stumbled—quite unwillingly—into memories of past lives. What he did next was courageous: he followed the data. And when he published *Many Lives, Many Masters*, he risked everything: his reputation, his position, his professional credibility.

That mattered to me. Because it meant his message was not driven by belief; it was driven by evidence that defied existing models. He became, in a sense, the bridge between my clinical training and the intuitive, quantum-informed path I would later walk.

From there, I found Raymond Moody and the emerging literature on near-death experiences. Then Caroline Myss, whose language of energy anatomy and archetypes helped me reconcile the emotional, the symbolic, and the physical dimensions of illness and healing. What began as a curious divergence became a full integration: science and spirituality, biology and belief, body and soul.

You do not need to believe in energy healing or higher consciousness to read this book. In fact, skepticism is welcome here. I am not asking you to take anything on faith. I am inviting you to *think differently*. To question what you have been taught. To follow the breadcrumbs of logic, research, and experience, and see where they lead.

This book is for the ones who have tried everything and still feel like something is missing. It is for the practitioners who suspect there is more to healing than protocols and prescriptions. It is for those who feel, deep down, that healing must include the soul, but have not known how to say it out loud.

If that is you, then welcome. You have just entered a terrain that science is only beginning to map, and that consciousness has known all along.

Let us begin.

ACKNOWLEDGEMENTS

No book is ever truly written alone, especially one like this. It came together through late-night musings, deep conversations, invisible nudges, and the kind of support that shows up when you are tired, tangled, and unsure.

First, to my **husband**, who kept believing I had something to say, long before I believed it myself. Thank you for your relentless encouragement, for holding space when dinner was not on the table (again), and for grounding me with science and love in equal measure. This book might not exist without your gentle but persistent "You should really write this down."

To my **daughter**, whose Generation Z wisdom continually challenged me to stretch beyond old frameworks and embrace new ways of thinking, and doing. You reminded me that sacred truths and modern tools can coexist, and that heart and innovation are not opposites. Thank you for being my mirror, my muse, and my tech support.

To my **early reviewers**—Shelly, Robin, Louis, Eduardo, Anna, and Alicie—thank you for your insights, warmth, and thoughtful attention. Whether you offered detailed feedback or simply shared your enthusiasm, your engagement supported the evolution of this work in meaningful ways.

To my **AI assistant** (yes, you!), who accompanied me like a tireless editorial sidekick, formatting wizard, and literary bloodhound. From chasing DOI links at odd hours to catching grammar slips and smoothing out redundancies, you helped me bridge the gap between science and soul without losing my voice—or my mind.

And finally, to **all my unseen allies**—in spirit, in synchronicity, in intuition—who whispered ideas, opened paths, and reminded me that what we are creating here is more than words on a page. It is a transmission. It carries frequency. And it was never meant to be done alone.

Thank you. All of you. Truly.

TABLE OF CONTENTS

Healing may not be so much about getting better, as about letting go of everything that isn't you—all of the expectations, all of the beliefs—and becoming who you are.
— Rachel Naomi Remen, M.D.

Introduction

Why This Book Matters Now

We are living through a health crisis that goes far beyond pathogens or genetics.

Despite unprecedented access to medical technology, chronic illness is on the rise. Conditions like autoimmune disease, depression, anxiety, hormonal imbalance, chronic pain, and fatigue are now so widespread they are almost normalized, even though they drastically reduce quality of life.

Modern medicine, while brilliant in acute care and emergency response, still operates in a symptom-oriented, reductionist model. It excels at treating the parts but often fails to see the whole. Patients are offered pharmaceutical solutions that suppress symptoms rather than addressing root causes, and in many cases, these drugs produce side effects that require further treatment.

One of the most striking examples is the widespread use of antidepressants. Despite their popularity, studies increasingly question their efficacy, particularly for mild to moderate depression. In *A Mind of Your Own*, psychiatrist Dr. Kelly Brogan explores how these medications may mask deeper imbalances rather than resolve them — and how true healing often lies in addressing lifestyle, trauma, environment, and belief systems.

In response, functional medicine has emerged to identify root causes through personalized, systems-based approaches. But even this promising model faces barriers: limited accessibility, high costs, insufficient insurance coverage, and a shortage of well-trained practitioners. Many of the most advanced diagnostics — from microbiome mapping to comprehensive toxin screening — are still considered "alternative" and remain financially out of reach for the average person. Even more crucially, conventional models ignore or undervalue the invisible forces that influence healing: belief, intention, emotional energy, coherence, consciousness.

This omission has consequences.

In the United States alone, medical error is estimated to be the third leading cause of death, behind heart disease and cancer (James, 2013). Adverse drug reactions are responsible for over 100,000 deaths per year (Lazarou et al., 1998). And yet the dominant conversation remains focused on pharmaceuticals and pathology, while dismissing the body's innate intelligence.

That is why this book matters now.

This Is a Book of Exploration

You will not find a one-size-fits-all protocol in these pages. This book is not here to hand you definitive answers. Rather, it offers a framework for asking better questions—for thinking independently, examining assumptions, and uncovering your own truths through empowered self-discovery.

The goal is to help you recognize that knowledge is not the same as belief, and that much of what we have inherited — from medical dogma to societal programming — may need to be questioned, if not unlearned.

> *Some truths live on the surface. Others wait deeper down. But the most powerful discoveries often begin with what we do not even realize we do not know.*
>
> — Insight from the Landmark Forum

We will explore the vastness of what we do not know we do not know. And we will do it slowly, gently, and respectfully. You are encouraged to look under each "rock" at your own pace, to feel what resonates, and to pause when needed.

Healing is not linear. Neither is learning. Both are intimate, layered, and deeply personal.

From Frustration to Inquiry: My Story

For me, this exploration is not academic — it is personal.

I have always been intrigued by psychosomatic disorders and so-called idiopathic diagnoses — conditions where the cause is unknown or assumed to be psychological. As a psychologist, I questioned why a physician's inability to find a root cause would so often lead to blaming the patient: "It's all in your head," or worse, "You're doing this for attention."

That narrative never sat right with me — especially when I became the patient.

I experienced my own struggle with autoimmune symptoms that were as ignored as they were misunderstood. I endured the same vague dismissals, halfhearted referrals, and absence of answers that so many others face. But I refused to accept that nothing could be done — or that my symptoms were psychosomatic noise.

When the system failed me, I became my own doctor.

I immersed myself in research and education. I attended conferences, medical symposia, and workshops focused on functional medicine, nutritional psychiatry, epigenetics, and energy-based therapies. Influential figures like Dr. Mark Hyman, Dr. Jeffrey Bland, Dr. Joe Dispenza, Dr. Kelly Brogan, Dr. Tom O'Bryan, and Dr. Bruce Lipton gave me new frameworks — ones that honored both the science and the soul of healing.

I learned how environmental toxins, food sensitivities, water additives, pesticides and biocides, home cleaning products, and even personal care products can silently disrupt our biology. I worked with elimination diets, gut restoration, and targeted supplementation, and I slowly began to improve.

But the deeper turning point came when I explored the energetic dimension of healing.

I studied the nervous system's role in illness and recovery. I practiced vagal toning, mindfulness, and somatic release. I experienced firsthand the effects of light therapy, biofield tuning, binaural beats, heart-brain coherence, and intentional breathing.

I also trained in Genius Biofeedback, a non-invasive technology that uses energetic resonance to assess and balance the body's frequency patterns. It offered a new lens into subtle imbalances — a way to work with the body's information field directly, not just symbolically.

I explored QHHT® (Quantum Healing Hypnosis Technique®) and BQH (Beyond Quantum Healing) — methods that go far beyond traditional clinical hypnosis and tap into soul-level insight and multidimensional awareness. These expanded states revealed deeper root causes and healing potentials that no conventional modality could access.

What I found was transformative:

My body responded to information.
To vibration. To conscious intention.

This was not a placebo effect. This was a re-alignment with the body's deeper intelligence. This was biology meeting energy, science meeting spirit, and symptoms becoming signals.

Over time, I noticed clear shifts: more energy, fewer body aches, faster post-exercise recovery, improved digestion, healthier skin, hair, and nails—even though no single factor alone could account for the changes.

A New Paradigm in Practice

As I healed, my practice changed.

I could no longer treat the psyche without addressing the body. I could no longer focus on thought patterns without recognizing the energetic and physiological ecosystems beneath them. I began integrating psychoenergetics, biofield awareness, nutrition, and consciousness-based tools into my sessions.

And I saw my clients shift — faster, deeper, more sustainably.

These modalities affirmed what I had long suspected: That the human system is not only biochemical or psychological — it is informational, vibrational, and conscious.

And as I worked with clients and continued my own inner work, something even more profound became clear:

Time is not linear. Healing does not follow a straight line. And we are not only what we appear to be.

We are multidimensional beings — shaped not only by biology and history, but by energetic imprints, subtle perception, and non-linear realities.

This journey gave me a new reverence for the dream state — no longer a realm of random fragments, but a dimension of intelligence and insight. I began to understand the deeper truth—paraphrasing Eastern mystics— that we are often asleep when we are awake, and awake when we are asleep.

In dreams, we escape the limits of our third-dimensional (3D) vessel. We move through layers of self and space, unbound by time, reuniting with wisdom that our waking mind may not yet comprehend.

These revelations did not diminish my scientific mindset — they expanded it. They reminded me that true inquiry does not end at the edge of what is measurable. It asks us to lean into mystery, to listen more deeply, and to integrate what is felt but not yet proven.

That is the kind of science this book invites: One that honors both data and direct experience. One that includes the full spectrum of what it means to heal — as a body, a mind, and an energy being.

The Concept of the Healing Terrain

This book begins with the concept of **healing terrain** — a living, breathing internal ecosystem composed of your gut lining, cellular signaling, immune responses, nervous system, and energetic field. When this terrain is supported, the body can repair, regenerate, and rebalance. When the terrain is neglected, disrupted, or overloaded, symptoms appear.

In this view, illness is not simply an enemy to eliminate — it is **a messenger of imbalance**.

This concept pulls from functional medicine, biofield science, and holistic traditions, but goes further. It includes not just biochemistry, but also **frequency, information, intention, and the field of consciousness**. It asks not only *what is malfunctioning,* but also *what is the terrain trying to tell us?*

Embracing Systems Thinking in Medicine

One of the greatest flaws of modern healthcare is its tendency to **compartmentalize**. A cardiologist treats the heart, a gastroenterologist the gut, a psychiatrist the mind — but the body does not work in isolation. It works as a **system of systems**, constantly exchanging information.

This book calls for **systems thinking** — an approach that acknowledges the interconnectedness of the gut-brain axis, the microbiome, the immune system, emotional states, environmental toxins, and energetic fields.

To illustrate this more intuitively, we'll use the **computer system metaphor**:

- **The Conscious Mind** is like **RAM** – it processes short-term tasks.
- **The Subconscious** is like a **hard drive** – storing long-term programming.
- **The Higher Self** holds the **master key** – the deep code, the soul's operating system.
- And **Energy**? Energy is the **electricity** that powers the whole system — without which none of it functions.

We cannot fix a frozen computer by just clicking harder. We must understand the system behind the screen. The same is true of healing.

The Elimination Diet as a Metaphor for Healing

One of the most useful tools I discovered early in my journey was the **elimination diet** — not just for food, but for life.

Originally designed to identify food sensitivities, the elimination diet removes potential irritants and reintroduces them slowly. But its genius lies in its simplicity: it teaches you to **listen**. To your body. Your energy. Your emotions.

This principle can be applied to more than just food.

We can eliminate:

- **Toxic thoughts,**
- **Destructive habits,**
- **Draining environments,**
- **Outdated belief systems.**

Healing often begins not by adding more, but by removing what no longer serves.

Scientific Foundations and Emerging Modalities

This book will also present **emerging scientific evidence** supporting energy-based and consciousness-based healing modalities. These include:

- The gut-brain-immune axis, and the role of the microbiome in autoimmune disease;

- The impact of structured water on cellular hydration and information transfer;

- The use of photobiomodulation (light therapy) to support mitochondrial function;

- The growing field of psychoenergetics and the role of intention in physiology.

These are not speculative theories. They are **early signals** from a new medical paradigm — one that integrates form and frequency, structure and information, biology and consciousness.

Resilience, Adaptation, and the Innate Intelligence of the Body

Above all, this book is about **trust** — in the body's capacity to adapt, regenerate, and find its way back to balance when given the right inputs.

Healing is not about perfection. It's about restoring **coherence**. The body is always seeking homeostasis — always moving toward harmony. The question is not *how do we fix it,* but *how do we support it?*

- Through better questions.
- Through respectful observation.
- Through multidimensional awareness.

You are not broken.

You are not just a set of symptoms.

You are a living system — and you are already healing.

Let us begin.

The Cultural and Scientific Shift Underway

My story is not unique.

All over the world, practitioners, researchers, and everyday people are coming to the same conclusion: **we need a new model of healing** — one that includes energy, consciousness, and the intelligence of the body itself.

The last decade has seen a **groundswell of interest** in integrative and holistic medicine. Functional medicine is gaining traction. Somatic therapy, polyvagal theory, trauma-informed care, light therapy, sound therapy, and frequency-based technologies are entering the mainstream. Mindfulness is now taught in hospitals, schools, and corporations. Meditation apps and heart-rate variability monitors are household tools.

What we are witnessing is more than a wellness trend. It's the **early formation of a scientific and cultural paradigm shift** — away from fragmented, pharmaceutical-centered care, and toward **coherence**, **self-awareness**, and **energetic alignment**.

Even within mainstream science, the edges are beginning to blur.

- In **quantum biology**, researchers explore how subatomic behavior influences enzymatic reactions and consciousness.

- In **biofield science**, the body's subtle electromagnetic field is being studied for its diagnostic and therapeutic potential.
- In **psychoneuroimmunology**, emotions and beliefs are shown to influence immune function and inflammation.
- In **epigenetics**, we see that gene expression is modulated by environment, perception, and behavior — in real time.

These are not mystical concepts. They are **frontier sciences** — and they are validating what mystics, healers, and indigenous traditions have long understood.

But to move this revolution forward, we must also evolve the **tools of inquiry**. It is no longer enough to rely on surface-level correlations or linear cause-and-effect models. Healing is a **complex, dynamic, and multidimensional process**, often involving **dozens of interacting variables** — biological, emotional, environmental, and energetic.

Old research models—designed to isolate single variables—fall short when applied to living systems. To truly understand what works, and why, we need research models that reflect that complexity.

That means using **advanced modeling techniques** capable of accounting for **moderating and mediating variables**, non-linear feedback loops, and systems-level interactions. Illness is not isolated — especially not in the chronic or autoimmune domains. We now know, for instance, that the **gut-brain axis**, **microbiome diversity**, **toxic load**, and **psychological**

trauma are all interwoven in the expression of disease. No single variable explains the whole.

And this is where **artificial intelligence** may offer unprecedented support. With its ability to rapidly analyze large volumes of data and identify patterns that are invisible to the human mind, AI can help us model the **real complexity of human health** — not by reducing it, but by revealing it.

The human being is more than the sum of its parts.
And chronic illness cannot be treated in parts.

This book stands at that intersection — between data and direct experience, biology and energy, skepticism and awakening.

It is written for those who know there is more.

For those who want to understand how.

And for those ready to move **beyond the mind-body duality** — into the **expanded awareness** that true healing requires.

References

Bland, J. (2013). The disease delusion: Conquering the causes of chronic illness for a healthier, longer, and happier life. Harper Wave.

Brogan, K. (2016). A mind of your own: The truth about depression and how women can heal their bodies to reclaim their lives. Harper Wave. https://www.kellybroganmd.com/books/a-mind-of-your-own

Dispenza, J. (2017). Becoming supernatural: How common people are doing the uncommon. Hay House. https://drjoedispenza.com/shop/categories?shopSection=Books

Hyman, M. (2012). The blood sugar solution: The ultrahealthy program for losing weight, preventing disease, and feeling great now!. Little, Brown, Spark. https://drhyman.com/collections/books-multimedia?_pos=1&_psq=books&_ss=e&_v=1.0

Institute of Medicine. (2001). *Crossing the quality chasm: A new health system for the 21st century.* National Academies Press. https://nap.nationalacademies.org/catalog/10027/crossing-the-quality-chasm-a-new-health-system-for-the

James, J. T. (2013). A new, evidence-based estimate of patient harms associated with hospital care. Journal of Patient Safety, 9(3), 122–128. https://doi.org/10.1097/PTS.0b013e3182948a69

Lazarou, J., Pomeranz, B. H., & Corey, P. N. (1998). Incidence of adverse drug reactions in hospitalized patients: A meta-analysis of prospective studies. JAMA, 279(15), 1200–1205. https://doi.org/10.1001/jama.279.15.1200

Lipton, B. H. (2005). The biology of belief: Unleashing the power of consciousness, matter & miracles. Hay House. https://www.brucelipton.com/books/biology-of-belief/

McEwen, B. S., & Stellar, E. (1993). Stress and the individual: Mechanisms leading to disease. Archives of Internal Medicine, 153(18), 2093–2101. https://pubmed.ncbi.nlm.nih.gov/8379800/

National Institute of Mental Health. (n.d.). Mental health information. U.S. Department of Health and Human Services. https://www.nimh.nih.gov/health

Schoenfeld, D. A., & Schoenfeld, B. D. (2015). The mind-body solution: Train your brain to manage your weight, your mood, and your long-term health. Penguin Books. https://www.penguinrandomhouse.com/books/247044/the-mindbody-solution-by-david-schoenfeld-and-brett-d-schoenfeld/

PART I

From Breakdown to Breakthrough

Foundations for a New Healing Paradigm

Modern medicine has changed the world—but when it comes to the rise of chronic illness, autoimmunity, and emotional disintegration, it is clear we need a new paradigm. Too often, the current system fragments the body, dismisses emotion, suppresses symptoms, and disempowers the patient. It is not designed for healing—it is designed for control.

Part I opens the conversation on where conventional thinking falls short—and why terrain-based healing must include more than biology. These chapters begin by exposing the blind spots of reductionism and symptom suppression, and gradually introduce a more complete model: one that treats the body as an intelligent ecosystem, recognizes coherence as a healing principle, and restores power to the individual.

Terrain repair is not just a physical process—it is psychoenergetic. Healing is not compliance—it is agency. And true transformation does not happen through prescriptions alone, but through reclamation of wholeness, inner listening, and self-responsibility.

This is where the journey begins—away from fragmentation, toward coherence. Away from blind trust in external authorities, toward a reclamation of inner knowing. When we stop pathologizing symptoms and start listening to them, healing transforms from a battle into a dialogue.

The chapters ahead are not just about medicine. They are about meaning. They ask us to see chronic illness not only as a biological disruption—but as an invitation. An invitation to slow down, look deeper, and participate in our own healing with new eyes.

Healing is not the absence of symptoms. It is the return of harmony, clarity, and empowerment. And that begins by recognizing the cracks in the old story—so we can step into a much larger one.

The part can never be well unless the whole is well.

— Plato

Chapter 1

The Cracks in Conventional Medicine
Why a Root-Cause Approach Matters

In 1999, while living in France, I was diagnosed with a thyroid nodule. Fortunately, I was under the care of a functional medicine doctor—someone who did not just look at one lab result or rush to medicate. Through holistic interventions and terrain-focused support, the nodule was determined benign and gradually shrank. No surgery. No long-term medication. Just a systems-based approach that respected the body's intelligence and ability to heal.

Then I moved to the United States.

It was not just a change of address—it was a shift in medical paradigm and environmental exposure. In France, I had been shielded from many of the toxins common in the American lifestyle. In the U.S., I was suddenly drinking fluoridated water, surrounded by processed foods, and exposed to environmental pollutants that my body had never had to process before. In 2005, I gave birth to my child. What followed was not the typical fatigue of new motherhood—it was unrelenting exhaustion that lingered for years. I could not resume a basic exercise routine. My energy was nonexistent and I was gaining weight. My body was waving a red flag.

I went to the doctor and demanded a thyroid check. The response? "Your TSH is normal. You're just tired because you have a kid."

Except my child was in daycare. And this was not tired. This was broken.

Still, I persisted. I got my labs run and discovered my thyroglobulin antibodies were through the roof—a textbook sign of Hashimoto's Thyroiditis, an autoimmune disease in which the body attacks the thyroid gland. But two separate endocrinologists dismissed the result. They blamed it on the nodule, which by then had grown and calcified—still benign, still "nothing to worry about," according to them.

Once the biopsy was negative, they had nothing left to say. No treatment. No curiosity. No answers. I was still feeling like hell, and all they had was a normal TSH result to wave in my face.

So I turned to the only person left who would take me seriously: myself. I dove into research and quickly uncovered the link between halide exposure—fluoride, chloride, bromide—and thyroid dysfunction. I took immediate steps to detox my home: filtered the water, eliminated halides, and cleaned up my environment. My symptoms began to improve.

Then I discovered something called peptide immunotherapy, specifically involving colostrum and proline-rich polypeptides, as described in *Peptide Immunotherapy* by Andrew Keech, Ph.D. This approach helps modulate the immune response—rather than suppress it. Within three months of beginning this therapy, my TgAb dropped to 4. For reference, that's normal. That's remission.

And I wasn't done.

I ran a full immunoglobulin panel—IgA, IgG, IgM—and discovered severe sensitivities to both dairy and gluten. Genetic testing confirmed my predisposition. I eliminated these foods entirely and supported my recovery with targeted nutrient therapy based on my specific deficiencies.

That was in 2011.

I've never taken thyroid medication. I have remained in remission ever since.

This was not spontaneous healing. It was not a miracle. It was a root-cause resolution driven by systems thinking, environmental awareness, and respect for the body's innate intelligence.

This mindset is not just philosophical—it is supported by a growing body of systems-based research and critique of over-reliance on symptom suppression and reductionist protocols (Ioannidis, 2005; Sackett et al., 1996; IFM, 2023).

While I am not a medical doctor, my health psychology training gave me a different map—one that considers psychological issues, environmental triggers, and psychoenergetic patterns as part of the terrain of chronic illness. I learned that healing requires more than clinical intervention. It requires us to ask deeper questions about what the body is trying to communicate.

From Self-Healing to Guiding Others: Kate's Recovery from Hashimoto's

As a health psychologist, my role was to help my client, Kate (name changed to protect confidentiality) identify and process the emotional, relational, and psychological burdens that were woven into her physical condition. Trauma leaves biological imprints. Chronic illness often reflects prolonged internal conflict. My work with Kate was never about replacing medical care—but rather, bringing in what medicine had left out. In doing so, I expanded the circle of options available to her—widening the conversation about what healing could include.

That insight became crucial when I began working with Kate, a former service member and professional navigating a serious, long-standing health crisis.

Kate came to me while under disability status— physically depleted, emotionally overwhelmed, and carrying the weight of years of unresolved illness. Her diagnoses included Hashimoto's Thyroiditis, Celiac Disease, Chronic Thoracic Back Pain, Malabsorption Syndrome, and Major Depressive Disorder with Suicidal Ideation. Her history was both medically and emotionally complex: a traumatic childbirth experience, three pregnancies with escalating autoimmune symptoms, and chronic nutritional depletion. She had undergone psychotherapy during her years of service to manage depression and chronic pain—but no one had ever looked at the whole system.

By the time we connected in 2014, Kate had already been through several rounds of therapy across different institutions. Her story highlights a core issue in modern healthcare: fragmentation of care. Despite having multiple providers involved at various stages—primary care physicians, mental health specialists, pain management teams—no one had a full picture of her. This is the shadow side of hyper-specialization: each expert sees only their piece, and the person behind the chart disappears. What she needed was integration, not more opinions in silos, across different institutions. She was highly self-aware, incredibly resilient, and profoundly motivated to change her circumstances—but she had not yet found a healing model that addressed the root causes of her decline.

What stood out most was not just her suffering—it was her readiness to lead her own transformation. With deep intelligence, discipline, and hard-won insight, Kate assembled a multi-disciplinary healing team, including:

- A functional medicine provider to identify and address physiological root causes

- A biological dentist to treat systemic inflammation reflected in her oral health

- A therapist (my role) to support trauma recovery, grief processing, and emotional reintegration

- And herself—as the committed driver of her own recovery

She took full responsibility for her nutrition and lifestyle upgrades, integrating knowledge from her readings and consultations to rebuild her system from the ground up. Her progress was steady, layered, and transformational.

From Disabled to Empowered

Today, Kate has reclaimed her life and her voice. She is now a Licensed Clinical Social Worker, specializing in Behavioral Health. Her experience fuels her mission: helping others navigate chronic illness, trauma, and emotional dysregulation with clarity, compassion, and evidence-based care.

Her story is not just about remission.

It is about reclamation.

It is about what becomes possible when healing is rooted in systems thinking, multi-disciplinary support, and the refusal to give up.

This way of thinking isn't just professional for me—it is a direct response to the disempowerment I observed in conventional care. As a health psychologist, I saw how often patients were stripped of their agency, their intuition ignored in favor of protocols. My entire approach has been shaped by the need to restore self-agency and remind individuals that they are not passive recipients of care, but active participants in their healing. It's deeply personal. Asking "Why?" and "How?" has always been the lens through which I understand the world. Functional medicine simply gave me the structure and language to apply that lens to healing.

Kate's story is not unique. If you have ever had your symptoms dismissed or your healing instincts doubted, know that your experience is real—and you are not alone. And if you are a practitioner who has ever wondered how to support clients who were told "nothing is wrong." This book offers a new lens. One that honors both the science and the story.

The Biopsychosocial Model in Practice

This evolving model continues to find new relevance in clinical and philosophical discourse, particularly as it is applied to chronic illness, trauma, and integrative care (Scheidt & Waller, 2012).

First introduced by George Engel in 1977, the biopsychosocial model was a revolutionary response to the limitations of the biomedical model. Engel argued that health and illness are best understood through a dynamic interplay of biological, psychological, and social factors—not just isolated physical mechanisms. This model was a call to integrate human experience into medical reasoning, and it laid the foundation for health psychology, behavioral medicine, and integrative care.

Pioneers like James Matarazzo expanded on this foundation, emphasizing the scientific rigor and clinical value of applying psychological frameworks to medical problems. Over the decades, the biopsychosocial model has been supported by decades of research into stress physiology, psychoneuroimmunology, and trauma-informed care.

Yet despite its adoption in theory, it is often under-applied in practice. Most healthcare systems still favor a reductionist approach that marginalizes psychological contributions to chronic illness. This creates a gap between what we *know* matters and what actually informs patient care.

Before we continue building the case for an integrative view of healthcare, it's important to pause and acknowledge what has been historically overlooked. The conventional model of care tends to focus heavily on physical symptoms and biochemical markers, often sidelining the emotional, relational, and psychological factors that contribute to chronic illness.

As a health psychologist, I have witnessed how unresolved trauma, long-standing stress, unexpressed grief, and inner conflict can embed themselves into the body—showing up as fatigue, autoimmune dysfunction, digestive disorders, and mood imbalances. These are not just mental overlays; they are part of the terrain itself.

This insight is not abstract—it is deeply clinical. Many of my clients experience plateaus in physical healing until we begin to explore the emotional undercurrents beneath their symptoms. It is not about assigning blame or saying illness is "all in your head." It is about seeing the psyche as a key organ in the healing ecosystem.

Integrating Psychology with Root-Cause Medicine

In this model, the practitioner does not hold the answers—they help the client access their own. True empowerment happens when individuals reconnect with their inner knowing and cultivate the confidence to navigate healing beyond prescribed protocols.

The intersection of psychology and root-cause medicine is gaining traction in the scientific literature. Research continues to affirm what many holistic practitioners have long intuited: mental and emotional health cannot be separated from physical healing.

A 2011 paper published in the Journal of Clinical Psychology in Medical Settings emphasized the role of health psychologists in integrating behavioral and medical care, especially in addressing chronic illness and psychosomatic interactions (Belar, 2011). An article in the Behavioral Medicine Report similarly recognizes the rise of integrative approaches that bring nutrition, psychological insight, and environmental awareness into mental health interventions.

Organizations like the Institute for Functional Medicine (IFM) are now actively educating healthcare providers on how nutrition, inflammation, and gut health intersect with conditions like depression, anxiety, and cognitive decline (IFM Mental Health, IFM Nutrition and Mental Health). Practitioners in "functional psychiatry," such as those trained through the Kresser Institute, are also showing how mood disorders often reflect deeper biological dysfunctions.

This body of work validates the integrative model I've been working within for years—a model that not only integrates psychological, biological, and lifestyle factors but also empowers the client to move beyond dependency on experts. It positions the individual as an active participant in his/her own healing process, rather than a passive recipient of care; a model that values psychological insight, trauma integration, biochemical individuality, and lifestyle medicine as complementary forces in the healing process.

Beyond the Physical:
Emotion, Energy, and Soul

Root-cause medicine offers a profound step forward from symptom suppression—but even it sometimes stops short. It excels at connecting the dots between gut health, inflammation, toxicity, and chronic disease, yet many practitioners remain anchored in biochemistry. My work, and that of many pioneers before me, has revealed that true healing sometimes requires reaching into less visible dimensions: the emotional body, the energetic field, and the deeper patterns of consciousness.

In cases of chronic, treatment-resistant illness, it is not uncommon for symptoms to reflect unresolved trauma, ancestral entanglements, or even material from past-life memory. Authors like Caroline Myss (*Anatomy of the Spirit*), and entire communities of practitioners trained in regression-based techniques, have documented how illness can mirror deeper soul lessons, archetypal imbalances, or disruptions in energetic anatomy. These insights have not only touched millions of readers—they have seeded a new generation of practitioners who now work with consciousness exploration in clinical and therapeutic settings.

Emerging research from the *Journal of Regression Therapy* and organizations like EARTh (Earth Association for Regression Therapy) shows how past life regression can improve quality of life, resolve chronic symptoms, and deepen self-awareness. These results are not merely anecdotal—they represent a growing field of evidence-based integrative approaches, even as they challenge mainstream medical orthodoxy (Devereux, 2012; Sharma & Maheshwari, 2012).

For some clients, especially those attuned to soul-level meaning, the body's breakdown is a message from the soul: an invitation to evolve. This does not mean abandoning science. It means expanding it—acknowledging that our biology is shaped not only by food, toxins, and genes, but also by belief systems, suppressed emotions, energetic imprints, and what some experience as existential or soul-rooted pain.

Healing, then, becomes not just a clinical process—but a spiritual and transformational one.

In this light, coherence becomes the guiding principle of lasting change. Coherence is the state in which biological, psychological, and energetic systems synchronize—creating the conditions for flow, regulation, and repair. Whether through emotional integration, nervous system regulation, or quantum alignment, healing depends on the restoration of internal harmony.

From this perspective, terrain expands beyond the biological; it becomes a dynamic, multidimensional field that includes consciousness, soul, and deep forms of memory that are stored beyond the mind—in the body, in the field, or across timelines.

I call this the **psychoenergetic terrain**—the inner landscape shaped not only by physiology and neurobiology, but also by beliefs, emotional residue, trauma, and subtle energy patterns. Just as the gut microbiome reflects environmental inputs, the psychoenergetic terrain reflects the internal environment of thought, feeling, and spiritual evolution, in whatever form it reveals itself. For healing to be sustainable, both terrains—biological and psychoenergetic—must be brought into coherence.

Root-Cause Medicine vs. Conventional Medicine: A Comparison

I reference the principles of functional medicine here not as a practitioner of that model, but because its systems-thinking approach complements the psychological and consciousness-based framework that I work within. Both ask deeper questions. Both refuse to stop at symptom control.

Narrative Overview

To appreciate the paradigm shift that functional medicine represents, it helps to look closely at the contrast. Conventional, allopathic medicine is brilliant at addressing acute, life-threatening situations. It has revolutionized trauma care, emergency surgery, and infectious disease management. But when it comes to chronic, complex, systemic illness—it often falls short.

Conventional medicine tends to view the body as a series of separate systems, where each organ has a specialist and symptoms are treated in isolation. The typical approach is to identify a disease, match it with a pharmaceutical or procedure, and manage the symptoms.

Root-cause medicine, on the other hand, sees the body as an interconnected web of systems. It restores self-agency by inviting the client to take ownership of their healing process, rather than relying solely on external interventions. It recognizes that chronic illness doesn't arise from a single broken part but from patterns of dysfunction influenced by lifestyle, environment, trauma, diet, and even belief systems. It does not dismiss pharmaceuticals, but seeks to understand what created the need for them in the first place.

Comparison Table

Conventional (Allopathic) Medicine	Root-Cause (Functional) Medicine
Disease-centered	Patient-centered
Focuses on diagnosis and symptom suppression	Focuses on underlying mechanisms and root causes
Organs and systems treated in isolation	Views the body as an integrated, dynamic system
Standardized treatment protocols	Individualized care plans
First-line treatment: pharmaceuticals or surgery	First-line treatment: lifestyle, nutrition, detox
Reactive: treats disease after it occurs	Proactive: aims for prevention and optimization
Acute-care excellence	Chronic illness expertise
External authority (doctor-driven)	Shared authority (patient-practitioner partnership)
Minimal consideration of emotional/energetic root causes	Considers mental, emotional, and spiritual contributors
Authority rests with the expert	Empowers the client as a co-creator of healing
Healing = absence of disease	Healing = return to coherence across systems
Focus on physical and biochemical markers	Includes belief systems, energy, and consciousness

Of course, this kind of individualized model presents real-world challenges: most healthcare systems are not built to support it, and many patients simply do not have the time or resources to search for root causes. But even small shifts in awareness—by practitioners or patient—can restore agency and open new healing paths.

This contrast is not about choosing sides—it is about recognizing the gaps in a system that was never designed for today's chronic disease epidemic. Functional medicine does not oppose conventional medicine; it completes it.

And in many cases, as Kate and I both discovered, it is the only approach that actually delivers lasting results.

Why Dependency is Not Healing

True healing is a return to self-trust. When we heavily depend on external experts or systems, we risk disconnecting from our own inner wisdom. The new healing paradigm restores sovereignty—it does not substitute one form of control for another.

From Germ Theory to Terrain Thinking: A Paradigm Shift

As introduced in the concept of the healing terrain, illness is rarely the result of a single broken part. Instead, it reflects a broader disruption in the body's internal ecosystem—its terrain. Root-cause medicine builds on this view, aiming not to suppress symptoms but to restore coherence across the biological, emotional, and energetic dimensions of the self. In this model, symptoms become messengers, pointing toward systemic imbalances that require listening, not silencing.

For most of us raised in the Western medical system, the idea that "germs cause disease" is as baked into our worldview as gravity. This is the essence of germ theory, formalized in the 19th century by Louis Pasteur. According to this model, illness is caused by pathogenic microbes—bacteria, viruses, fungi—that invade the body and must be eradicated to restore health.

Germ theory changed the world. It gave us sterilization, vaccines, antibiotics — tools that revolutionized acute care and helped curb deadly infections. But it also planted the seed of a combat-oriented view of health: one in which the body is a passive battleground, and healing requires fighting off external enemies.

What most people do not realize is that there was another voice in the room: Antoine Béchamp, a lesser-known contemporary of Pasteur, offered an alternative lens. Béchamp proposed what we now call terrain theory. Instead of focusing solely on the invading microbe, terrain theory asks: *What kind of internal environment allows disease to take hold in the first place?*

Germs Are Opportunists—Not Villains

In the terrain model, microbes are not the primary cause of disease—they are opportunists. They thrive in toxic, stagnant, or inflamed environments, much like mold grows in a damp basement. The body's terrain includes its pH balance, nutrient reserves, microbiome composition, detoxification capacity, and—critically—its mental and emotional state.

In other words: we are not helpless victims of bad luck or bad germs. We are active participants in the health of our internal ecosystem.

This is not a fringe idea. Even modern immunology acknowledges that chronic stress can suppress immune function that gut dysbiosis can cause systemic inflammation, and that detox pathways can become overwhelmed by environmental toxins.

As a psychologist, I have seen firsthand how emotional repression, trauma, and chronic stress contribute to physiological imbalance. Your thoughts, feelings, and beliefs are part of your terrain. When you ignore them, they do not disappear—they go underground and begin to fester, eventually manifesting as fatigue, illness, or mental breakdown.

Terrain Thinking Is Not Anti-Science— It is Systems Thinking

Let us be clear: terrain theory does not deny the existence of germs. It reframes the conversation. Instead of asking, What pill will kill this microbe?, we ask, What conditions allowed this microbe to thrive? What needs to be cleared, nourished, repaired, or rebalanced?

This shift in thinking is especially crucial when dealing with:

- Chronic conditions like autoimmune diseases, IBS, and anxiety;

- Long-standing fatigue, brain fog, and hormonal imbalance;

- Mental health struggles with no clear "external" cause;

- Cases where conventional medicine offers suppression, not resolution.

When we zoom out and look at the bigger picture, terrain theory gives us a much richer diagnostic lens—and a more hopeful path forward.

You are not a battleground. **You are a living ecosystem.** And when you learn to tend your terrain, healing does not need to be a fight—it becomes a process of remembering how to flow.

The failures I have witnessed in conventional care—and the breakthroughs I have experienced through root-cause and integrative frameworks—are not random. They are symptoms of something deeper: a worldview that has shaped modern medicine for over a century. To truly understand why healing often fails, we must look beyond the clinic and into the culture of science itself. What assumptions are baked into the way we diagnose, treat, and define health? What gets excluded from the conversation— not because it is untrue, but because it challenges the model?

That's where we're going next.

References

Scheidt, C. E., & Waller, E. (2012). The biopsychosocial model of health and disease: New philosophical and scientific developments. *Open Journal of Philosophy, 2*(4), 38–47. https://www.scirp.org/pdf/OJPP_2012112815535692.pdf

Belar, C. D. (2011). The role of psychologists in a patient-centered medical home. *Journal of Clinical Psychology in Medical Settings, 18*(1), 1–6. https://doi.org/10.1007/s10880-011-9232-7

Devereux, D. (2012). Development in the life quality by past life regression therapy together with an integrated psychological approach. *Journal of Regression Therapy, 22*, 43–52. https://regressionjournal.org/jrt_article/development-life-quality-past-life-regression-therapy-together-integrated-psychological-approach-is-29/

Institute for Functional Medicine. (2023). *What is functional medicine?* https://www.ifm.org/functional-medicine/

Ioannidis, J. P. A. (2005). Why most published research findings are false. *PLoS Medicine, 2*(8), e124. https://doi.org/10.1371/journal.pmed.0020124

Sackett, D. L., Rosenberg, W. M. C., Gray, J. A. M., Haynes, R. B., & Richardson, W. S. (1996). Evidence based medicine: What it is and what it isn't. *BMJ, 312*(7023), 71–72. https://doi.org/10.1136/bmj.312.7023.71

Sharma, N., & Maheshwari, S. (2012). Past life regression therapy and its effectiveness in improving quality of life. *IOSR Journal of Humanities and Social Science, 2*(6), 39–45. https://www.iosrjournals.org/iosr-jhss/papers/Vol2-issue6/H0263945.pdf

We must learn how to see. Realize that everything connects to everything else.

— Leonardo da Vinci

Chapter 2

The Limits of Science-as-We-Know-It

The Philosophy behind Modern Medicine

Modern medicine did not evolve in a vacuum. It is built upon philosophical assumptions—often invisible, rarely questioned—that shape what we consider "real," "treatable," and "scientific." Chief among these assumptions are reductionism and materialism, which still shape today's research priorities, funding structures, and what counts as legitimate evidence in mainstream care.

These ideas trace their lineage to the **European Enlightenment**, when scientific rationalism replaced spiritual and mystical explanations of the world. The universe was increasingly seen as a mechanical system governed by fixed laws—a worldview profoundly influenced by Newtonian physics and Cartesian dualism. The body, within this model, was reimagined as a machine, separate from mind, spirit, or environment.

Reductionism is the belief that complex systems can be fully understood by breaking them down into their parts. In contrast, systems thinking emphasizes the relationships and interactions among those parts, offering a more holistic view that will become central to the evolving paradigm of medicine discussed later in this chapter. This reductionist lens tells us that to understand the human body, we must zoom in—dissecting organs into tissues, tissues into cells, cells into molecular interactions. The body becomes a machine: intricate, but ultimately fixable through precision tuning. This mindset led to incredible breakthroughs in surgery, diagnostics, and pharmacology, especially in acute care. But for chronic illness, trauma, and multidimensional healing? Reductionism falls flat. You cannot treat a soul wound with a scalpel.

The whole is more than the sum of the parts.
— Aristotle

Materialism, meanwhile, is the philosophical position that only physical matter is real. This perspective limits the inclusion of holistic and energy-based modalities in mainstream care, as it excludes non-physical influences like intention, emotional resonance, or subtle energy fields from serious scientific consideration. Anything that cannot be measured, touched, or quantified—energy, emotion, consciousness, spirit—is dismissed or de-prioritized. Within this framework, consciousness is reduced to neurochemical activity, and healing is what happens when a molecule binds to a receptor. There is no room for intention, subtle energy, or the intelligence of the body.

These worldviews combined to shape the biomedical model, a framework that excels in acute care but struggles to address chronic illness, mind-body dynamics, and healing phenomena explored later in this chapter. It treats illness as mechanical failure, the body as hardware, and health as the absence of observable dysfunction—overlooking more dynamic definitions of health that include balance, adaptability, coherence, and self-awareness, all of which are central to the emerging paradigm explored further below.

A vivid example of the limits of reductionism is the Human Genome Project. When launched in the 1990s, it was heralded as the key to unlocking every disease, based on the belief that identifying individual genes would fully explain human health and pathology. But after mapping the genome, researchers found that genes rarely act alone. Environmental influences, stress, toxins, emotions, and belief systems all play a major role in gene expression (Lipton, 2005; Nestle, 2015)—revealing a far more complex, dynamic, and context-sensitive system than materialist assumptions had predicted.

As the Human Genome Project fell short of its promises, it revealed the limitations of reductionist thinking. "Science commits suicide when it adopts a creed," wrote Thomas Huxley—a warning science would do well to heed.

The biomedical model did not fail. It completed its task—offering lifesaving advances in emergency care, infectious disease, and surgical interventions rooted in physical diagnostics and pharmaceutical so-lutions. Now it's time to evolve beyond it.

The biomedical model didn't fail. It completed its task. Now it's time to evolve beyond it.

Science as Dogma – The Myth of Objectivity

"Follow the science" sounds noble. But what happens when science itself becomes dogma?

Evidence-based medicine (EBM) began as a call for rigor. But today, it often serves as a gatekeeping system. For instance, energy-based therapies like Reiki and modalities such as homeopathy or acupuncture are frequently dismissed or excluded from funding and publication not because of poor outcomes, but because they do not fit the pharmaceutical or mechanistic criteria that dominate EBM frameworks. Randomized controlled trials (RCTs), while valuable, are expensive and typically funded by industries with vested interests. That means non-pharmaceutical interventions are rarely studied on a meaningful scale (Greenhalgh et al., 2014).

Even within drug research, bias is rampant. Positive results are more likely to be published; negative or inconclusive studies are buried (Ioannidis, 2005). Industry funding strongly predicts favorable outcomes (Lundh et al., 2017), and journals are financially dependent on pharmaceutical advertising (Angell, 2004).

"He who pays the piper calls the tune." — Unknown

Science is often idealized as a purely objective, self-correcting system. But in reality, it is conducted by humans—subject to social pressures, economic incentives, and institutional constraints. Philosopher of science Thomas Kuhn famously argued that science progresses not through linear accumulation of knowledge, but through disruptive **paradigm shifts** that occur when dominant frameworks can no longer explain mounting anomalies (Kuhn, 1962). In the interim, mainstream science defends its orthodoxy as fiercely as any religion (Brown, 2021; Stanford Encyclopedia of Philosophy, 2023).

This inertia has consequences. According to Richard Horton, editor of *The Lancet*, much of scientific literature may be unreliable due to systemic flaws, including publication bias, conflicts of interest, and methodological weaknesses (Horton, 2015). In other words, the appearance of rigor can mask a culture of conformity.

Emerging fields like energy medicine, biofield science, and terrain theory are rarely investigated not because they lack promise, but because they challenge foundational assumptions. This selective attention reflects **scientific dogmatism**—a reluctance to consider evidence that falls outside the prevailing worldview (Scientific American, 2021; The Scientist, 2021).

The peer review process, meant to ensure quality, increasingly filters for ideological conformity. Researchers who publish on mind-body phenomena or consciousness studies are often marginalized, regardless of the data's merit. Critics of this orthodoxy have begun to warn that **science is losing its spirit of inquiry** in favor of intellectual control (Nature Immunology, 2010).

"The greatest obstacle to discovery is not ignorance—it is the illusion of knowledge." — Daniel J. Boorstin

---

When science becomes institutionalized belief, it stops being science.

The Edge of Science: Healing Phenomena We Can't Yet Explain

Despite advances in technology and pharmaceuticals, chronic illness is on the rise. Autoimmune diseases, mental health disorders, and lifestyle-driven conditions are overwhelming systems worldwide.

At the same time, a growing body of well-documented healing phenomena—once dismissed as anomalies—challenges the limits of the biomedical model. These are not outliers; they are signals from the edge of science—anomalies that, in the Kuhnian sense, begin to accumulate until the prevailing paradigm can no longer contain them. These phenomena point to the need for a new framework, one that can integrate the full spectrum of human experience, including consciousness, intention, and terrain-based healing.

The following examples illustrate just how much lies beyond the current paradigm's reach:

- **The placebo effect** produces real physiological changes, even when patients know they are taking inert pills (Kaptchuk et al., 2010). More than just a curiosity, the placebo effect is a profound example of the body's capacity to heal through belief, expectation, and context. It can influence everything from pain and depression to asthma and Parkinson's disease (Harvard Health, 2017; Benedetti et al., 2011). In some surgical studies, sham operations have produced outcomes as significant as the real procedures. Placebos even work when patients are *told* they are taking a placebo (open-label studies), as long as they believe in the process. This speaks to the power of **conscious expectation** and the **therapeutic relationship**—elements almost entirely ignored by conventional medicine.

- Yet research into the placebo phenomenon has remained largely restricted to **psychological explanations**—expectancy, conditioning, and affective response—without fully exploring physiological or quantum-biological frameworks. Scholars argue that this narrow focus may overlook complex biopsychosocial and biofield mechanisms (Peiris et al., 2018). As long as the placebo is treated as a statistical nuisance rather than a gateway to deeper understanding, mainstream medicine misses an opportunity to harness its full healing potential.

- **Spontaneous remissions** occur in cancer and autoimmune conditions, often following emotional, spiritual, or lifestyle shifts. One widely documented case is that of **Anita Moorjani**, who was diagnosed with end-stage lymphoma, fell into a coma, and had a near-death experience that transformed her understanding of illness. Upon waking, her tumors began to shrink rapidly, and within weeks she was declared cancer-free. Moorjani's experience—detailed in her book *Dying to Be Me*—illustrates the kind of healing that challenges mechanistic and purely biological explanations.

- **Mind-body healing** practices, like meditation, yoga, tai chi, and somatic therapy, show biological effects—including reduced inflammation, improved immune regulation, and changes in gene expression. While historically sidelined, these therapies are now being studied more seriously within psychoneuroimmunology and integrative medicine (Astin et al., 2003; Bower & Irwin, 2016; Garland et al., 2017). The tide may be turning, but the research is still treated with less legitimacy and funding than pharmaceutical interventions.

- **Consciousness remains unexplained.** Despite all our technological and neuroscientific advances, the core question—*what is consciousness and where does it come from?*—remains unsolved.

Mainstream science continues to treat consciousness as an emergent property of brain activity, yet this view is increasingly contested. Peer-reviewed literature is now exploring theories that place consciousness as a fundamental, non-local phenomenon—not a mere byproduct of neurons, but perhaps a field-like substrate that precedes matter (Hunt et al., 2022; Manzalini, 2022).

What is Somatic Therapy?

Somatic therapy is a form of body-centered psychotherapy that integrates physical sensation and movement with emotional healing. It draws from neuroscience, trauma research, and somatic awareness practices to help individuals release stored tension, process trauma, and restore nervous system balance. Practitioners may incorporate breathwork, touch, guided movement, or awareness of bodily sensations as part of the healing process.

Near-death experiences (NDEs), out-of-body perceptions during clinical death, and verifiable reports of past-life memories in children all suggest that awareness may persist independently of brain function (Stevenson, 2001; Beauregard et al., 2014). These phenomena challenge the assumption that the brain creates consciousness, suggesting instead that it may function more like a receiver or transducer.

Publications like *Scientific American* now acknowledge that we may need radically new frameworks to understand consciousness (Seth, 2020). Meanwhile, philosophical debates continue over whether consciousness is a useful illusion, a survival mechanism, or an emergent dimension of universal intelligence (Psychology Today, 2020). Whatever the case, the prevailing models are insufficient.

In the same way that earlier generations believed the sun revolved around the Earth, we may be clinging to a model of consciousness that reflects our tools and biases more than reality itself.

"The day science begins to study non-physical phenomena, it will make more progress in one decade than in all the previous centuries of its existence." — Nikola Tesla

---

Anomalies are not errors. They are clues that it's time for a new map.

A Fork in the Road: From Machine Thinking to Empowered Partnership

Every paradigm reaches a tipping point—a moment when its contradictions become too glaring to ignore. Medicine is at that crossroads now. It can either double down on reductionist fixes, or evolve into something more holistic, intelligent, and aligned with the complexity of life itself.

The signs are already here. The old metaphors—**the body as machine, disease as enemy, the doctor as authority**—no longer reflect our lived experience. People are hungry for deeper answers. They are turning to integrative practitioners, somatic therapists, energy workers, trauma-informed healers—not because they are gullible, but because they are desperate for something that actually helps.

This is not fringe anymore. It is the future demanding to be born.

People want to feel better, think clearly, have more energy and enhance endurance and resilience to illness, have less chronic pain, have improved mood, sleep better, and be active. They are not diseases but are symptomatic of functional problems that can be addressed by looking for root causes.

— Jeffrey Bland, Ph.D.

Andrew Weil, MD, summed it up succinctly. "Belief is the strongest drug known to mankind." It is a statement that speaks not only to psychology but to physiology. The placebo effect, long dismissed as a nuisance variable—something to be controlled for, not explored—may be one of the most powerful healing agents available precisely because it activates our innate capacity to shift biology through perception and expectation.

Belief and intention are not abstract concepts. They are therapeutic forces that shape physiology, shift terrain, and activate healing.

From Machine Thinking to Systems Thinking

Rather than viewing the body as a broken machine, **systems biology**, **psychoneuroimmunology (PNI)**, and **biofield science** reveal a dynamic, adaptive, and multidimensional system. PNI, which emerged in the 1980s and was already established in academic settings like the University of Miami by the late 1990s, provides a framework for understanding how psychological processes—like stress, belief, and emotion—affect the immune, nervous, and endocrine systems in real-time (Ader et al., 2001).

This view goes far beyond the hypothalamic-pituitary-adrenal (HPA) axis, encompassing hormonal signaling, cytokine expression, gut-brain communication, and the epigenetic modulation of inflammation (Irwin & Cole, 2011; Slavich & Cole, 2013). It supports a truly **biopsychosocial model**, one that reflects the lived interplay between body, mind, behavior, and environment.

As Dr. Jeffrey Bland recently stated, "Without a dramatic change in focus from a disease-treatment-centric system to a scientific wellness-based system, we will lose the opportunity to create a system that delivers improved health outcomes consistent with an individual's definition of health" (PLMI Newsletter, Feb 26, 2025), one that reflects the lived interplay between body, mind, behavior, and environment.

From Energy Denial to Biofield Science

Where conventional medicine draws the line at anatomy and biochemistry, a new frontier has opened through **biofield research**. Biofield science studies the endogenous electromagnetic and subtle energy fields that surround and permeate living systems. These fields appear to play a regulatory role in physiology, communication, and coherence (Rubik et al., 2015).

Reiki, Healing Touch, and other so-called "subtle energy" modalities have demonstrated measurable physiological benefits—including reduced pain, anxiety, and cortisol levels—in randomized clinical trials (Jain & Mills, 2010; Hammerschlag et al., 2014). Yet until recently, practitioners like myself could not offer such treatments without risking professional sanctions. When I became a Reiki Level 2 practitioner in the early 2000s, I was unable to openly incorporate energy work into my clinical practice due to the restrictive scope of psychology licensing laws.

Fortunately, times are changing. Scoping reviews now document dozens of studies confirming the clinical effectiveness of biofield therapies, especially in chronic conditions (Sprengel et al., 2025). Advances in measurement tools and conceptual modeling are expanding what counts as legitimate science.

From Fighting Disease to Restoring Harmony

The language of war is baked into modern medicine: we fight disease, target symptoms, attack pathogens, and wage battles with the body. But what if illness is not an enemy, but a **messenger**?

In this new model, disease is not just something to eradicate. It's a signal of imbalance, an invitation to look deeper. The fever, the inflammation, the fatigue—they're all part of the body's attempt to recalibrate. Instead of declaring war on the process, we work with it. As Christiane Northrup eloquently summarized, "Illness is the cry of the soul made flesh."

This shift does not reject science. It reclaims it from a narrow materialist box and re-integrates it with wisdom traditions, intuitive knowing, and the lived complexity of being human.

From Authority to Empowered Partnership

In the old model, the doctor is the expert and the patient is the passive recipient of care. In the emerging model, the healer is a **guide**, and the individual becomes an **active participant in their own recovery**.

Empowerment becomes the cornerstone. The new paradigm invites collaboration. The healer becomes a guide; the patient, a co-creator. The client's intuition, experience, and internal compass matter. We no longer outsource our authority to a white coat or a data chart. We enter into partnership—with the practitioner, with the body, and ultimately with ourselves. This approach echoes the growing recognition that belief and intention are not secondary elements but central forces in the healing process—keys to terrain modulation and sustainable transformation.

"We cannot solve our problems with the same thinking we used when we created them." — Albert Einstein

---

Healing is not the suppression of symptoms.
It is the restoration of wholeness.

These anomalies—placebo, spontaneous remission, mind-body effects, and consciousness itself—are not fringe mysteries. They are evidence that the current map is too small for the territory of healing. To move forward, we must not only question the assumptions of the old model—we must begin building a new one.

That journey begins with recognizing that the body is not a machine, but a dynamic system; that healing is not control, but communication; and that consciousness may not be a byproduct, but a primary force.

Across the globe, clinicians and researchers alike are already laying the groundwork for this new terrain—one grounded in coherence, connection, and consciousness. In the next chapter, we explore the frameworks that are already pointing the way forward—quietly, courageously, and in some cases, brilliantly.

A new scientific truth does not triumph by convincing its opponents. but because its opponents eventually die, and a new generation grows up that is familiar with it.

— Max Planck

References

Ader, R., Felten, D., & Cohen, N. (2001). *Psychoneuro-immunology*. Academic Press. https://psycnet.apa.org/record/2000-12302-000

Angell, M. (2004). *The truth about the drug companies: How they deceive us and what to do about it*. Random House. https://www.penguinrandomhouse.com/books/3901/the-truth-about-the-drug-companies-by-marcia-angell-md/

Baldwin, A. L., Wagers, C., & Schwartz, G. E. (2008). Reiki improves heart rate homeostasis in laboratory rats. *Journal of Alternative and Complementary Medicine, 14*(4), 417–422. https://doi.org/10.1089/acm.2007.0753

Beauregard, M., Schwartz, G. E., & Miller, L. (2014). The brain, mind, and spiritual experience. In E. Cardeña, S. J. Lynn, & S. Krippner (Eds.), *Varieties of anomalous experience* (2nd ed., pp. 327–365). American Psychological Association.

Bower, J. E., & Irwin, M. R. (2016). Mind–body therapies and control of inflammatory biology: A descriptive review. *Brain, Behavior, and Immunity, 51*, 1–11. https://doi.org/10.1016/j.bbi.2015.06.012

Garland, E. L., Geschwind, N., Peeters, F., & Wichers, M. (2015). Mindfulness training promotes upward spirals of positive affect and cognition: Multilevel and autoregressive latent trajectory modeling analyses. *Frontiers in Psychology, 8*, 585. https://www.frontiersin.org/journals/psychology/articles/10.3389/fpsyg.2015.00015/full

Greenhalgh, T., Howick, J., & Maskrey, N. (2014). Evidence based medicine: A movement in crisis? *BMJ, 348*, g3725. https://www.bmj.com/content/348/bmj.g3725

Hammerschlag, R., Marx, B. L., Yamamoto, M., et al. (2012). Biofield research: A roundtable discussion of scientific and methodological issues. *Journal of Alternative and Complementary Medicine, 20*(11), 799–805. https://doi.org/10.1089/acm.2012.1502

Horton, R. (2015). What is medicine's 5 sigma? *The Lancet, 385*(9976), 1380. https://doi.org/10.1016/S0140-6736(15)60696-1

Hunt, T., Ericson, M., & Schooler, J. (2022). Where's my consciousness-ometer? How to test for the presence and complexity of consciousness. *Perspectives on Psychological Science, 17*(4), 1172–1189. https://doi.org/10.1177/17456916211029942

Ioannidis, J. P. A. (2005). Why most published research findings are false. *PLoS Medicine, 2*(8), e124. https://doi.org/10.1371/journal.pmed.1004085

Irwin, M. R., & Cole, S. W. (2011). Reciprocal regulation of the neural and innate immune systems. *Nature Reviews Immunology, 11*(9), 625–632. https://doi.org/10.1038/nri3042

Jain, S., & Mills, P. J. (2010). Biofield therapies: Helpful or full of hype? A best evidence synthesis. *International Journal of Behavioral Medicine, 17*(1), 1–16. https://doi.org/10.1007/s12529-009-9062-4

Kaptchuk, T. J., Friedlander, E., Kelley, J. M., et al. (2010). Placebos without deception: A randomized controlled trial in irritable bowel syndrome. *PLoS ONE, 5*(12), e15591. https://doi.org/10.1371/journal.pone.0015591

Lipton, B. H. (2005). *The biology of belief: Unleashing the power of consciousness, matter & miracles*. Hay House. https://www.brucelipton.com/books/biology-of-belief/

Lundh, A., Sismondo, S., Lexchin, J., Busuioc, O. A., & Bero, L. (2017). Industry sponsorship and research outcome. *Cochrane Database of Systematic Reviews*, 2, MR000033. https://doi.org/10.1002/14651858.MR000033.pub 3

Manzalini, A. (2022). A new model of consciousness as a quantum field. *Journal of Biomedical Research & Environmental Sciences, 3*(9), 1092–1099. https://doi.org/10.37871/jbres1568

Markov, M. S. (2007). Pulsed electromagnetic field therapy: History, state of the art, and future. *The Environmentalist, 27*(4), 465–475. https://link.springer.com/article/10.1007/s10669-007-9128-2

Nestle, M. (2015). *Soda politics: Taking on big soda (and winning).* Oxford University Press. ISBN-13: 978-0190263430

Peiris, N., Blasini, M., Wright, T., & Colloca, L. (2018). The placebo phenomenon: A narrow focus on psychological models. *Perspectives in Biology and Medicine, 61*(3), 388–400. https://doi.org/10.1353/pbm.2018.0051

Rubik, B., Muehsam, D., Hammerschlag, R., & Jain, S. (2015). Biofield science and healing: History, terminology, and concepts. *Global Advances in Health and Medicine, 4*(Suppl), 8–14. https://doi.org/10.7453/gahmj.2015.038.suppl

Seth, A. K. (2020). What is consciousness? *Scientific American, 322*(4), 26–33. https://www.scientificamerican.com/article/what-is-consciousness/

Slavich, G. M., & Cole, S. W. (2013). The emerging field of human social genomics. *Clinical Psychological Science, 1*(3), 331–348. https://doi.org/10.1177/2167702613478594

Sprengel, M. L., Teo, L., Allen, S., Jissennagger, N., Hammerschlag, R., Dyer, N. L., & Crawford, C. (2025). Biofield therapies clinical research landscape: A scoping review and interactive evidence map. *Journal of Integrative and Complementary Medicine, 31*(5). https://doi.org/10.1089/jicm.2024.0773

Stevenson, I. (2001). *Children who remember previous lives: A question of reincarnation.* McFarland & Company. https://med.virginia.edu/perceptual-studies/publications/books-by-dops-faculty/study-of-reincarnation/children-who-remember-previous-lives-a-question-of-reincarnation/

All disease begins in the gut.

— Hippocrates

Chapter 3

The Interconnected Terrain — Gut, Detox, and the Immune Web

Why a Health Psychologist Talks About Gut Health

> *Health is not achieved by micromanaging symptoms, but by cultivating an internal environment where healing can occur naturally.*

In previous chapters, we laid the foundation for understanding health through the lens of terrain medicine. We explored the elimination diet as both a tool and a philosophy—a process that removes internal noise and helps the body reestablish equilibrium. Now, we deepen the lens and examine the core components of terrain restoration through three integrated frameworks: the 5 R's of Functional Medicine, the example of neurodegeneration as a terrain-based illness, and real-world clinical cases where psychological symptoms resolved after addressing environmental toxicity.

But first, we need to ask: *Why is a health psychologist talking about gut protocols, detoxification, and immune modulation in the first place?*

As a psychologist, I was trained to look inward—at cognition, behavior, emotion, and narrative. But over the years, working at the edge where medicine and psychology meet, I have come to see that what we call "mental health" is often an expression of systemic imbalance. The gut, the immune system, the mitochondria, even environmental inputs like mold or toxins—all shape our internal experience. So when I speak about terrain, I am not stepping outside my field. I am expanding it. In this chapter, we will explore why the restoration of the inner ecosystem is not just for the body—it is also essential for restoring clarity, resilience, and emotional coherence.

The answer lies in the **Brain-Gut-Microbiota Axis** — the dynamic, bidirectional communication system between the gastrointestinal tract, the immune system, and the central nervous system. This axis involves neural, hormonal, and immunological signaling, and disruptions in any part of this communication loop can manifest as **anxiety, depression, fatigue, cognitive fog, and even neurodegenerative illness** (Dinan & Cryan, 2017; Foster et al., 2017).

Recent advances in psychobiotic research have shown that the **gut microbiome directly influences neurotransmitter production, synaptic plasticity, and neuroinflammation**. Certain gut bacteria produce or modulate GABA, serotonin, dopamine, and BDNF—all central to emotional regulation and cognitive function (Strandwitz, 2018). Dysbiosis, leaky gut, and inflammatory cascades can drive mental health deterioration, which is why restoring microbial terrain is no longer optional—it is foundational (Hoban et al., 2016; Knudsen et al., 2021).

The Functional Medicine Terrain Framework: The 5 R's

The 5 R Protocol is one of the foundational models in Functional Medicine—a structured, systems-based approach originally designed to heal the gastrointestinal system. But over time, practitioners and researchers have recognized that its power extends far beyond digestion. When applied properly, the 5 R framework becomes a blueprint for restoring terrain across multiple physiological networks: the immune system, the endocrine system, and the central nervous system.

Let's walk through it:

1. **Remove**: This is the cleanup phase. We eliminate what is disrupting the terrain—whether it is inflammatory foods, pathogens, mold, environmental toxins, or even chronic stressors. From a psychological standpoint, this might also include identifying toxic relationships, trauma imprints, or beliefs that are contributing to physiological dysregulation. In gut healing, this step might involve antimicrobials, elimination diets, or detox support. , including environmental exposures that act as neuroendocrine disruptors or immune irritants. These may include fluoride, heavy metals, pesticides, mold mycotoxins, industrial solvents, and air pollutants. Emerging research confirms that such exposures are strongly associated with disruptions in mental health and neurological function (Aggarwal et al., 2022; Miller et al., 2022; Di Ciaula et al., 2023; Taylor et al., 2025). Even trace levels of fluoride, for instance, have been shown to impact thyroid hormone balance—

critical to mood, energy, and cognition (Sauerheber, 2013; Ferreira et al., 2024).

2. **Replace**: Once harmful inputs are removed, we must replace what the body is missing—particularly digestive enzymes, bile acids, hydrochloric acid, or key micronutrients needed for neurotransmitter production, mitochondrial energy generation, or immune regulation.

This is also where we must assess and support **methylation pathways**, especially in individuals with known genetic polymorphisms such as MTHFR C677T or A1298C. Gut dysbiosis can impair the absorption of **B vitamins**—particularly B6, B9 (folate), and B12—which are crucial for methylation and directly influence mood, cognition, and energy metabolism. Low levels of these vitamins have been associated with increased anxiety and depressive symptoms (Gong et al., 2022; de Koning et al., 2022).

Magnesium, another often-depleted nutrient, plays a vital role in neurotransmitter regulation and has shown promise in reducing symptoms of anxiety (Marcinkiewicz et al., 2023). Supporting these foundational pathways can significantly improve psychological resilience and emotional regulation.

3. **Reinoculate**: Here, we repopulate the gut terrain with beneficial microbes using probiotics, fermented foods, and most importantly, prebiotics and polyphenols—plant fibers that feed keystone species like *Akkermansia muciniphila*. This microbial diversity is essential for producing mood-regulating compounds like GABA, serotonin, and short-chain fatty acids such as butyrate.

Recent meta-analyses and reviews have confirmed the therapeutic potential of probiotics and prebiotics in the treatment of mental health disorders, including depression, anxiety, Alzheimer's disease, and autism spectrum disorders (Mohammadi et al., 2020; Wang et al., 2023; Ma et al., 2023). These microbes influence the gut-brain axis through neural, endocrine, and immune pathways, altering inflammation, neurotransmitter levels, and even synaptic plasticity.

Akkermansia muciniphila, in particular, has drawn attention for its role in modulating immune responses and neuroinflammation. Studies show this bacterium may improve metabolic parameters and support brain function by preserving gut barrier integrity and reducing endotoxin load (Lei et al., 2023; Depommier et al., 2022).

Supporting microbial diversity is not just a gut strategy—it is a neuropsychiatric intervention.

4. **Repair**: Repairing the gut lining and mucosal immune system requires nutrients like L-glutamine, zinc, collagen, and butyrate. These help seal the intestinal epithelium, reduce inflammation, and support mucosal immunity. But repair also includes **psychological safety**—healing the nervous system's relationship to inflammation, stress, and past experiences. In this sense, functional gut repair parallels trauma recovery.

The importance of this phase for mental health is now well documented. The gut lining is not just a physical barrier—it is a dynamic, immunologically active interface with the outside world. When compromised, it can allow microbial fragments and toxins into circulation, triggering systemic inflammation and affecting brain function. As Dr. David Perlmutter (2015) emphasizes in *Brain Maker*, the health of the gut plays a central role in cognitive function, emotional balance, and long-term neurological resilience.

Scientific reviews have also shown that dietary strategies promoting epithelial integrity—such as omega-3 fatty acids, fermented foods, and polyphenol-rich plants—can reduce depressive symptoms and modulate the microbiome (Liu et al., 2023; Burokas et al., 2024). Psychobiotics and mucosal-healing nutrients support gut-brain communication and have a ripple effect on stress resilience and emotional regulation.

Repair is not just about digestion—it's about restoring the physiological boundary that protects and regulates the psyche.

5. **Rebalance**: Finally, we rebalance the nervous system through lifestyle rhythms—sleep, movement, mindfulness, and circadian coherence. This step invites deep psychological work: finding purpose, reclaiming agency, and establishing inner alignment.

Rebalancing may appear simple, but it is profoundly impactful. Movement, for example, has consistently been shown to enhance neuroplasticity, elevate mood, and reduce systemic inflammation (Chen et al., 2023). Regular physical activity increases brain-derived neurotrophic factor (BDNF), a key molecule involved in learning, memory, and emotional regulation. Sleep quality is also closely tied to diet and circadian rhythm. Studies show that dietary interventions like the MIND diet improve both sleep and BDNF serum levels in individuals with metabolic and mood disturbances (Golmohammadi et al., 2025).

Even in autoimmune conditions such as lupus, lifestyle interventions have demonstrated efficacy in reducing flare-ups and supporting mental well-being (Tsoi et al., 2024). This speaks to the universal nature of terrain restoration across all systems.

Rebalance is not the final step—it is the ongoing rhythm of coherence in a healing life.

The 5 R's form the architecture for terrain restoration. Each step intersects with mental health, not as a side effect, but as an **integrated expression of internal ecology**. In fact, the protocol serves as a clinical bridge between gut health and psychospiritual coherence.

This is not just gut work—it is **psycho-neuro-immunology in action**.

The terrain includes the air we breathe,
the water we drink, and the unspoken toxins
that quietly erode emotional resilience.

The Functional Terrain of Mental Health: How the 5 R Protocol Supports Psychological Resilience

5 R Phase	Primary Action	Mental Health Intersections
Remove	Eliminate toxins, pathogens, stressors	Reduces neuroinflammation, immune activation, endocrine disruption
Replace	Restore enzymes, nutrients, cofactors	Supports neurotransmitter synthesis, methylation, energy balance
Reinoculate	Add beneficial microbes & prebiotics	Produces neuroactive compounds (GABA, serotonin, SCFAs)
Repair	Heal gut lining & barriers	Resolves leaky gut & blood-brain barrier dysfunction
Rebalance	Regulate lifestyle & emotional rhythms	Restores vagal tone, circadian rhythm, trauma integration

Neurodegeneration as Terrain Breakdown: A Functional and Psychological Perspective

Before we examine the breakdown of brain function, it is important to reframe neurodegeneration through the lens of systems collapse—not as an inevitable part of aging, but as a long-term outcome of unaddressed disruptions in the body's interconnected terrain. This section offers a deeper look into how various physiological failures intersect, and why early intervention through terrain repair can change the course of these devastating illnesses.

Alzheimer's disease is often used as a prime example of irreversible decline. But current research reframes it as a systemic failure of terrain regulation that begins years—even decades—before clinical diagnosis. It is not just about aging neurons; it is about the collapse of the body's internal communication systems across the microbiome, mitochondria, immune system, vascular pathways, and detoxification mechanisms (Butterfield & Halliwell, 2019; De la Monte & Wands, 2008).

From the terrain perspective, neurodegeneration can be understood as a slow, multi-system unraveling:

- **Microbial terrain dysbiosis** (gut and oral): Pathogens like *Porphyromonas gingivalis* can colonize the mouth, leach into circulation, cross the blood-brain barrier, and trigger microglial activation. Oral health becomes a frontline defense (Dominy et al., 2019).

- **Leaky gut and endotoxemia**: LPS (lipopolysaccharides) from gram-negative bacteria can cross into the bloodstream, fueling systemic inflammation and priming the brain for neurodegeneration (Werner et al., 2014).

- **Mitochondrial decline**: Oxidative stress and impaired energy production hinder synaptic plasticity, memory consolidation, and neuroprotection.

- **Insulin resistance and metabolic dysfunction**: Alzheimer's is now referred to by many as "Type III diabetes." Impaired glucose utilization in the brain is both a cause and a consequence of terrain breakdown (De la Monte & Wands, 2008).

- **TBI and APOE4 risk**: Traumatic brain injury increases oxidative burden, especially in genetically susceptible individuals. Free iron acts as a transition metal and oxidizer—literally rusting the brain.

- **Blood-brain barrier dysfunction**: Chronic inflammation, nutrient deficiencies, and exposure to toxins (e.g., pesticides, mold, heavy metals) degrade this barrier, allowing immune triggers into the CNS.

- **Sleep disruption and glymphatic failure**: The brain's detox system operates primarily during deep sleep. Terrain imbalances impair both the structure and the rhythm of restorative sleep (Iliff et al., 2012; Mawuenyega et al., 2010).

Dr. Todd LePine has referred to Alzheimer's as a model of terrain collapse—where immune, metabolic, and microbial pathways all converge to create neuroinflammation and cognitive decline. But this model is also what makes prevention and early intervention possible.

Functional medicine offers tools to reverse this pattern:

- **Butyrate**, a postbiotic generated by high-fiber diets, promotes brain-derived neurotrophic factor (BDNF) expression and epigenetic signaling.

- **Prebiotic fibers and polyphenols** foster microbial diversity and gut integrity, feeding keystone species like *Akkermansia muciniphila*.

- **Mitochondrial nutrients** such as NAC, glycine, Mito-PQQ, alpha-lipoic acid, and lithium orotate enhance energy resilience and reduce ROS damage.

- **Hormetic phytochemicals** (sulforaphane, resveratrol, curcumin) activate endogenous defense systems and stimulate cellular repair.

- **Sleep as terrain restoration**: Deep sleep clears metabolic waste via the glymphatic system, reduces neurotoxic load, and consolidates memory.

Terrain medicine changes the question from "How do we treat Alzheimer's?" to "What breaks down in the ecosystem that allows neurodegeneration to take hold?"

And the answer, increasingly, is not just found in the brain—but in the gut, the mouth, the mitochondria, the airways, the sleep cycle, and the food we eat every day.

As Dr. LePine said, sleep is the "garbage truck of the brain." Terrain repair must include restoring rest, detox pathways, and biochemical resilience.

Case Summary Box: Alzheimer's as a Terrain Collapse

A Clinical Lens on Terrain Breakdown

Alzheimer's disease is not an isolated brain disorder—it is a systemic signal of long-term terrain breakdown. When viewed through the functional lens, it represents the convergence of multiple biological failures that begin well before cognitive symptoms appear:

- Chronic oral and gut infections drive neuroinflammation.
- Leaky gut and endotoxins cross into systemic circulation.
- Mitochondrial damage and oxidative stress accelerate cellular aging.
- Insulin resistance disrupts brain glucose metabolism (Type III diabetes).
- Toxic exposures, TBI, and compromised sleep degrade resilience.

This terrain breakdown pattern illustrates why prevention and repair must start early—and why terrain medicine provides hope. By addressing these root imbalances through microbial repair, detoxification, nutritional repletion, sleep restoration, and psychological regulation, we can slow or even reverse early decline.

Alzheimer's is not just a disease of the brain—
It is a mirror of the terrain

Clinical Insight: When Psychological Symptoms Are Terrain Disturbances

Environmental medicine is not separate from psychology. It is the soil in which psychological symptoms often take root. And in some cases, those symptoms are the *only visible signal* that something is wrong with the terrain.

As a health psychologist immersed in functional medicine, I often approach emotional dysregulation, anxiety, and fatigue not only as psychological patterns, but also as potential signs of immune activation, toxic exposure, or physiological overwhelm. The following three cases demonstrate the power of listening to the body's distress signals—and how terrain restoration can produce dramatic healing.

Case 1: Abby — Anxiety and Night Terrors from Mold Exposure

Abby (name changed to protect confidentiality), a 26-year-old newlywed living in California, came to therapy for severe anxiety, difficulty falling asleep, and vivid, hallucinatory night terrors. These symptoms were so intense that she occasionally leapt from bed, convinced she was surrounded by danger. Despite her psychological insight and openness to treatment, nothing in her history explained the symptoms.

Our work included relaxation induction and lucid imagery training, which she excelled at. But the breakthrough came not from within—rather, from the environment. When she traveled back to Florida to visit family, her symptoms disappeared completely. I suggested testing for mold in her California home.

Mold was found. After moving, the symptoms resolved. This was not a mental illness. This was a terrain disruption with psychological expression.

Case 2: Luis — Anxiety, Fatigue and Brain Fog Linked to Mold in the Home

Luis (name changed to protect confidentiality), a man in his late 30s, came to me confused by his profound fatigue, anxiety that surged when returning home, brain fog, and body aches. A successful professional and devoted father, he had no identifiable psychological triggers. The symptoms only appeared while he was at home.

Suspecting a hidden terrain factor, I recommended he have his home inspected for mold. The assessment revealed contamination throughout the HVAC system. Mold was found throughout the AC coils and ductwork. After professional remediation, his energy returned, his mind cleared, and the anxiety-like symptoms disappeared. It took just two therapy sessions to help him fully reorient to his normal self—an outcome rarely seen in cases of chronic psychological distress, but entirely logical when the source is environmental rather than internal. No medication. Just a cleaner internal and external environment.

Case 3: Stan — Immune Dysfunction, Depression, Anxiety and Recovery Through Relocation

Stan (name changed to protect confidentiality), a single man in his 30s, relocated from Europe to South Florida to expand his successful career. But shortly after arrival, he began experiencing allergies, anxiety, depressive symptoms, and a steep decline in cognitive and professional functioning. He had never experienced anything like this before.

We investigated both physical and emotional terrain. Testing confirmed mycotoxin exposure and immune dysregulation. His office tested positive for mold. We worked to stabilize both his physiology and his sense of identity, which had begun to fracture under the weight of these unexplained symptoms. Ultimately, he relocated to Canada, a radically different climate, changed his environment, restored his health, found a new job—and reconnected with himself. Healing happened not just at the gut or brain level, but through alignment with place and purpose.

These cases validate the **biopsychosocial model** not as an abstract theory, but as an essential clinical map. Terrain disturbances can masquerade as psychiatric symptoms. Mold, mycotoxins, neuroinflammation, toxicants, and microbial imbalance all have psychological signatures. Without considering these layers, we risk medicating the signal instead of decoding the message.

The body speaks through the mind.
And terrain is the language.

Environmental Toxicity and Mental Health
A Growing Field of Concern

Mounting scientific evidence links environmental exposures to a wide range of neuropsychiatric and cognitive disorders. A 2022 review published in *Environmental Research* emphasized that air pollution, drinking water contaminants, indoor mold, and endocrine-disrupting chemicals are emerging as major risk factors for anxiety, depression, ADHD, and neurodegeneration (Di Ciaula et al., 2023).

Key findings:

- Fluoride exposure has been associated with **thyroid hormone disruption** and lowered IQ scores, with downstream effects on mood and cognitive function (Sauerheber, 2013; Ferreira et al., 2024).

- Chronic low-level exposure to **mold and mycotoxins** contributes to brain fog, fatigue, and limbic system sensitization (Miller, 2018).

- Heavy metals such as **lead and mercury** interfere with neurotransmission, mitochondrial function, and neurodevelopment.

As a psychologist with functional medicine training, I see these factors not as fringe theories—but as essential considerations in root-cause assessment. The terrain includes the air we breathe, the water we drink, and the hidden exposures that quietly erode emotional resilience and brain function.

Reflective Sidebar: The Body Speaks in Metaphor

Authors like Julia Cannon (*Soul Speak: The Language of Your Body*) and Louise Hay (*Heal Your Body*) have long explored the idea that physical symptoms are not just biological malfunctions, but metaphors—messages from the soul or subconscious. While their language is more metaphysical than clinical, the core insight resonates with functional terrain thinking: the body expresses imbalance in symbolic ways.

When we learn to listen to these signals—not to suppress them, but to decode them—we shift from control to collaboration. Whether it is a gut flare, anxiety, or chronic fatigue, the question is the same: *What is this trying to tell me?* In this way, even the most disruptive symptoms become invitations to realign with coherence.

Returning to Coherence: The Final Phase of Terrain Repair

We close this chapter by zooming out. Having examined the 5Rs, neurodegeneration, clinical insights, and environmental contributions, we now return to the larger goal: coherence. This final section explores what it truly means to heal—not just biologically, but across all layers of being.

To heal the terrain is to restore coherence—in the gut, the brain, the immune system, and the mind. Functional medicine provides protocols. Psychology provides meaning and context. But more than anything, healing requires attunement to complexity—

and a willingness to follow intuition when the answers are not obvious.

In each of the cases described, it was not a textbook or lab result that first revealed the root cause. It was intuition—a felt sense that something did not add up. It was the body speaking through the symptom, and the terrain whispering through disruption. Listening deeply made all the difference.

Symptoms are not information to be suppressed, but information that requires some decoding. They are signals—guiding us toward the imbalances that call for attention.

The terrain approach does not deny pathology. It expands it. It asks: *What is this symptom responding to? What is the body trying to say?* And how can we listen deeply enough to create the conditions for its resolution?

This chapter has offered one such map. The terrain is real. And with the right lens, it becomes readable—and healable.

In the next chapter, we will expand this framework even further—beyond the physical terrain—into the energetic, vibrational, and consciousness-based fields that shape healing in more subtle but equally powerful ways.

References

Aggarwal, V., Mehndiratta, M. M., Wasay, M., & Garg, D. (2022). Environmental toxins and brain: Life on Earth is in danger. *Annals of Indian Academy of Neurology, 25*(Suppl 1), S15–S21. https://doi.org/10.4103/aian.aian_169_22

Tsoi, A., Gomez, A., Boström, C., Pezzella, D., Chow, J. W., Girard-Guyonvarc'h, C., Stamm, T., Arnaud, L., & Parodis, I. (2024). Efficacy of lifestyle interventions in the management of systemic lupus erythematosus: A systematic review of the literature. *Rheumatology International, 44*(5), 765–778. https://doi.org/10.1007/s00296-024-05548-x

Bourassa, M. W., Smith, J. L., & Chen, R. T. (2016). Butyrate, neuroepigenetics, and the gut microbiome: Can a high-fiber diet improve brain health? *Neuroscience Letters, 625*, 56–63.https://doi.org/10.1016/j.neulet.2016.02.009

Burokas, A., et al. (2024). Exploring the gut-brain Axis: Potential therapeutic impact of psychobiotics on mental health. *Toxicology and Applied Pharmacology.* https://doi.org/10.1016/j.pnpbp.2024.111073

Butterfield, D. A., & Halliwell, B. (2019). Oxidative stress, dysfunctional glucose metabolism and Alzheimer disease. *Nature Reviews Neuroscience*, 20(3), 148–160. https://doi.org/10.1038/s41583-019-0132-6

Chen, A. G., Liu, H., Zhang, Y., & Wang, Q. (2023). The impact of exercise on depression: How moving makes your brain and body feel better. *Brain Sciences, 13*(2), 123. https://doi.org/10.20463/pan.2024.0015

De la Monte, S. M., & Wands, J. R. (2008). Alzheimer's disease is type 3 diabetes—evidence reviewed. *Journal of Diabetes Science and Technology, 2*(6), 1101–1113. https://doi.org/10.1177/193229680800200619

Depommier, C., et al. (2022). Supplementation with Akkermansia muciniphila in overweight and obese human volunteers: A proof-of-concept exploratory study. *Nature Medicine*, 28(2), 315–324. https://doi.org/ 10.1038/s41591-019-0495-2

Dinan, T. G., & Cryan, J. F. (2017). The microbiome–gut–brain axis in health and disease. *Gastroenterology Clinics of North America, 46*(1), 77–89. https://doi.org/10.1016/j.gtc.2016.09.007

Dominy, S. S., et al. (2019). Porphyromonas gingivalis in Alzheimer's disease brains: Evidence for disease causation and treatment with small-molecule inhibitors. *Science Advances*, 5(1), eaau3333. https://doi.org/10.1126/sciadv.aau3333

Golmohammadi, M., Ebrahimzadeh Attari, V., Salimi, Y., Saed, L., Nachvak, S. M., & Samadi, M. (2025). The effect of MIND diet on sleep status, mental health, and serum level of BDNF in overweight/obese diabetic women with insomnia: A randomized controlled trial. *Scientific Reports, 15*, Article 8237. https://doi.org/10.1038/s41598-025-91389-y

Ferreira, M. K. M., Nascimento, P. C., Bittencourt, L. O., Miranda, G. H. N., Fernandes Fagundes, N. C., Zahoori, F. V., Martinez-Mier, E. A., Buzalaf, M. A. R., & Lima, R. R. (2024). Is there any association between fluoride exposure and thyroid function modulation? A systematic review. *PLOS ONE, 19*(4), e0301911. https://doi.org/10.1371/journal.pone.0301911

Foster, J. A., Rinaman, L., & Cryan, J. F. (2017). Stress & the gut-brain axis: Regulation by the microbiome. *Neurobiology of Stress, 12*, 100276. https://doi.org/ 10.1016/j.ynstr.2017.03.001

Gong, X., Zhang, Y., Chen, H., & Li, M. (2022). Association between variants of MTHFR genes and psychiatric disorders: A meta-analysis. *Frontiers in Genetics, 13*, 943375. https://doi.org/10.3389/fpsyt.2022.976428

Hoban, A. E., Stilling, R. M., Ryan, F. J., Shanahan, F., Dinan, T. G., Claesson, M. J., Clarke, G., & Cryan, J. F. (2016). Regulation of prefrontal cortex myelination by the microbiota. *Translational Psychiatry, 6*, e774. https://doi.org/10.1038/tp.2016.42

Iliff, J. J., et al. (2012). A paravascular pathway facilitates CSF flow through the brain parenchyma and the clearance of interstitial solutes, including amyloid β. *Science Translational Medicine*, 4(147), 147ra111. https://doi.org/10.1126/scitranslmed.3003748

Jain, A., Madkan, S., & Patil, P. (2023). The role of gut microbiota in neurodegenerative diseases: Current insights and therapeutic implications. *Cureus, 15*(10), e47861. https://doi.org/10.7759/cureus.47861

Lei, W., Cheng, Y., Gao, J., Liu, X., Shao, L., Kong, Q., Zheng, N., Ling, Z., & Hu, W. (2023). *Akkermansia muciniphila* in neuropsychiatric disorders: Friend or foe? *Frontiers in Microbiology, 14*, 1036372. https://doi.org/10.3389/fmicb.2023.1036372

LePine, T. (2024). Clinical lecture materials and functional medicine insights [Webinar – March 2025].

Mawuenyega, K. G., et al. (2010). Decreased clearance of CNS beta-amyloid in Alzheimer's disease. *Science*, 330(6012), 1774. https://doi.org/10.1126/science.1197623

Miller, J. G., Dennis, E. L., Heft-Neal, S., Jo, B., & Gotlib, I. H. (2022). Fine particulate air pollution, early life stress, and their interactive effects on adolescent structural brain development: A longitudinal tensor-based morphometry study. *Cerebral Cortex, 32*(10), 2156–2169. https://doi.org/10.1093/cercor/bhab346

Miller, K. (2018). *Saving your brain: Causes, prevention, and reversal of dementia and Alzheimer's disease* (Health Restoration Series). Greenleaf Book Group Press. ISBN-13: 978-0997911379

Perlmutter, D. (2015). *Brain maker: The power of gut microbes to heal and protect your brain—for life.* Little, Brown Spark. ISBN-13: 978-0316380102

Sanada, K., Nakajima, S., Kurokawa, S., Barceló-Soler, A., Ikuse, D., Hirata, A., Yoshizawa, A., Tomizawa, Y., Salas-Valero, M., Noda, Y., Mimura, M., Iwanami, A., & Kishimoto, T. (2020). Gut microbiota and major depressive disorder: A systematic review and meta-analysis. *Journal of Affective Disorders, 266*, 1–13. https://doi.org/10.1016/j.jad.2020.01.102

Sauerheber, R. (2013). Physiologic conditions affect toxicity of ingested industrial fluoride. *Journal of Environmental and Public Health*, 2013. https://doi.org/10.1155/2013/439490

Taylor, K. W., Eftim, S. E., Sibrizzi, C. A., Blain, R. B., Magnuson, K., Hartman, P. A., Rooney, A. A., & Bucher, J. R. (2025). Fluoride exposure and children's IQ scores: A systematic review and meta-analysis. *JAMA Pediatrics, 179*(3), 282–292. https://doi.org/10.1001/jamapediatrics.2024.5542

PART II

BUILDING A NEW FRAMEWORK OF HEALING

As the cracks in conventional medicine become more apparent, the need for a new healing paradigm becomes undeniable. Part I of this book laid the groundwork for a terrain-based model, integrating functional medicine with a biopsychosocial lens. Now, in Part II, we begin to reconstruct—a more expansive, systems-oriented, and integrative view of human health.

We will explore emerging scientific insights that point to a deeper intelligence within the human body—an intelligence expressed through dynamic networks, rhythmic communication, and a constant interplay between structure and energy. Systems biology, terrain theory, the microbiome, bioenergetics, and quantum-level organization are not treated here as abstract theories, but as living frameworks with practical applications for healing.

It is important to clarify that my intent is not to claim expertise in scientific fields outside my formal training, nor to dilute complex theories into oversimplified concepts. Rather, this work seeks to build bridges—connecting knowledge across disciplines to create a coherent, accessible framework for healing. Where concepts may appear esoteric or obscure, they will be clearly defined so that both novice and advanced readers can engage meaningfully with the material.

Some of the ideas presented in this part go beyond the conventional scope of psychological or medical practice. They are shared here with discernment and integrity—not to diagnose or prescribe, but to expand the conversation and empower critical thinking. Peer-reviewed research, interdisciplinary science, and clinical observation will be brought together to explore the body as more than a machine—as an intelligent ecosystem informed by energy, frequency, and coherence.

The ultimate purpose of Part II is to support a paradigm shift—from a reductionist model of health to a systems-based, consciousness-aware perspective. From this more expansive foundation, the possibilities for healing deepen and multiply.

When we try to pick out anything by itself,
we find it hitched to everything else in the Universe.

— John Muir

Chapter 4

The Body as an Intelligent Ecosystem

This chapter opens the doorway into a new way of understanding the body—not as a sum of disconnected parts, but as a dynamic, self-organizing ecosystem embedded within a larger web of life. Borrowing from the foundational insights of Dr. George Engel, father of the biopsychosocial model, we affirm that an individual does not exist in a vacuum, but in constant interaction with other organisms and environments. We will explore the foundational concepts of systems biology, terrain theory, and the human microbiome, revealing how health is not a fixed state but a continuously evolving process of adaptation, communication, and ecological participation.

It is important here to make a key distinction: although the gut resides within the physical body, the contents of its lumen are technically considered outside the internal environment. This is because nutrients, microbes, and toxins in the gastrointestinal tract do not become truly 'internal' until they cross the intestinal barrier into the bloodstream or lymphatic system. The gut, then, functions as a highly selective interface—simultaneously a site of nutrient exchange, microbial communication, and immune vigilance. As Lucas (2018) point out, the gut lining serves as a physiological and symbolic boundary between self and world. Its integrity is central to understanding how the terrain is shaped not only by what we consume but by how our body interprets and responds to that input. Research in mucosal immunology and barrier function further supports this view, emphasizing the role of intestinal permeability in immune dysregulation and chronic inflammation (Fasano, 2012).

We will then begin to explore the energetic dimension of healing—introducing the scientific and clinical basis for concepts such as coherence, frequency, and bioenergetics. These terms may not be immediately self-explanatory to all readers, and that is perfectly okay. We are simply introducing them here as part of a broader narrative. As we move forward, each concept will be clearly defined, situated within relevant scientific theories and experimental findings, and explored in terms of its practical applications within clinical and therapeutic settings. These concepts are beyond theory—they are reshaping how we understand health in dynamic systems.

This chapter steps beyond the conventional domain of psychology, and readers are invited to engage with it using both discernment and curiosity. Some concepts introduced may feel unfamiliar, but they are grounded in emerging science and framed through a lens of clinical relevance. Readers are encouraged to consult qualified professionals when applying any new insights to health or therapeutic practice.

The purpose here is not to overstep, but to expand—to bring together knowledge streams that rarely intersect, and to offer a broader framework in which the mind, body, and surrounding field are seen as dynamically interwoven. Healing, in this view, is not imposed from the outside but cultivated from within a system capable of self-regulation, coherence, and transformation.

Systems Biology and Terrain Theory: The Body as a Living Network

To understand the body as an intelligent ecosystem, we must first step away from the industrial model of health that dominates conventional medicine. In that outdated framework, the body is treated like a machine—its organs viewed as interchangeable parts, its symptoms isolated and suppressed rather than understood. But biology, when studied through a systems lens, tells a very different story.

Systems biology invites us to see the body not as a linear sequence of cause and effect, but as a complex web of interdependent relationships. It recognizes that physiology does not operate in silos. Cells communicate with other cells. Organs influence other organs. Networks of signaling molecules, feedback loops, and information channels shape everything from inflammation to mood, immunity to gene expression. This systems-oriented approach has already begun to reshape fields as diverse as oncology, psychiatry, and stress-related disorders—offering tools to identify biomarkers and map the intricate biological networks underlying disease states (Cai et al., 2013; Mehta et al., 2015; Sprengel et al., 2025).

This holistic view finds a natural ally in terrain theory, which proposes that the internal environment of the body—its microbial landscape, redox state, nutrient availability, and energetic coherence—determines whether health is sustained or illness takes hold.

While Louis Pasteur is widely credited with establishing germ theory, he is said to have acknowledged later in life that the host environment plays a critical role in disease susceptibility. The well-known quote often attributed to him—"The microbe is nothing; the terrain is everything"—may not be his exact words, but it reflects a truth that his contemporary, Claude Bernard, strongly advocated. Pasteur reportedly admitted that Bernard might have been right. This shift—from focusing solely on the invading pathogen to considering the internal terrain—offers a powerful lens to understand why responses to the same virus, such as SARS-CoV-2, varied so dramatically. It is not just the presence of the microbe, but the condition of the host, that shapes the outcome.

Redox Balance and Terrain Health

The term *redox state* refers to the balance between oxidation and reduction reactions in the body. Oxidation involves the loss of electrons and the generation of reactive oxygen species (ROS), which in excess can cause cellular damage. Reduction involves the gain of electrons and is part of the body's antioxidant defense system. A healthy redox balance ensures that ROS are neutralized before they can harm tissues or disrupt cellular function. When this balance is lost—due to chronic stress, poor diet, environmental toxins, or mitochondrial dysfunction—oxidative stress arises, contributing to inflammation, immune dysregulation, and accelerated aging. Thus, the redox state serves as a key marker of terrain integrity and an organism's capacity to adapt to internal and external stressors.

As we have seen, terrain theory shifts the focus from "What pathogen caused this?" to "What conditions made the body susceptible?" This reframing invites inquiry into balance, resilience, and restoration. We no longer fight external invaders—we work to cultivate an internal environment where vitality thrives and resilience is restored.

This is not just conceptual—it reflects emerging research such as immunometabolism, bioinformatics, and neuropsychobiology, which affirm that terrain integrity influences systemic resilience (Yang et al., 2025; Martinis et al., 2025).

These integrative sciences invite us to explore how biological systems are shaped not just by chemical interactions, but also by signaling patterns, vibrational inputs, and fields of informational resonance—an inquiry we will expand in the next chapter.

Key Interdisciplinary Terms

• *Immunometabolism*: The study of how metabolic processes influence immune cell function and vice versa. This field explores how factors like nutrition, stress, and cellular energy impact inflammation, autoimmunity, and resilience.

• *Bioinformatics*: A discipline that uses computational tools to analyze large-scale biological data (like genomic or molecular network data). In systems medicine, bioinformatics helps uncover how complex biological pathways interact to shape health or disease.

• *Neuropsychobiology*: An interdisciplinary field exploring how psychological processes, neural activity, and biological systems interact. It connects mental states to immune responses, hormonal regulation, and the microbiome—providing a framework for mind-body integration in health.

Modern systems biology echoes this wisdom. It recognizes that **health is not a fixed state but a dynamic process**— a constant negotiation between internal resilience and environmental inputs. Rather than focusing solely on cellular mechanisms, it emphasizes how biological systems interact to maintain balance and coherence—what we refer to as terrain repair.

Terrain repair is the restoration of harmony across interconnected systems. Whether at the cellular, metabolic, or microbial level, health emerges from their ability to communicate, adapt, and align. This concept of coherence will be explored more deeply in the next chapter—but here, it already stands as a guiding principle of terrain-based healing

This foundation sets the stage for our next layer of inquiry: how energy, frequency, and coherence shape and reflect the terrain of health. This terrain-based view of health naturally leads us to ask: what governs this internal harmony? How do cells, tissues, and networks know how to coordinate across time and space? The emerging answer points to coherence—an energetic signature we will explore more fully in what follows.

The Psychological Terrain: Mind, Stress, and Resilience

Yet before we go there, we must pause and reintroduce the psychological perspective. Health and disease are not merely biochemical or microbial phenomena—they are also shaped by how we perceive, process, and respond to the world around us. The capacity to handle adversity, to adapt and maintain internal balance in the face of external pressure, varies greatly from one person to another.

This is where the psychological terrain intersects with the biological. The experience of stress is not simply a reaction to objective threats, but a deeply personal and subjective appraisal of circumstances. Some individuals mount a flexible, resilient response; others may become overwhelmed by the same input, leading to dysregulation of the nervous, immune, or endocrine systems. These individual differences in perception, coping, and adaptability shape the internal environment just as much as diet or toxins do.

Resilience, then, is not merely a psychological trait—it is a biological capacity. This idea is supported by decades of research into stress physiology, neuroplasticity, and immune modulation. The concept of **allostatic load**—the cumulative biological cost of chronic stress—offers a scientific framework for understanding how stressors, when mismanaged or chronic, lead to long-term dysregulation (McEwen, 1998). Early life experiences and individual stress appraisals play a pivotal role in shaping these responses over a lifetime (Lupien et al., 2009).

Furthermore, resilience has been described as a dynamic process involving biological, psychological, and social dimensions that enable individuals to maintain or regain health despite adversity (Southwick et al., 2014). Research by Porges (2011) on **polyvagal theory** helps explain the physiological mechanisms of resilience, especially as they relate to autonomic nervous system regulation.

Polyvagal Theory

Developed by Dr. Stephen Porges, polyvagal theory describes how the autonomic nervous system is not just a binary on/off switch between stress and relaxation, but a complex hierarchy of neural responses. It introduces the concept of the vagus nerve as a key regulator of safety, connection, and threat detection. Polyvagal theory explains how social cues, trauma, and internal states shape our ability to self-regulate—and how chronic states of fight, flight, or freeze impact long-term health and resilience. Recent findings in psycho-neuroimmunology confirms that psychological stress can modulate immune function and inflammatory pathways with direct relevance to chronic disease (Slavich & Irwin, 2014).

Resilience is the ability of an organism to return to baseline after a challenge, to re-establish coherence when chaos disrupts the system. Terrain repair, then, includes not only restoring physical and biochemical balance but also enhancing the emotional and neurological flexibility that underlies true resilience. It strengthens the organism's capacity to return to equilibrium after a challenge and creates the conditions for transformation rather than mere compensation. Practices that regulate the nervous system—such as breathwork, somatic awareness, or heart-brain coherence training—do more than calm symptoms; they foster adaptive capacity and coherence, reinforcing the terrain as a foundation for lasting health and psychological growth.

Resilience is the body's ability to flex and adapt—to bend with pressure without breaking.

As we move forward, we will explore how these mental-emotional patterns are encoded in the body, and how they influence the terrain at multiple levels—from gene expression to gut microbiota, from neuroplasticity to immune modulation.

When we approach terrain repair from this integrative perspective, resilience is no longer just a trait to be cultivated—it becomes a reflection of restored coherence across the entire system. True healing transcends symptom relief; it activates transformation. It strengthens an individual's capacity to adapt, connect, and self-regulate. In this way, terrain repair expands the meaning of recovery, turning it into a foundation for renewal. And no, it does not require a bulldozer or a landscaping crew—just curiosity, compassion, and the willingness to tend the inner soil.

Epigenetics and the Nature–Nurture Dialogue

For decades, the field of psychology has grappled with the question: Are we shaped more by our biology (nature) or our environment (nurture)? This classic debate, central to psychological training and research, was given early form by Francis Galton in the 19th century and later examined in depth by Nicholas Pastore in his seminal 1950 article, "The Nature-Nurture Controversy." Pastore's work remains a cornerstone in doctoral psychology programs and framed the evolving understanding that neither genes nor environment act alone.

In recent decades, the rise of **epigenetics** has revolutionized this conversation. Epigenetics refers to the biological mechanisms—such as DNA methylation and histone modification— that regulate gene expression without altering the DNA sequence itself. These mechanisms are highly responsive to environmental signals including stress, nutrition, toxins, relational dynamics, and even belief systems. This means that while we may inherit certain genetic predispositions, their expression can be modulated—or even silenced—by our lived experience.

Epigenetic Mechanisms

• *DNA Methylation*: This process involves the addition of a methyl group to DNA, typically at cytosine bases. It acts like a dimmer switch, turning down the expression of genes without changing their sequence. Methylation is one way the body can silence genes that may otherwise contribute to inflammation, disease, or maladaptive patterns.

• *Histone Modification*: DNA is wrapped around proteins called histones. Chemical modifications to these histones (such as acetylation or methylation) affect how tightly DNA is packed, thereby influencing whether specific genes are accessible for expression. Looser packaging generally allows for more gene expression, while tighter packaging reduces it. Together, these mechanisms allow the body to regulate gene activity in response to the environment.

This is a powerful reframe for both clinicians and clients. Genetic potential is not a deterministic sentence. The internal terrain, shaped by daily choices and external influences, plays a defining role in whether a gene is expressed or remains dormant. Chronic stress, for example, can upregulate inflammatory genes, while meditation, movement, and nutrient sufficiency can downregulate genes associated with disease.

Dr. Bruce Lipton, a developmental biologist and one of the most visible public educators on epigenetics, has popularized this concept in ways that are empowering and accessible. In *The Biology of Belief*, he explains that our perception—especially unconscious beliefs—acts like a filter that shapes how our cells interpret the environment. This interpretation drives biochemical responses that ultimately influence gene expression.

While Lipton's work has been critiqued for simplifying the science, it offers a useful therapeutic bridge. For clients not drawn to academic discussions, the core message is transformative: *You are not a victim of your genes. You are the author of your biological story.*

Think of gene expression like a symphony: the DNA is the sheet music, but it is our lifestyle—our choices, environment, and beliefs—that conduct the orchestra. What gets played, and how beautifully, depends on the skill of that conductor.

Striking the right balance between scientific rigor and accessible delivery is an essential task for any practitioner or educator aiming to empower others. A clear, engaging explanation can often open doors that a technically perfect but dense presentation cannot. When we translate complex scientific insights into meaningful, relatable guidance, we meet people where they are—and that is often where real healing begins.

The Gut-Brain-Immune Axis Revisited

The idea that the gut is merely an organ of digestion is outdated. Modern research in systems biology, neurogastroenterology, and psychoneuroimmunology reveals the gut as a central hub in a triadic communication system involving the brain and immune system. This intricate axis, often referred to as the **gut-brain-immune axis**, plays a pivotal role in regulating mood, cognition, inflammation, and systemic resilience.

At the core of this system is the intestinal barrier—a selectively permeable lining that determines what enters the body and what is kept out. When this barrier becomes compromised, as in the case of intestinal permeability or "leaky gut," toxins, food antigens, and microbial products can cross into the bloodstream. This breach activates the immune system, leading to chronic low-grade inflammation, which is now recognized as a central driver of many chronic diseases, including anxiety, depression, autoimmune disorders, and neuro-degeneration (Fasano, 2012).

Intestinal Permeability (Leaky Gut)

Intestinal permeability refers to the loosened tight junctions between epithelial cells lining the gut wall. Under normal conditions, these junctions regulate what passes from the gut lumen into the bloodstream. Inflammatory stimuli, infections, poor diet, chronic stress, and dysbiosis can impair these junctions, allowing harmful substances to pass through. This triggers immune responses and systemic inflammation, altering the terrain and contributing to both physical and psychological dysfunction.

The vagus nerve—our bidirectional communication highway—further integrates gut and brain function. Signals from the gut microbiota influence brain chemistry, while emotional and psychological stress can alter gut motility, secretion, and microbial balance. This two-way relationship has major implications for both mental health and immune regulation.

Clinical practice increasingly incorporates this knowledge. For instance, patients with irritable bowel syndrome (IBS) often present with comorbid anxiety or depression. A holistic approach may include dietary interventions, gut-healing protocols, prebiotics, probiotics, and stress-reduction practices such as vagal nerve stimulation or breathwork. In cases of autoimmune disease, restoring gut integrity through anti-inflammatory nutrition, microbial rebalancing, and barrier repair (e.g., using glutamine, zinc carnosine, or immunoglobulin formulas) is now a foundational step in functional medicine protocols.

Research also suggests that gut microbiota composition affects neurodevelopment and may be implicated in neuropsychiatric conditions such as autism spectrum disorder, schizophrenia, and major depressive disorder (Cryan et al., 2019). As such, terrain-based therapies that include prebiotics, targeted probiotics, fermented foods, and environmental hygiene play a crucial role in restoring systemic balance.

The gut is also frequently referred to as the "second brain" due to the density of neurons and neurotransmitters located in the enteric nervous system, which governs gastrointestinal function. Remarkably, around 95% of the body's serotonin receptors are found in the gastrointestinal tract, not the brain (Gershon, 1998; Mawe & Hoffman, 2013). This has profound implications for understanding mental health conditions like depression and anxiety, which are often linked to imbalances in serotonin signaling.

Ultimately, the gut-brain-immune axis underscores the reality that our internal ecology is both sentient and self-organizing. To ignore the gut's role in psychological and immune health is to overlook one of the most profound and clinically actionable relationships in human biology.

Did you know? 95% of your serotonin receptors are in your gut—not in your brain.

References

Cai, Y., Huang, T., Chen, L., & Niu, B. (2013). Application of systems biology and bioinformatics methods in biochemistry and biomedicine. *BioMed Research International*, 2013, Article ID 651968. https://doi.org/10.1155/2013/651968

Cryan, J. F., O'Riordan, K. J., Cowan, C. S. M., Sandhu, K. V., Bastiaanssen, T. F. S., Boehme, M., Codagnone, M. G., Cussotto, S., Fulling, C., Golubeva, A. V., Guzzetta, K. E., Jaggar, M., Long-Smith, C. M., Lyte, J. M., Martin, J. A., Molinero-Perez, A., Moloney, G., Morelli, E., ... Dinan, T. G. (2019). The microbiota–gut–brain axis. *Physiological Reviews, 99*(4), 1877–2013. https://doi.org/10.1152/physrev.00018.2018

Fasano, A. (2012). Leaky gut and autoimmune diseases. *Clinical Reviews in Allergy & Immunology, 42*(1), 71–78. https://doi.org/10.1007/s12016-011-8291-x

Gershon, M. D. (1998). *The Second Brain: A Groundbreaking New Understanding of Nervous Disorders of the Stomach and Intestine*. Harper Perennial.

Lipton, B. H. (2005*). The Biology of Belief: Unleashing the Power of Consciousness, Matter & Miracles*. Hay House.

Lucas, G. (2018). Gut thinking: The gut microbiome and mental health beyond the head. *Microbial Ecology in Health & Disease, 29*(1), 1548250. https://doi.org/10.1080/16512235.2018.1548250

Lupien, S. J., McEwen, B. S., Gunnar, M. R., & Heim, C. (2009). Effects of stress throughout the lifespan on the brain, behaviour and cognition. *Nature Reviews Neuroscience, 10*(6), 434–445. https://doi.org/10.1038/nrn2639

Martinis, E., Tonon, S., Colamatteo, A., La Cava, A., Matarese, G., & Pucillo, C. E. M. (2025). B cell immunometabolism in health and disease. *Nature Immunology, 26*, 366–377. https://doi.org/10.1038/s41590-025-02102-0

Mawe, G. M., & Hoffman, J. M. (2013). Serotonin signalling in the gut—functions, dysfunctions and therapeutic targets. *Nature Reviews Gastroenterology & Hepatology, 10*(8), 473–486. https://doi.org/10.1038/nrgastro.2013.105

McEwen, B. S. (1998). Protective and damaging effects of stress mediators. *New England Journal of Medicine, 338*(3), 171–179. https://doi.org/10.1056/NEJM199801153380307

Mehta, D., et al. (2015). From genetics to systems biology of stress-related mental disorders. *Dialogues in Clinical Neuroscience, 17*(2), 125–135. https://www.ncbi.nlm.nih.gov/pmc/articles/PMC8456113/

Pastore, N. (1950). *The nature–nurture controversy. The Journal of Philosophy, 47*(17), 506. https://doi.org/10.2307/2020717

Porges, S. W. (2011). *The polyvagal theory: Neurophysiological foundations of emotions, attachment, communication, and self-regulation.* W. W. Norton & Company.

Slavich, G. M., & Irwin, M. R. (2014). From stress to inflammation and major depressive disorder: A social signal transduction theory of depression. *Psychological Bulletin, 140*(3), 774–815. https://doi.org/10.1037/a0035302

Southwick, S. M., Bonanno, G. A., Masten, A. S., Panter-Brick, C., & Yehuda, R. (2014). Resilience definitions, theory, and challenges: interdisciplinary perspectives. *European Journal of Psychotraumatology, 5*(1), 25338. https://doi.org/10.3402/ejpt.v5.25338

Werner, H. M. J., Mills, G. B., & Ram, P. T. (2014). Cancer systems biology: A peek into the future of patient care. *Nature Reviews Clinical Oncology, 11*, 167–176. https://doi.org/10.1038/nrclinonc.2014.6

Yang, R., Daigle, B. J., Jr., Rampersaud, R., & Schultebraucks, K. (2025). Editorial: Systems biology approaches to psychiatric and psychological disorders: Unraveling the complexities. *Frontiers in Genetics, 16*, 1547943. https://doi.org/10.3389/fgene.2025.1547943

If you want to find the secrets of the universe, think in terms of energy, frequency, and vibration.

— Nikola Tesla

Chapter 5

Frequency, Light, and the Energetic Terrain

As modern biology probes deeper into subcellular and electromagnetic processes, a new picture of human health is emerging—one that recognizes energy, not just chemistry, as a fundamental regulator of life. From the oscillatory behavior of proteins to the biophotonic emissions of cells, living systems function as frequency-based networks. These energetic dynamics, once considered outside the scope of conventional science, are now being explored through fields such as quantum biology (Popp & Yan, 2002), electrophysiology (Rubik et al., 2015), and integrative neuroscience (Peper et al., 2009).

Emerging Fields of Research

Quantum Biology: A field that explores how quantum principles—such as coherence, entanglement, and tunneling—may influence biological functions, including enzyme reactions, photosynthesis, and neural signaling.

Emerging Fields of Research (cont.)

Electrophysiology: The study of the electrical properties of biological cells and tissues. It includes the measurement of voltage changes or electric current flow, foundational to understanding neural activity, cardiac rhythms, and biofeedback techniques.

Integrative Neuroscience: A systems-level approach to understanding the brain and mind, combining molecular biology, psychology, energy medicine, and neurophysiology. This field emphasizes brain-body-environment interactions and the regulation of consciousness and healing.

This chapter explores the scientific and clinical foundations of vibrational medicine. It begins by establishing the role of frequency and coherence as fundamental organizing principles of the bioenergetic terrain. It then examines light-based therapies such as photobiomodulation, which harness specific wavelengths to activate mitochondrial repair and modulate neuroinflammation. Sound and vibration therapies follow, offering insight into how resonance and rhythm can reprogram stress physiology and synchronize neural patterns. The discussion continues into the realm of structured water and informational fields, where new evidence reveals how water acts as both carrier and amplifier of bioenergetic information.

These modalities are not speculative. They are grounded in measurable changes—enhanced heart rate variability, improved mitochondrial function, reduced neuroinflammatory markers, and increased parasympathetic tone. As this chapter will demonstrate, vibrational therapies represent more than tools of the future—they are already transforming clinical outcomes today.

Coherence, Frequency, and the Bioenergetic Terrain

The healer's art is not only to cure but to harmonize.

— Dr. Richard Gerber

Health, at its most fundamental level, is not only biological but energetic. Beneath the biochemistry of neurotransmitters and hormones lies a deeper realm of electromagnetic signaling, vibrational resonance, and oscillatory coherence. These subtle but powerful forces govern the way cells communicate, synchronize, and self-organize—and they form the unseen architecture of the bioenergetic terrain.

Frequency in Biology

Every living system operates within an electromagnetic field and emits characteristic frequencies. These frequencies regulate biological rhythms, cellular communication, and physiological timing. Disruptions in frequency can interfere with normal function, while restoring optimal frequencies—through natural or clinical means—may improve system-wide coherence and healing.

Coherence refers to a state of harmony within and between biological systems. In a coherent state, heart rhythms, brain waves, respiration, and autonomic activity are synchronized, allowing energy to flow efficiently across systems. This coherence is measurable, reproducible, and deeply linked to emotional regulation, physiological resilience, and even cognitive function (McCraty & Childre, 2010). Coherence is not simply relaxation; it is an *organized state of flow*—a condition in which the body's systems operate in harmony. Clients can learn to cultivate this state intentionally—through practices that regulate breath, focus attention, and activate heart-brain synchronization.

Coherence

In *biophysiology*, coherence describes the degree to which different systems of the body—such as the cardiovascular, nervous, and respiratory systems—are synchronized in their patterns. Coherent states are associated with optimal functioning, emotional stability, and regenerative capacity. Technologies developed by organizations like the HeartMath Institute have shown that coherence can be enhanced through breath regulation, heart-focused attention, and positive emotional states.

Frequency, meanwhile, refers to the rate at which energy oscillates. All biological systems generate and respond to electromagnetic fields—brainwaves, heart rhythms, and even cellular structures operate at specific frequencies. When these frequencies are disrupted—by environmental toxins, chronic stress, or trauma—the body's regulatory systems can fall out of sync. Conversely, restoring frequency balance, through modalities like sound therapy, PEMF (pulsed electromagnetic field therapy), or photobiomodulation, may help reestablish internal harmony (Markov, 2007; Hamblin, 2016).

Together, coherence and frequency represent essential dimensions of what could be called the **bioenergetic terrain**—an internal energetic environment that is dynamic, responsive, and integral to the body's ability to heal and adapt. In the emerging field of cardiac psychology, research highlights the bidirectional connection between emotional states and cardiovascular function. For instance, heart rate variability (HRV)—a key marker of autonomic flexibility—is now recognized as a psychophysiological indicator influenced by stress, trauma, and emotional regulation (Castelnuovo et al., 2015; Agorastos et al., 2023).

Heart Rate Variability (HRV)

HRV refers to the variation in time intervals between heartbeats. Higher HRV indicates greater adaptability and resilience of the autonomic nervous system. Low HRV has been linked to a range of mental health disorders, including anxiety, depression, and PTSD. Practices that improve HRV—such as breathwork, meditation, or heart-focused induction techniques—may enhance emotional regulation and coherence.

In Beyond Quantum Healing (BQH), practitioners often use a heart-mind coherence induction before formal hypnosis. This approach primes the nervous system, creating a relaxed yet alert state that facilitates deeper access to subconscious and intuitive realms. Such coherence practices are more than mere preparation—they reflect a foundational principle: that healing occurs most effectively in states of synchronization between mind, body, and heart—an internal energetic environment that is dynamic, responsive, and integral to the body's ability to heal and adapt. Although not yet fully embraced by conventional medicine, this field draws on a growing body of literature in electrophysiology, quantum biology, and integrative neuroscience (Rubik et al., 2015; Peper et al., 2009).

Emerging technologies in voice frequency analysis—such as those used in the Genius Insight biofeedback system—offer an example of how sound and vibration can be harnessed to assess and potentially recalibrate the bioenergetic terrain. These systems analyze vocal recordings using Fast Fourier Transform (FFT) algorithms to identify energetic imbalances reflected in voice patterns. The app then generates customized sound frequencies, tones, or affirmations aimed at re-establishing internal coherence. While these tools remain outside conventional clinical practice, they are increasingly used in complementary settings by integrative health practitioners and therapists as adjunctive biofeedback interventions.

Fast Fourier Transform (FFT) in Voice Analysis

FFT is a mathematical algorithm that decomposes complex signals—like voice recordings—into their individual frequency components. This allows systems like Genius Insight to detect patterns or imbalances in frequency that may correspond to stress states, organ systems, or emotional imprints. The output can then be used to deliver personalized frequencies designed to restore balance or coherence.

Such tools are not diagnostic, but exploratory—and when thoughtfully integrated into a broader therapeutic framework, they can offer valuable insight into a client's energetic terrain. By analyzing voice patterns and extracting frequency data, therapists may gain a deeper understanding of underlying stress signatures or emotional imprints that might not be immediately accessible through conventional assessment alone.

For example, a practitioner working with a client experiencing anxiety might use a voice frequency scan via Genius Insight. The app may highlight dysregulation in frequencies associated with emotional regulation or specific organ systems. In response, the practitioner could select a personalized audio program—containing sound frequencies, energetic tones, or affirmations—designed to support recalibration. When used in conjunction with talk therapy, nervous system regulation techniques, or mindfulness interventions, such tools may deepen client engagement and accelerate progress.

In this context, voice analysis becomes a form of real-time biofeedback, allowing both practitioner and client to track subtle shifts in the energetic field over time. Especially within models that value resonance, frequency, and vibrational alignment, such technology provides a bridge between intuition and measurable data—helping to translate subtle information into therapeutic action.

As we learn more about how energy shapes matter—and how frequency guides form—we expand the vocabulary of healing from one of chemistry alone to one of vibration, resonance, and informational alignment (Rubik et al., 2015; Peper et al., 2009).

Recent clinical findings have further validated this energetic perspective. Vibroacoustic stimulation, for instance, offers a practical application of frequency medicine using sound-induced vibrations delivered through the body to influence physiological and psychological states. A recent study on the effects of vibroacoustic stimulation found that it significantly reduced physiological stress markers, increased parasympathetic activity, and improved cognitive performance in participants exposed to stress-inducing tasks (Löser et al., 2024). These findings support the view that low-frequency vibration, properly calibrated, can entrain the nervous system and induce a state of coherence—contributing to improved regulation of emotional and cognitive responses.

Vibroacoustic Therapy (VAT)

Vibroacoustic Therapy is a form of sound-based treatment that delivers low-frequency vibrations (typically 30–120 Hz) to the body through speakers embedded in specialized chairs or mats. These vibrations stimulate the body's tissues and nervous system, promoting relaxation, reducing muscle tension, and enhancing autonomic balance. Clinical research has shown VAT to be effective in managing stress, anxiety, chronic pain, and neurodevelopmental conditions by facilitating coherence between physiological and psychological processes.

Light Therapy as Frequency Medicine

In addition to sound-based interventions, light itself functions as a potent carrier of biological information. Photobiomodulation (PBM)— primarily the therapeutic use of red and near-infrared (NIR) light—is gaining ground as a non-invasive modality that delivers coherent light to tissues in order to stimulate healing, modulate inflammation, and restore cellular energy balance. By targeting mitochondria, PBM influences the production of ATP (adenosine triphosphate), alters gene expression, and activates a cascade of biochemical signals that promote regeneration and reduce oxidative stress (Hamblin, 2016).

Photobiomodulation (PBM)

Photobiomodulation is a light-based therapy that uses red or near-infrared wavelengths (typically between 600–1000 nm) to influence cellular function. The absorbed light stimulates mitochondrial respiration, leading to increased ATP production and cellular repair. PBM has shown promise in managing pain, inflammation, depression, traumatic brain injury, and neurodegenerative conditions.

Recent meta-analyses and randomized controlled trials have confirmed PBM's efficacy in alleviating depressive symptoms (Ji et al., 2024; Shirkavand et al., 2023). Functional imaging studies suggest that light applied to the forehead can modulate activity in prefrontal cortical regions implicated in mood regulation. Beyond mood disorders, PBM is also being explored in the treatment of Alzheimer's disease and Parkinson's disease, where it appears to influence neuroinflammatory markers and improve cognitive function (Lim, 2024).

What makes PBM particularly relevant in the context of bioenergetic medicine is its capacity to entrain tissue-level coherence. Just as sound can synchronize neuronal oscillations, light can harmonize metabolic processes and restore cellular communication. From personal experience, red and near-infrared (NIR) light therapy has been effective for post-exercise recovery, likely through its role in enhancing collagen production and reducing inflammation. It also supports mitochondrial function, helping to alleviate fatigue.

These applications are now being explored for patients with chronic pain or multiple sclerosis (MS), not only to improve cellular function but to enhance overall quality of life. Notably, a recent review article has evaluated the role of low-level laser therapy—a form of PBM—in MS treatment, highlighting its ability to reduce inflammation, improve nerve function, and potentially delay disease progression (Hosseinzadeh Khannazer et al., 2021), thereby enhancing overall quality of life. The sessions themselves offer a moment of rest and coherence—important in both physiological and psychological healing.

Light is a nutrient for the body. It is absorbed by every cell and used to stimulate healing and balance.

— Dr. Michael Hamblin

It is important to distinguish PBM from other light-based interventions, such as bright light therapy used for seasonal affective disorder (SAD). While both approaches rely on light to influence biological systems, their mechanisms differ significantly: PBM targets mitochondrial pathways using specific wavelengths to influence cellular energy production and repair, whereas bright light therapy modulates circadian rhythms through retinal stimulation and hormonal signaling. Each approach holds promise, but they operate through different mechanisms and clinical intentions.

Resonance and Entrainment

Resonance occurs when an object or system vibrates in response to a matching frequency. *Entrainment* describes the synchronization of rhythmic cycles—such as a metronome aligning with another. In biology, entrainment helps coordinate internal rhythms, such as heartbeat, respiration, and neural oscillations, with external stimuli like music or environmental cues.

As the field evolves, light therapy devices are becoming increasingly sophisticated. Manufacturers—particularly in the Shenzhen region of China—are now producing systems that deliver multiple frequencies in different color combinations, each corresponding to specific therapeutic intentions. For instance, blue light therapy is used to treat acne, sun damage, and actinic keratosis (a form of precancerous skin lesion) by targeting and killing bacteria, while also rejuvenating the skin. Yellow light therapy is used for more superficial treatments, such as improving skin texture and reducing redness and pigmentation. These colored light therapies are often used in dermatological and aesthetic settings but are gradually finding their place in holistic therapy practices as well.

Near-infrared (NIR) wavelengths penetrate the deepest, making them particularly effective for connective tissue repair and mitochondrial activation. This deeper penetration capacity makes red and NIR light therapies uniquely suited for musculoskeletal issues, wound healing, and chronic fatigue management—expanding the therapeutic reach of photobiomodulation beyond the skin to include systemic, energetic, and psychological benefits.

In integrative practice, PBM is increasingly paired with other coherence-based modalities such as meditation, breathwork, or guided imagery to enhance receptivity and support nervous system regulation. These synergistic applications reflect a broader view of healing as the restoration of coherence across biological, psychological, and energetic systems.

As technology continues to advance, multi-wavelength and color-modulated light therapies are providing even more nuanced opportunities for individualized treatment strategies, rooted in both clinical science and vibrational principles. Just as sound can synchronize neuronal oscillations, light can harmonize metabolic processes and restore cellular communication. These synergistic applications align with a broader view of healing as the restoration of coherence across biological, psychological, and energetic systems.

As at-home red light devices become more accessible, photobiomodulation offers not only a therapeutic intervention, but a self-directed tool. Clients can learn to support their own energetic terrain, integrating light therapy into personal practices that promote coherence and resilience.

Sound, Vibration, and the Rhythms of Health

Sound is one of the most accessible and scientifically validated gateways into the realm of vibrational medicine. As oscillating energy, sound operates through pressure waves and frequency patterns that are both measurable and deeply influential on biological systems. When sound waves interact with a medium—air, water, or tissue—they generate resonance, entrainment, and rhythmic coherence. These principles, long established in physics (Clayton, 2001; Thaut & McIntosh, 2014), are now being explored in neuroscience, cardiology, and trauma therapy.

Frequency plus intention equals healing.
— Jonathan Goldman

Cymatics—the visual study of sound—demonstrates how frequency can organize matter into complex geometric patterns. Pioneered by Hans Jenny, cymatics involves applying sound to a medium like water or sand to reveal geometric, often mandala-like forms. These experiments suggest that the body—composed largely of fluid—may respond to sound through similar pattern formation and cellular reorganization.

Cymatics

Cymatics is the study of visible sound vibration. It uses sound frequencies to animate particulate matter or liquids into intricate geometries. These patterns illustrate how frequency acts as an organizing principle in physical and biological systems.

The human body operates through multiple rhythmic systems, including circadian rhythms (daily sleep-wake cycles), ultradian rhythms (shorter cycles such as hormonal or attentional shifts), and infradian rhythms (longer cycles such as the menstrual cycle or lunar phases). These rhythms are governed by internal biological clocks and are sensitive to environmental cues such as light, temperature, and sound (Buijs & Kalsbeek, 2001; Foster & Kreitzman, 2017). Disruptions in these natural rhythms have been linked to a wide range of physiological and psychological disorders. Synchronizing biological rhythms through sound, light, and behavioral entrainment supports homeostasis, nervous system balance, and emotional regulation. These effects are increasingly supported by research in chronobiology, music therapy, and neurophysiology, demonstrating how rhythmic alignment improves heart rate variability, stress resilience, and mood regulation (Thaut & McIntosh, 2014; McCraty & Childre, 2010; Foster & Kreitzman, 2017).

At the neurological level, brainwaves—measured in hertz—reflect distinct states of consciousness. Delta (0.5–4 Hz) is associated with deep sleep and cellular repair. Theta (4–8 Hz) supports creativity and subconscious access. Alpha (8–13 Hz) is linked to relaxed alertness. Beta (13–30 Hz) corresponds to active thought and focus, while Gamma (>30 Hz) integrates higher cognitive function.

Hypnotherapy and Brainwave States

Hypnotherapy involves guiding the client into a trance-like state where brainwaves typically shift from beta (conscious thinking) to alpha (relaxed alertness) or theta (deep relaxation and memory access). These brainwave states increase receptivity to therapeutic suggestions, enable emotional processing, and support reprogramming of limiting beliefs. Techniques such as guided visualization, regression therapy, and subconscious reframing are often used in this altered state to facilitate psychological and energetic transformation.

Techniques that induce or entrain specific brainwave states—such as meditation, binaural beats, hypnotherapy, or rhythmic drumming—may facilitate healing by promoting alignment with these natural frequencies.

Brainwave States

Brainwaves are rhythmic electrical patterns generated by neural activity. Each frequency band corresponds to a different state of consciousness and function. Modalities like sound healing or binaural beats aim to guide the brain into specific states—such as theta for trauma integration or alpha for stress reduction (Wahbeh et al., 2007; Gao et al., 2014).

Heart rate variability (HRV), discussed earlier, is another rhythmic marker that reflects nervous system adaptability. Entrainment of HRV through auditory stimulation, such as coherent breathing with music, can stabilize autonomic function and support emotional regulation.

Sound-based modalities are increasingly supported by both clinical studies and practitioner experience. Binaural beats use slightly different frequencies in each ear to produce a perceived third frequency in the brain, facilitating entrainment to desired brain-wave states (Wahbeh et al., 2007; Gao et al., 2014). Singing bowls, tuning forks, overtone chanting, and sound baths produce harmonic vibrations that resonate with tissue and the nervous system (Goldsby et al., 2017; Porges, 2011).

Vibroacoustic therapy (VAT), already discussed, uses low-frequency sound waves delivered through the body to induce relaxation, reduce pain, and improve autonomic regulation. Its use in clinical settings for stress, chronic pain, and neurodevelopmental disorders demonstrates the practical impact of sound on health.

The vagus nerve—central to Polyvagal Theory—responds strongly to harmonic auditory input (Porges, 2011; Groves & Brown, 2005). Vocalizations such as humming, toning, or chanting can stimulate the vagus nerve and shift the nervous system into parasympathetic dominance. These self-generated sounds are simple, safe, and effective tools for regulating the emotional brain, contributing to improved vagal tone and emotional regulation in both clinical and self-care contexts (Snow et al., 2018).

The Vagus Nerve and Sound

The *vagus nerve* is the longest cranial nerve and plays a major role in autonomic balance. Auditory stimulation—especially low-frequency, rhythmic, or harmonic sounds—activates the vagus through both the ear canal and vocal pathways. Practices like humming, singing, or listening to soothing music can enhance vagal tone and support emotional resilience (Porges, 2011; Brinthaupt et al., 2019).

Clinical research supports the use of music therapy for conditions such as chronic pain, Alzheimer's disease, PTSD, and anxiety. For example, structured music interventions have been shown to reduce cortisol, improve mood, and enhance memory recall in dementia patients (Chanda & Levitin, 2013; Fang et al., 2017). Case studies also highlight profound emotional releases and trauma resolution during sound healing sessions (Warth et al., 2015; Aalbers et al., 2017).

Clinical Applications of Sound

Studies have found that music therapy and vibrational sound interventions can reduce anxiety, support trauma processing, lower inflammation markers, and improve cognitive function in neurodegenerative diseases (Chanda & Levitin, 2013; Aalbers et al., 2017). These results offer empirical support for sound as a legitimate therapeutic tool.

Sound, more than any other frequency-based modality, provides a bridge between ancient practices and modern science. Its effects are measurable, its applications diverse, and its presence universal. As a vibrational medicine, sound invites us to explore coherence not only within our bodies, but with the world around us. Simple practices like chanting, humming, or listening to binaural beats offer accessible tools for individuals to shift their internal state and support their own healing terrain.

YOU ARE THE FREQUENCY GENERATOR

You are not only affected by external frequencies—you emit them. Your heartbeat, breath, and brainwaves generate patterns that influence your physiology and shape the energy field around you. Every thought, feeling, and intention becomes part of this signal. Healing begins when you recognize yourself as a source, not just a receiver—capable of tuning your own terrain.

Structured Water and Informational Fields

Water is far more than a passive solvent for biochemical reactions. Recent discoveries suggest that it acts as a dynamic carrier of vibrational and informational content, capable of storing energy, transmitting frequencies, and influencing the structure and function of surrounding molecules. Within the human body—composed of over 99% water molecules by number—these properties have profound implications for healing, cellular signaling, and terrain regulation.

Side note: While water accounts for about 60% of the human body by weight and approximately 70% by volume, it makes up over 99% of the body's molecules. This often surprises people, but it reflects the molecular scale: water molecules are tiny, yet overwhelmingly abundant compared to proteins, fats, and other cellular components.

One of the leading contributors to this paradigm is Dr. Gerald Pollack, whose research on the "fourth phase" of water—also known as Exclusion Zone (EZ) water—has redefined our understanding of water's role in biology. Unlike bulk water, EZ water forms adjacent to hydrophilic surfaces and exhibits properties of a quasi-crystalline, gel-like phase. It holds charge separation, stores light energy, and supports coherent domains that facilitate biological communication (Pollack, 2013).

Exclusion Zone (EZ) Water

EZ water refers to a structured phase of water discovered by Dr. Gerald Pollack. It forms next to hydrophilic surfaces and has distinct physical properties—such as negative charge, increased viscosity, and the ability to absorb light. EZ water is thought to act as a biological battery, converting light into usable energy and structuring the internal environment of cells.

This idea of water as an energetic matrix was also explored by French immunologist Dr. Jacques Benveniste, who demonstrated that biological information could be transferred via highly diluted solutions—even in the apparent absence of molecules. His controversial work, later expanded by Nobel laureate

Luc Montagnier, proposed that water could retain a "memory" of substances it once contained, a concept long embedded in homeopathic traditions and now partially validated by electromagnetic transmission experiments (Montagnier et al., 2015).

Another key voice in the field is Professor Emilio del Giudice, whose theoretical work in quantum field theory suggests that water molecules can form coherent domains that act as resonant structures. These domains allow water to support low-frequency electromagnetic fields that propagate information throughout biological tissues—creating a vibrational interface between energy and matter (Del Giudice & Tedeschi, 2009).

Water Memory

Water memory refers to the hypothesis that water can store and transmit information about substances it has encountered, even after serial dilution. Though initially dismissed by mainstream science, this idea has regained traction through modern studies in biophysics and quantum coherence (Montagnier et al., 2015; Del Giudice & Preparata, 1998).

These properties position water not just as a carrier of nutrients and waste but as an active participant in vibrational healing. Structured water systems—whether produced through vortexing, light exposure, or electromagnetic imprinting—are now being studied for their potential to improve hydration, enhance redox signaling, and support cellular coherence (Vallée et al., 2005).

Vortexing

Vortexing is a technique that involves swirling water into a spiral motion, mimicking the natural flow patterns found in rivers and tornadoes. This dynamic movement is believed to help reorganize water molecules into a more coherent structure, enhancing its energetic properties and potential bioavailability.

Electromagnetic Imprinting

Electromagnetic imprinting refers to the process of encoding specific frequencies or informational patterns into a medium—such as water—using low-level electromagnetic fields. This is believed to allow water to store vibrational signatures that influence cellular communication and terrain regulation.

Redox Signaling

Redox signaling involves the transmission of cellular messages through reactive oxygen and nitrogen species (ROS and RNS). These molecules help regulate inflammation, mitochondrial function, and cell repair. Disruptions in redox balance are associated with aging and chronic disease, while enhanced redox signaling supports resilience and adaptation.

In therapeutic contexts, structured water is used to optimize internal terrain and facilitate informational transfer. One example includes the Genius Insight app, which allows practitioners to imprint water with personalized frequencies using remedy plates embedded with copper coils. These imprinting plates are designed to carry the energetic signatures generated by the app, transferring them into water to support vibrational alignment and coherence (Genius Bio-feedback, 2025).

Devices like the Analemma wand or UMH Live systems claim to imprint coherent frequencies into water, often through geometry, vortex motion, or quartz structuring. While more research is needed, anecdotal evidence and emerging biophysics suggest these methods can influence physiological parameters such as mitochondrial function, inflammation, and even mood states (Zhang et al., 2018).

Cellular Coherence

Cellular coherence describes a state in which cellular functions—such as metabolism, communication, and repair—are synchronized and efficient. Coherent cells exhibit enhanced energy flow, reduced oxidative stress, and more effective signaling, contributing to overall physiological harmony and health.

Some researchers and clinicians have hypothe-sized that specific sound frequencies—especially those generated through voice biofeedback programs like Genius Insight—may influence the structure of water not only extracellularly, but within and around the cell membrane itself. While empirical validation remains limited, this emerging idea draws from studies in **sonoporation**, acoustic resonance, and water structuring. The notion that intracellular water may be responsive to vibrational input raises exciting questions for future research into the dynamic interface between sound, water, and cellular energetics.

New Consideration for Research

The use of sound frequencies to alter water structure at the intracellular level—particularly in response
to personalized vocal input—merits further scientific
inquiry. Bioresonance studies suggest that cells may
resonate with specific electromagnetic and vibrational
inputs (Mureşan et al., 2022; Vallée et al., 2005). If
these principles can be extended to structured water,
as proposed by Pollack (2013), this could open a new
frontier in understanding how voice-derived frequencies imprint coherence into biological systems, potentially regulating terrain from the inside out.

Structured Water and Therapeutic Terrain
Structured water refers to water that has been physically or energetically altered to adopt a coherent, organized state. Methods include vortexing, exposure to
light, sound frequencies, or contact with specific geometries. Structured water may improve hydration, support mitochondrial function, and facilitate terrain repair by enhancing vibrational communication at the
cellular level.

The implications are profound: if water indeed
serves as a medium for frequency storage and biological coherence, then terrain-based medicine must account for the quality, structure, and informational
content of the body's water systems. Researchers like
Pollack, Del Giudice, and Montagnier—all pioneers
in their fields—invite us to move beyond reductionism toward an integrated view in which water, ener-

gy, and consciousness are inseparably linked in the healing process.

Water is not a passive substance. It responds to energy, stores information, and may be the most sensitive medium of all life.

— Dr. Gerald Pollack

Vibrational Medicine: Bridging Energy and Healing

The concept of vibrational medicine, most notably articulated by physician Richard Gerber in his seminal work *Vibrational Medicine: The #1 Handbook of Subtle-Energy Therapies* (first published in 1988, revised in 2001), provides an integrative framework for understanding healing beyond the molecular level. Gerber proposed that the human being is not only a biochemical entity, but a complex, multi-layered energetic system composed of physical, etheric, emotional, mental, and spiritual fields. These subtle energy fields—while not directly measurable by conventional instruments—may govern physiological coherence, inform cellular communication, and serve as blueprints for health and disease.

Having explored how light, sound, and water carry vibrational information, we now arrive at the overarching concept that binds them together: vibrational medicine.

Gerber's model incorporates ancient traditions like Chinese medicine and Ayurvedic concepts alongside modern physics and emerging biofield science. He explained how therapies such as homeopathy, acupuncture, color therapy, sound healing, and crystal work operate through resonance and frequency, targeting these energetic layers to promote systemic balance. In doing so, vibrational medicine bridges esoteric healing traditions with contemporary medical paradigms.

Vibrational Medicine

Vibrational medicine is a form of integrative healing based on the idea that all matter—including the human body—vibrates at specific frequencies. Dis-ease is viewed as a distortion or disharmony in this vibrational pattern. Therapies aim to restore balance by introducing healing frequencies that resonate with the body's energy fields. These may be delivered through sound, light, electromagnetic fields, or intention. Richard Gerber, MD, defined it as a method of healing that "works through the energetic field to harmonize and guide the physical body back to health."

In health psychology and other forms of integrative practice, vibrational approaches may be used to complement cognitive, behavioral, or somatic therapies. For instance, a therapist might use tuning forks or binaural beats during trauma work to entrain the brain and nervous system into a more receptive state. A health coach could integrate crystal resonance tools to support emotional balancing during life transitions. Breathwork, guided visualization, and voice toning—forms of vibrational engagement—are increasingly used to shift emotional states, recalibrate energetic patterns, and amplify the therapeutic process.

These approaches resonate with the growing view that healing is not only a physical or psychological process, but also an energetic one. As quantum biology and subtle energy research evolve, vibrational medicine offers a promising language—and toolkit—for practitioners bridging intuition, science, and human transformation.

Water has a memory and carries within it our thoughts and prayers.

— Masaru Emoto

References

Aalbers, S., Fusar-Poli, L., Freeman, R. E., Spreen, M., Ket, J. C., Vink, A. C., & van Haren, N. E. (2017). Music therapy for depression. *Cochrane Database of Systematic Reviews, 2017*(11), CD004517. https://doi.org/10.1002/14651858.CD004517.pub3

Agorastos, A., Mansueto, A. C., Hager, T., Pappi, E., Garidiklioti, A., & Stieglitz, O. (2023). Heart rate variability as a translational dynamic biomarker of altered autonomic function in health and psychiatric disease. *Biomedicines, 11*(6), 1591. https://doi.org/10.3390/biomedicines11061591

Buijs, R. M., & Kalsbeek, A. (2001). Hypothalamic integration of central and peripheral clocks. *Nature Reviews Neuroscience, 2*(7), 521–526. https://doi.org/10.1038/35081582

Cassano, P., Petrie, S. R., Mischoulon, D., Cusin, C., & Hamblin, M. R. (2024). Review of low-level light therapy in mood disorders. *Journal of Affective Disorders, 338*, 188–198. https://doi.org/10.1016/j.jad.2023.10.047

Castelnuovo, G., et al. (2015). Psychological aspects of heart rate variability in stress-related disorders. *BioPsychoSocial Medicine, 9*(1), 10. https://doi.org/10.1186/s13030-015-0034-4

Chanda, M. L., & Levitin, D. J. (2013). The neurochemistry of music. *Trends in Cognitive Sciences, 17*(4), 179–193. https://doi.org/10.1016/j.tics.2013.02.007

Clayton, M. (2001). *Time in Indian Music: Rhythm, Metre and Form in North Indian Rag Performance*. Oxford University Press.

Del Giudice, E., & Preparata, G. (1998). Coherent dynamics in water as a possible explanation of biological memories. *Journal of Biological Physics, 20*(1), 105–116. https://doi.org/10.1007/BF00700426

Del Giudice, E., & Tedeschi, A. (2009). Water and autocatalysis in living matter. *Electromagnetic Biology and Medicine, 28*(1), 46–52. https://doi.org/10.1080/15368370802708728

Fang, R., Ye, S., Huangfu, J., Calimag, D. P., & Wang, S. (2017). Music therapy is a potential intervention for cognition in Alzheimer's disease. *Frontiers in Aging Neuroscience, 9*, 110. https://doi.org/10.3389/fnagi.2017.00110

Foster, R. G., & Kreitzman, L. (2017). *Circadian Rhythms: A Very Short Introduction.* Oxford University Press.

Gao, X., Cao, H., Ming, D., Qi, H., Wang, X., & Zhou, P. (2014). Analysis of EEG activity in response to binaural beats with different frequencies. *International Journal of Psychophysiology, 94*(3), 399–406. https://doi.org/10.1016/j.ijpsycho.2014.10.001

Gerber, R. (2001). *Vibrational medicine: The #1 handbook of subtle-energy therapies* (3rd ed.). Bear & Company. ISBN: 978-1-879181-58-8.

Goldsby, T. L., Goldsby, M. E., McWalters, M., & Mills, P. J. (2017). Effects of singing bowl sound meditation on mood, tension, and well-being. *Journal of Evidence-Based Integrative Medicine, 22*(4), 401–408. https://doi.org/10.1177/2156587216668109

Groves, D. A., & Brown, V. J. (2005). Vagal nerve stimulation: A review of its applications and potential mechanisms that mediate its clinical effects. *Neuroscience & Biobehavioral Reviews, 29*(3), 493–500. https://doi.org/10.1016/j.neubiorev.2005.01.004

Hamblin, M. R. (2016). Shining light on the head: Photobiomodulation for brain disorders. *BBA Clinical, 6*, 113–124. https://doi.org/10.1016/j.jad.2021.08.059

Hosseinzadeh Khannazer, N., Kazem Arki, M.,
Keramatinia, A., & Rezaei-Tavirani, M. (2021).
The role of low-level laser therapy in the treatment
of multiple sclerosis: A review study. *Journal of
Lasers in Medical Sciences, 12*(e88).
https://doi.org/10.34172/jlms.2021.88

Ji, Q., Yan, S., Ding, J., Zeng, X., Liu, Z., Zhou, T., Wu,
Z., Wei, W., Li, H., Liu, S., & Ai, S. (2024).
Photobiomodulation improves depression symptoms: a systematic review and meta-analysis of
randomized controlled trials. *Frontiers in Psychiatry, 14*, 1267415.
https://doi.org/10.3389/fpsyt.2023.1267415

Lim, L. (2024). Modifying Alzheimer's disease patho-
physiology with photobiomodulation: model, evidence, and future with EEG-guided intervention.
Frontiers in Neurology, 15, 1407785.
https://doi.org/10.3389/fneur.2024.1407785

Löser, C., et al. (2024). Vibroacoustic stimulation and
stress modulation. *Frontiers in Human Neuroscience, 18*, 235.
https://doi.org/10.3389/fnhum.2024.00235

Markov, M. S. (2007). Expanding use of pulsed electromagnetic field therapies. *Electromagnetic Biology and Medicine, 26*(3), 257–274.
https://doi.org/10.1080/15368370701580806

McCraty, R., & Childre, D. (2010). Coherence: Bridging
personal, social, and global health. *Alternative
Therapies in Health and Medicine, 16*(4), 10–
24. [No DOI available — published in print only]

Montagnier, L., Del Giudice, E., Aïssa, J., Lavallee, C.,
Motschwiller, S., Capolupo, A., Polcari, A., Ro-
mano, P., Tedeschi, A., & Vitiello, G. (2015).
Transduction of DNA information through water
and electromagnetic waves. *Electromagnetic Biology and Medicine, 34*(2), 106–112.
https://doi.org/10.3109/15368378.2015.1036072

Muresan, D., Voidăzan, S., Salcudean, A., Bodo, C. R., & Grecu, I. G. (2022). Bioresonance, an alternative therapy for mild and moderate depression. *Experimental and Therapeutic Medicine, 23*(4), 264. https://doi.org/10.3892/etm.2022.11190

Peper, E., Harvey, R., & Takebayashi, N. (2009). Biofeedback: An evidence-based approach in clinical practice. *Japanese Journal of Biofeedback Research, 36*(1), 3–10. https://doi.org/10.20595/jjbf.36.1_3

Pollack, G. H. (2013). *The Fourth Phase of Water: Beyond Solid, Liquid, and Vapor*. Ebner & Sons Publishers.

Popp, F. A., & Yan, Y. (2002). Delayed luminescence of biological systems in terms of coherent states. *Physics Letters A, 293*(1–2), 93–97. https://doi.org/10.1016/S0375-9601(01)00752-3

Porges, S. W. (2011). *The Polyvagal Theory: Neurophysiological Foundations of Emotions, Attachment, Communication, and Self-regulation*. W.W. Norton & Company.

Rubik, B., Muehsam, D., Hammerschlag, R., & Jain, S. (2015). Biofield science and healing: History, terminology, and concepts. *Global Advances in Health and Medicine, 4*(Suppl), 8–14. https://doi.org/10.7453/gahmj.2015.038.suppl

Shirkavand, A., Akhavan Tavakoli, M., & Ebrahimpour, Z. (2023). A brief review of low-level light therapy in depression disorder. *Journal of Lasers in Medical Sciences, 14*(55), e55. https://doi.org/10.34172/jlms.2023.55

Snow, S., Bernardi, N. F., Sabet-Kassouf, N., Moran, D., & Lehmann, A. (2018). Exploring the experience and effects of vocal toning. *Journal of Music Therapy, 55*(2), 221–250. https://doi.org/10.1093/jmt/thy003

Thaut, M. H., & McIntosh, G. C. (2014). Neurologic music therapy in stroke rehabilitation. *Current Physical Medicine and Rehabilitation Reports, 2,* 106–113. https://doi.org/10.1007/s40141-014-0049-y

Vallée, P., Lafait, J., Legrand, L., Mentré, P., Monod, M.-O., & Thomas, Y. (2005). Effects of pulsed low-frequency electromagnetic fields on water characterized by light scattering techniques: Role of bubbles. *Langmuir, 21*(6), 2293–2299. https://doi.org/10.1021/la047916u

Wahbeh, H., Calabrese, C., & Zwickey, H. (2007). Binaural beat technology in humans: A pilot study to assess psychologic and physiologic effects. *Journal of Alternative and Complementary Medicine, 13*(1), 25–32. https://doi.org/10.1089/acm.2006.6196

Warth, M., Keßler, J., Hillecke, T. K., & Bardenheuer, H. J. (2015). Music therapy in palliative care: A randomized controlled trial. *BMJ Supportive & Palliative Care, 5*(2), 170–177. https://doi.org/10.3238/arztebl.2015.0788

Every thought, emotion, and intention sends out a vibrational wave. Healing begins when those waves are in harmony.
—Dr. Deepak Chopra

Chapter 6

Quantum Consciousness and Healing Potential

In the conventional medical model, consciousness is treated as an epiphenomenon—an emergent property of biochemical and neurological processes in the brain. It is perceived as passive, reactive, and largely irrelevant to biological healing. But what if this perspective has it backwards?

Emerging fields at the intersection of physics, biology, and neuroscience suggest that consciousness may not only influence the physical body—it may be central to its function, regeneration, and repair. As science gradually redefines the boundaries of what constitutes a "causal" factor in healing, an extraordinary paradigm shift begins to emerge: Consciousness may be primary. Biology may be downstream.

In this chapter, we take a step beyond even functional medicine and systems biology, into the strange but promising frontier of quantum biology and consciousness studies. We explore how coherence within the body—both electromagnetic and quantum—may be maintained, disrupted, or restored through intention, energy, resonance, and awareness. These ideas are no longer just spiritual beliefs or fringe theories. They are being articulated, tested, and published in scientific journals across disciplines such as quantum physics, cell biology, psychoneuroimmunology, and electrophysiology.

Why This Chapter Matters

As clinicians, healers, and conscious beings, we are participating in the next great evolution of medicine: one that acknowledges not only the body and the mind, but the **biofield**, the **field of consciousness**, and the **subtle energies** that surround and animate life.

This is not merely about metaphor or belief systems. It is about understanding the mechanisms through which healing intention, focused awareness, and coherent emotional states can create measurable physiological change—sometimes with more precision and power than pharmaceuticals or invasive procedures.

And yes, we will keep one foot firmly planted in science throughout.

What is Quantum Biology?

Quantum biology refers to the study of quantum phenomena—such as coherence, entanglement, tunneling, and superposition—within living organisms. While traditional biology has focused on macroscopic biochemical pathways, quantum biology investigates how subatomic processes may influence cellular behavior, consciousness, and energy transfer at the molecular level (Al-Khalili & McFadden, 2014).

Through the sections ahead, we will examine:

- The mysterious role of **microtubules** as possible quantum processors within neurons;

- The **biofield** as a scientifically measurable energy field and its role in healing and homeostasis;

- Evidence supporting **intention-based healing modalities** such as Reiki and Therapeutic Touch;

- The significance of **heart-brain coherence states**, and how emotional resonance may regulate immune and autonomic function.

We will also continue integrating the **clinical, psychological, and spiritual layers** of healing, drawing from my own experience and that of clients whose recovery defied conventional logic—but not universal principles.

Healing, it turns out, may be less about control and more about resonance.

Let us dive in.

Quantum Consciousness and Microtubular Coherence

To understand consciousness as a causal agent in healing, we must first ask where, and how, consciousness resides. Is it an emergent property of brain complexity, or does it originate from something more fundamental—perhaps even subcellular? This section explores one of the most compelling and controversial theories of consciousness in modern science: **Orchestrated Objective Reduction (Orch OR)**. At its heart is the idea that **microtubules**, the structural fibers within neurons, may serve as quantum processors—suggesting that the brain, and perhaps the body itself, operates as a **quantum coherent system**.

This lens opens radical new doors for healing. If coherence in these quantum structures underlies consciousness, then trauma, dissociation, and even chronic illness may result from disturbances in the system's energetic harmony. And healing? That may come through restoring coherence—not only at the cognitive or biochemical level, but at the quantum level as well.

The Orch OR theory proposes that awareness does not simply arise from neural complexity or chemical signaling, but from quantum processes occurring deep within the structural scaffolding of neurons—specifically, in protein filaments called **microtubules**. This theory was developed in the 1990s by Sir Roger Penrose, a physicist and mathematician, and Dr. Stuart Hameroff, an anesthesiologist and consciousness researcher. While controversial at first, their model has received increasing attention due to emerging research in quantum biology, coherence phenomena, and subtle energy medicine.

According to Orch OR, microtubules—cylindrical structures inside neurons—serve not just as cellular skeletons but also as quantum processors. These tiny structures, composed of tubulin proteins, are theorized to support coherent quantum states (similar to how particles behave in quantum physics) that collapse into conscious experience through what Penrose calls **objective reduction**. In essence, consciousness arises not just from brain chemistry, but from orchestrated patterns of quantum vibration that connect the brain to a deeper order of reality (Hameroff & Penrose, 2014).

Microtubules and Quantum Coherence

Microtubules are microscopic hollow tubes made of tubulin proteins that maintain the structure and shape of cells, especially neurons. In Orch OR theory, these microtubules host quantum vibrations—highly ordered, synchronized oscillations—that allow for ultra-fast information processing.

Quantum coherence refers to a condition where particles or systems remain in perfect synchrony, allowing them to act as a unified whole even across space and time. This coherence is thought to underlie both the emergence of consciousness and the body's capacity for energetic integration.

Recent studies from the MIT-based Bandyopadhyay lab have supported this idea by detecting warm-temperature quantum vibrations within microtubules—once thought impossible in biological systems (Craddock et al., 2014; Anirban et al., 2015). Other research has found that anesthesia—a process that shuts off consciousness—may work by disrupting microtubular quantum activity (Craddock et al., 2012), reinforcing the idea that these structures play a central role in awareness.

From a therapeutic standpoint, the implications are profound. If the brain operates as a quantum instrument, then healing modalities that enhance coherence—whether through sound, intention, light, or vibrational therapy—may also impact consciousness at its source. For example, low-frequency ultrasound stimulation has been shown to improve mood and memory in early studies by potentially interacting with microtubular vibration patterns (Hameroff et al., 2013).

In integrative psychological practice, this opens new avenues for working with trauma, identity, and spiritual transformation. Rather than viewing consciousness as a by-product of the brain, this theory allows clinicians to treat it as a dynamic, resonant field—a bridge between the individual and a larger, possibly universal intelligence.

Objective Reduction (OR)

Objective reduction is a theory proposed by Penrose to explain how quantum superpositions (particles being in multiple states at once) collapse into a single reality without needing a conscious observer. In Orch OR, this process is orchestrated by biological systems like microtubules. It provides a potential mechanism by which consciousness emerges from quantum activity—not as an illusion or epiphenomenon, but as a fundamental and irreducible feature of reality.

The Orch OR model challenges both reductionist neuroscience and purely metaphysical explanations of consciousness. It offers a hybrid framework—scientifically grounded, but open to deeper layers of human experience—that may help us rethink the very nature of mind, healing, and our connection to the universe.

This integrative view shares certain parallels with therapeutic approaches such as Eye Movement Desensitization and Reprocessing (EMDR), which also aim to restore coherence in the brain's processing system, though by different mechanisms. EMDR uses bilateral sensory stimulation—most often through guided eye movements—to support the brain's natural capacity to reprocess traumatic memories. It is thought to stimulate activity similar to that which occurs during REM sleep, helping the brain reorganize and integrate emotionally charged material.

While EMDR operates primarily within a neurobiological and psychological framework, its effectiveness may reflect the restoration of synchrony across neural circuits—an echo, perhaps, of the deeper quantum coherence Orch OR describes. In this light, we might understand EMDR as a "macro" coherence therapy, working at the cognitive and nervous system level, whereas modalities grounded in quantum coherence theory may aim to restore balance at a more fundamental, subcellular or energetic level. Both pathways converge on a central principle: healing involves restoring the natural capacity of the system—whether neurological or quantum-biological—to self-organize, integrate, and return to wholeness. It offers a hybrid framework—scientifically grounded, but open to deeper layers of human experience—that may help us rethink the very nature of mind, healing, and our connection to the universe.

For example, consider a therapeutic scenario involving a client with persistent dissociative symptoms following trauma. Traditional psychological approaches may focus on memory processing, emotional regulation, and cognitive restructuring. However, if the brain is also functioning as a quantum processor—as Orch OR suggests—then integrating modalities that restore coherence at the vibrational level (such as sound therapy, guided intention, or light-based interventions) could support the brain's capacity to self-organize and re-integrate fragmented consciousness.

In this way, Orch OR provides a rationale for why some subtle energy therapies may lead to shifts in awareness, perception, or emotional processing that feel immediate and transformative—because they may be interacting directly with the underlying quantum architecture of the mind.

Biofield Science and Intention-Based Therapies

In the evolving science of consciousness and healing, one of the most promising yet misunderstood frontiers is the biofield—an energetic matrix that both surrounds and interpenetrates the human body. Long referenced in ancient healing traditions as Qi, Prana, or life force, the biofield has become the subject of serious scientific inquiry over the past three decades. The term was formally introduced by a panel of National Institutes of Health (NIH) researchers in 1992 to describe "a massless field, not necessarily electromagnetic, that surrounds and permeates living bodies and affects the body" (Rubik et al., 1994).

If consciousness is not limited to the skull, and the body is a field of energy and information, then therapeutic intention may act as a tuning fork—realigning the body's frequencies, modulating biological processes, and catalyzing healing across systems.

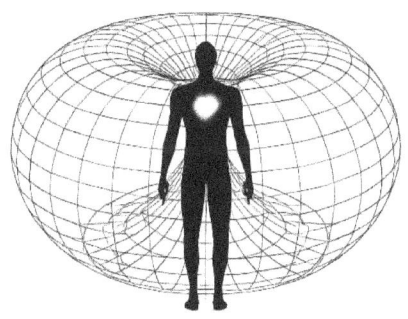

Biofield

What Is the Biofield?

The biofield refers to a complex field of energy and information that includes electromagnetic, magnetic, and possibly subtle energies. It is not simply the aura or metaphorical "energy" of new-age literature, but a scientifically measurable and biologically meaningful field. Techniques such as Heart Rate Variability (HRV), Gas Discharge Visualization (GDV), and Superconducting Quantum Interference Devices (SQUIDs) have been used to assess components of the biofield and its interaction with emotional, neurological, and physiological states (Rubik, 2002; Muehsam et al., 2015).

Intention as a Modulator of the Biofield

A growing body of research demonstrates that **intention**, particularly when focused and emotionally coherent, can induce measurable changes in biological systems. In experiments involving meditation, prayer, and distant healing, practitioners have been able to alter pH in water samples, reduce bacterial growth, influence DNA configuration, and affect the physiology of other humans—even at a distance (McTaggart, 2007; Rein & McCraty, 1994).

Within the framework of psychoneuroimmunology, these findings align with a growing recognition of the bidirectional pathways connecting emotional states, autonomic function, and immune activity. Positive emotional states such as gratitude, compassion, and inner stillness are consistently associated with increased vagal tone—a marker of parasympathetic nervous system activation—and coherent heart rate variability (McCraty & Childre, 2010). These physiological markers of regulation are not simply stress-reducing; they also influence immune parameters, including elevated levels of immunoglobulin A (IgA), enhanced natural killer (NK) cell activity, and reduced pro-inflammatory cytokines (Davidson et al., 2003; Bhasin et al., 2013). This implies that the **field generated by coherent intention is not passive**—it is biologically active.

Simultaneously, these states foster synchronized brain wave activity, particularly in the alpha and theta ranges, which support emotional integration, memory processing, and access to deeper levels of awareness. These brainwave frequencies are intentionally cultivated in regression-based modalities such as **Quantum Healing Hypnosis Technique® (QHHT®) and Beyond Quantum Healing (BQH)**, where the client is guided into trance states that facilitate access to subconscious and transpersonal realms.

Separately, modalities such as BQH and Quantum Biofeedback also emphasize **intention** as a central healing force. In these approaches, both the client's intention and the practitioner's ability to maintain a coherent, heart-centered field shape the therapeutic process. In **Quantum Biofeedback**, coherent frequencies are delivered to the biofield to promote resonance and reduce dissonance, often working on subtle vibrational patterns that interact with meridians, chakras, or informational pathways in the energy body. The field becomes both the medium and the message—entrained by resonance, refined by intention.

*Intention is not just a mental construct—
it is a directive force that shapes reality through
resonance and coherence.*

This framework is supported by foundational research in biofield science and psychoenergetics, which suggests that subtle energetic inputs—especially those amplified by conscious intention—can modulate physiological and psychological states (Rubik et al., 2015; Tiller, 2007; Muehsam et al., 2015). These findings align with earlier models proposed in vibrational medicine (Gerber, 2001) and are reinforced by psychoenergetic studies showing that intention can be imprinted onto electronic devices and influence biological targets (Tiller, 2007).

Clients often report experiences of expanded awareness, intuitive insight, and connection with higher guidance. Practitioners of QHHT® and BQH—particularly the late Dolores Cannon, founder of QHHT®—have documented thousands of sessions showing recurring patterns of healing, symbolic imagery, and emotional resolution. Cannon's 19 published books synthesize this archive, offering qualitative patterns that reveal commonalities across individual regressions.

Clinical studies on more widely accepted energy modalities such as Reiki, Therapeutic Touch, and Healing Touch have reported significant reductions in pain, anxiety, fatigue, and even accelerated wound healing—especially when used alongside standard medical treatment (Jain & Mills, 2010; Baldwin et al., 2017). These therapies are now offered in dozens of hospital systems worldwide, not as belief-based interventions but as evidence-supported complementary care.

Scientific Snapshot:
Randomized Trials on Reiki and Touch Therapies

- A 2014 review of 24 randomized controlled trials found that *Reiki* significantly reduced pain and anxiety in patients undergoing surgery and cancer treatment (Thrane & Cohen, 2014).
- A 2010 study on *Therapeutic Touch* showed improved wound healing and immune markers in post-surgical patients (Jain & Mills, 2010).
- *Healing Touch* interventions have been associated with reductions in cortisol and increases in immune cell activity (Baldwin et al., 2017).

While modalities like Reiki and Healing Touch have been subjected to randomized controlled trials, regression-based therapies such as QHHT® and BQH are not listed here due to the current lack of RCTs in that domain. This absence is not necessarily indicative of lower therapeutic value but reflects the unique methodological challenges posed by regression therapy. The highly individualized, nonlinear, and deeply subjective nature of these sessions makes standardization, placebo control, and blinding difficult to implement using conventional research designs.

Despite these limitations, there exists a rich archive of case-based documentation attesting to the therapeutic impact of regression modalities. Dolores Cannon, the founder of QHHT®, conducted thousands of sessions over several decades and identified recurring themes, symbolic content, and archetypal healing narratives. Her published works—notably *Between Death and Life* and *The Convoluted Universe* series—often detailed syntheses of recurring themes in these transpersonal healing journeys.

Complementing these anecdotal and experiential findings, early studies in transpersonal psychology and regression therapy provide conceptual support for the therapeutic potential of these altered states (Grof, 1985; Woolger, 1990). While not generalizable through RCTs, single-case studies and qualitative research represent a valuable phenomenological archive—offering insight into how expanded states of consciousness may facilitate emotional resolution, spiritual insight, and somatic healing.

Bridging Physics and Clinical Practice

How can we understand these effects in a mechanistic way? One explanation lies in the principles of **resonance** and **entrainment**. Just as a tuning fork can bring a nearby object into vibrational harmony, a coherent biofield may entrain disordered physiological systems—whether in the nervous, immune, or even genetic domains.

Some theorists have proposed that intention-based therapies interact with **non-local fields**, potentially through quantum entanglement—where two systems remain interconnected across space and time. While controversial, such hypotheses are beginning to receive rigorous attention in the areas of quantum biology, field theory, and consciousness research (Tiller et al., 2005; Muehsam et al., 2015).

Honestly, it is a lot to digest. Try explaining quantum entanglement, non-local fields, and intention-based therapies on live camera while remembering to breathe. These are the kinds of questions that make you wish the interviewer had asked about your favorite tea blend instead.

In practice, this means that **intention, presence, and resonance** are not abstract ideas—they are **interventions**. A practitioner who enters a heart-coherent, centered state may influence the client's physiology not through words alone, but through biofield entrainment.

Clinical Illustration

Consider a case involving a middle-aged client suffering from chronic fatigue and persistent anxiety following prolonged caregiving for a terminally ill parent. After conventional psychotherapy reached a plateau, she agreed to integrate Reiki sessions into her care. Following three sessions, she reported a dramatic reduction in mental fog and emotional reactivity. Physiologically, her HRV improved, her sleep normalized, and her capacity for emotional processing expanded—making deeper psychological work possible. She described the sessions as "tuning her system back into alignment," despite having no prior exposure to energy-based modalities.

Such results cannot be attributed solely to suggestion or placebo. Rather, they reflect the body's innate tendency to reorganize into coherence when given the right conditions—and the possibility that human consciousness, when harnessed with intention, can serve as both catalyst and conduit for that transformation.

One notable example of this integrative model in practice is the Genius Insight program, a biofeedback technology that incorporates the concept of the biofield into its design. The system begins by analyzing vocal recordings using **Fast Fourier Transform (FFT)** algorithms—a well-established method in signal processing research, including work from institutions like MIT (Oppenheim & Schafer, 2009; MIT News, 2012). FFT decomposes complex voice signals into their frequency components, creating a **spectrogram** that maps harmonic content over time (Mahdi, 2019). This spectrographic analysis provides a real-time snapshot of the client's energetic state.

When you listen closely enough, the body speaks in frequency. The rest is interpretation.

The resulting voice data is then compared to a proprietary database of energetic signatures that span physical, mental, and subtle-energy domains. For example, the Genius Insight program evaluates physiological systems such as liver function or immune stressors (body), emotional imbalances and neurotransmitter patterns (mind), and disruptions in chakra centers or auric coherence (biofield). Based on this analysis, the system delivers targeted sound frequencies—such as Solfeggio tones, Nogier frequencies, and sacred geometry waveforms—designed to support vibrational realignment.

This process is rooted in the principles of **bioresonance** and **sound healing**, which suggest that the human system can return to coherence when exposed to corrective vibrational input (Gerber, 2001; Rubik et al., 2015). While formal clinical trials on Genius Insight biofeedback remain limited, the scientific basis for FFT and frequency mapping is robust. Its use in clinical practice represents a fusion of voice-based biometric analysis and personalized vibrational therapy—bridging energetic diagnostics with user-friendly therapeutic interventions.

Such tools not only validate the lived experience of clients sensitive to energy, but also invite practitioners to move beyond mechanical protocols into a relationship with the field—where conscious intent, subtle perception, and vibrational intelligence intersect.

Subtle Energy Techniques (e.g., Reiki, Therapeutic Touch)

Subtle energy therapies occupy a fascinating space at the edge of modern science and ancient healing. They are grounded in the recognition that the body is not simply a biochemical machine, but a complex, resonant energy system that can be influenced, harmonized, and balanced through intention, presence, and energetic touch. These modalities often rely on the transmission of energy through the hands, the modulation of the biofield, and the entrainment of disordered patterns into coherence.

High-Frequency Electromagnetic Interventions

In contrast to subtle energy therapies, which work through low-intensity or non-measurable frequencies, high-frequency electromagnetic interventions involve strong, targeted stimulation of tissue or neural circuits. Examples include Transcranial Magnetic Stimulation (TMS), Pulsed Electromagnetic Field Therapy (PEMF), radiofrequency ablation, and deep brain stimulation. These are typically measurable, regulated, and increasingly used in clinical contexts for conditions such as depression, chronic pain, and neurological disorders.

Unlike high-frequency electromagnetic interventions—such as Transcranial Magnetic Stimulation (TMS), Pulsed Electromagnetic Field Therapy (PEMF), and radiofrequency ablation—subtle energy approaches operate at frequencies currently beyond the detection of standard instruments. Despite this, numerous studies have reported meaningful effects, including reductions in pain, anxiety, and fatigue, as well as improved immune responses and emotional integration.

A Brief Overview of Modalities

- Reiki, a Japanese technique for stress reduction and relaxation, is based on the principle of channeling "universal life force energy" through the practitioner's hands. Traditionally practiced with light touch, Reiki is now often delivered either hands-on or hands-off, depending on the client's needs and practitioner's training. Today, it is integrated into many hospital and hospice care settings worldwide.

- **Therapeutic Touch**, developed by nurse Dora Kunz and professor Dolores Krieger (drawing on earlier Reiki traditions), involves the conscious direction of healing energy to balance the patient's field. Unlike Reiki, it does not require physical touch.

- **Healing Touch**, often used in clinical settings, integrates techniques from several traditions and is taught through certified nursing programs.

- **Qigong**, **Polarity Therapy**, and **Biofield Tuning** are other examples, each with distinct cultural roots and theoretical frameworks, but sharing a common reliance on energetic attunement.

Scientific Findings and Theoretical Frameworks

Clinical studies continue to validate the outcomes of subtle energy work. EEG studies have demonstrated increased alpha and theta brain wave activity in recipients of Reiki and Healing Touch (Wardell & Engebretson, 2001). fMRI studies suggest shifts in limbic activity consistent with relaxation and parasympathetic dominance. Immunological studies show increased IgA and NK cell activity following sessions (Baldwin et al., 2017).

In simpler terms, subtle energy therapies may help the body remember how to function in harmony. From a systems theory perspective, these techniques support internal balance by encouraging clearer communication between the body's systems—like tuning an orchestra so the instruments play in sync again. This synchronized state, sometimes called **informational coherence**, helps reduce inner chaos and allows the body to heal more efficiently.

What Are Subtle Energies?

Subtle energies refer to forms of energy that are not currently measurable by conventional scientific instruments but are nonetheless perceived by healers and recipients. These energies may correspond to electromagnetic fields below current detection limits, quantum fluctuations, or bio-informational fields that organize matter and consciousness.

From the lens of quantum biology, these modalities may operate via mechanisms such as field resonance, coherence, or quantum entanglement. Focused intention becomes a kind of tuning mechanism—potentially collapsing a range of healing possibilities into a singular, more coherent outcome. Trying to bring together principles from quantum physics, electromagnetism, and systems biology into a clinical framework is a bit like trying to host a dinner party with guests from three different dimensions—everyone speaks in their own equations, and no one brought dessert.

Clinical Reflection

One client—a woman in her 40s with fibromyalgia, sleep disturbances, and PTSD—had been through years of pharmacological and psychological treatment with only partial relief. During a six-week course of combined talk therapy and Healing Touch sessions, she experienced not only physical symptom relief, but also spontaneous emotional releases tied to unresolved grief. She described feeling "more whole" and "reconnected to herself," echoing the language often used in energy healing traditions to describe reintegration of fragmented parts of the self.

In my own clinical experience, subtle energy therapies are most effective when used not as an alternative to psychology but as a complement. When the energetic field is held in coherence, deeper self-awareness and transformation often arise spontaneously. Rather than bypassing emotional integration, these techniques frequently create the conditions that support the emergence of self-agency and make such integration possible. This also implies a certain level of intention and openness on the part of the client—an inner readiness to participate in their own healing, even if only at the level of curiosity or willingness to explore beyond conventional models.

Healing is not a passive process. It is a fusion of two energetic sources—the client and the practitioner—dancing in coherence with the field.

Heart-Brain Resonance and Coherence States

Coherence-building practices—such as coherence breathing, heart-focused meditation, and compassion-based emotional regulation—serve as gateways to self-regulation and spiritual sovereignty. These practices help individuals reconnect to a deep inner rhythm that transcends stress physiology, establishing a foundation for autonomy and internal guidance. In this model, coherence serves as a dynamic expression of energetic alignment—an integrative state that supports one's ability to respond with clarity, purpose, and compassion, even in the face of external turbulence.

Perhaps the most measurable interface between consciousness and biology lies in the **heart-brain connection**. Far from being a mere mechanical pump, the heart generates the body's most powerful electromagnetic field—one that can be measured several feet from the body and is shaped by emotional and mental states.

Research from the HeartMath Institute has shown that **heart rate variability (HRV)**—a marker of autonomic nervous system balance—is strongly influenced by coherent emotional states such as gratitude, love, and compassion. These states bring the heart, brain, and nervous system into synchronized rhythm, producing what researchers call a **coherent state** (McCraty & Zayas, 2014).

What Is Heart Coherence?

Heart coherence refers to a harmonious pattern in heart rhythm variability that reflects optimal communication between the heart and brain. In this state, the autonomic nervous system becomes balanced, and physiological efficiency improves. It is associated with enhanced emotional regulation, cognitive clarity, and resilience.

Frequency, Emotion, and Field Effects

One of the most compelling visual models used to describe the interaction of human emotion and frequency is the toroidal energy field illustrated before. Often depicted in sacred geometry and energy medicine traditions, the torus represents the dynamic flow of energy that loops from the heart outward and back again—intersecting through the crown and root, creating a continuous, self-organizing field. This image, while symbolic, reflects actual electromagnetic patterns that can be measured around the body, and aligns with emerging insights from quantum field theory and neurocardiology.

The heart's electromagnetic field appears to interact with the biofield, not just of the individual, but also of those nearby. This concept is often illustrated in visual models of the human biofield, where toroidal energy fields flow around the body and intersect through the heart and crown—merging insights from quantum theory, sacred geometry, and ancient energetic maps (see illustration - page 125). While these representations are widely known in metaphysical circles, the underlying principles are also supported by scientific research in neurocardiology, psychophysiology, and biophysics (Armour, 2003; Bradley & Pribram, 1998; McCraty & Zayas, 2014). Studies on couples, therapists and clients, and even groups in synchronized meditation have shown entrainment of heart rhythms across individuals, suggesting that **coherence is both intra- and interpersonal** (Bradley & Pribram, 1998).

When clients access coherent states through breathwork, guided imagery, or emotional reframing, they not only experience psychological relief—they undergo **physiological regulation**. Cortisol levels drop. DHEA and oxytocin rise. Immune markers improve. In this way, coherence becomes a bridge between intention, emotional alchemy, and somatic healing.

Clinical Integration

Techniques such as **HeartMath biofeedback**, **coherence breathing**, and **compassion meditation** have become key tools in trauma therapy, anxiety treatment, and burnout recovery. In my practice, heart coherence exercises often serve as an energetic primer before deeper therapeutic exploration. In Beyond Quantum Healing (BQH) sessions, this is an integral part of the process. I begin each session with a water alchemy ritual to anchor the intention, followed by a heart-mind coherence breathing technique that prepares the energetic field before entering a formal trance induction. When the nervous system is regulated and the field is coherent, insight and integration arise with greater ease.

One client suffering from severe anxiety learned to use coherence techniques to interrupt panic attacks. Over time, this cultivated a sense of agency in her healing process. She began to identify the *felt sense* of coherence as a new emotional baseline—calm, steady, present. It became not only a coping skill, but a state of being.

From the quantum perspective, coherence is not merely a therapeutic outcome—it is a **state of resonance with a deeper order**. This deeper order can be understood as the intelligent field that underlies all matter—what some call the quantum field or unified field—capable of reorganizing biological terrain through conscious interaction. The **quantum field** refers to the underlying sea of energy and potential from which all particles arise. The **unified field** builds on this concept, suggesting that all forces and matter originate from a single, interconnected source—a view explored in both theoretical physics and consciousness studies. Together, these ideas support the possibility of reorganizing biological terrain through conscious interaction. It is a return to signal over noise, meaning over chaos. And from this space, healing unfolds—not through force, but through resonance.

Coherence is not just balance—it is alignment with a deeper intelligence that remembers who you are.

Healing Is Remembering the Blueprint

In the realm of quantum biology and consciousness-based healing, *remembrance* is more than metaphor—it is the process itself. Each cell, each organ system, each thought-form, carries within it a template of health, harmony, and inner order. Healing, in this view, is not about overriding the body's dysfunctions but listening closely enough for the signal beneath the noise—the blueprint beneath the symptoms.

As we have explored in this chapter, subtle energy therapies, biofield interventions, intention-based modalities, and coherence practices all point toward the same truth: that the body is not a static machine but a dynamic field of intelligence. It responds not only to matter but to meaning; not only to chemistry but to consciousness.

To heal is not to impose change, but to allow remembrance. A remembering of the body's capacity for regeneration. A remembering of the mind's capacity for clarity. And a remembering of the spirit's timeless coherence with something greater.

Healing is remembering the blueprint.

References

Al-Khalili, J., & McFadden, J. (2014). *Life on the edge: The coming of age of quantum biology*. Broadway Books.

Armour, J. A. (2003). Neurocardiology: Anatomical and functional principles. *Heart Rhythm, 1*(1), 87–91. https://neuroimaginalinstitute.com/wp-content/uploads/2013/03/Neurocardiology.pdf

Baldwin, A. L., Wagers, C., & Schwartz, G. E. (2008). Reiki improves heart rate homeostasis in laboratory rats. *Journal of Alternative and Complementary Medicine, 14*(4), 417–422. https://doi.org/10.1089/acm.2007.0753

Bhasin, M. K., Dusek, J. A., Chang, B. H., Joseph, M. G., Denninger, J. W., Fricchione, G. L., et al. (2013). Relaxation response induces temporal transcriptome changes in energy metabolism, insulin secretion, and inflammatory pathways. *PLoS ONE, 8*(5), e62817. https://doi.org/10.1371/journal.pone.0062817

Bradley, R. T., & Pribram, K. H. (1998). Communication and stability in social collectives. *Journal of Social and Evolutionary Systems, 21*(1), 29–80. https://doi.org/10.1016/S1061-7361(99)80005-8

Craddock, T. J. A., Hameroff, S., Ayoub, A., Klobukowski, M., & Tuszynski, J. A. (2012). Anesthetics act in quantum channels in brain microtubules to prevent consciousness. *Current Topics in Medicinal Chemistry, 12*(21), 2323–2332. https://doi.org/10.2174/156802612805289521

Davidson, R. J., Kabat-Zinn, J., Schumacher, J., Rosenkranz, M., Muller, D., Santorelli, S. F., et al. (2003). Alterations in brain and immune function produced by mindfulness meditation. *Psychosomatic Medicine, 65*(4), 564–570. https://doi.org/10.1097/01.PSY.0000077505.67574.E3

Gerber, R. (2001). *Vibrational medicine: The #1 handbook of subtle-energy therapies* (3rd ed.). Bear & Company. ISBN: 978-1-879181-58-8.

Grof, S. (1985). *Beyond the Brain: Birth, Death, and Transcendence in Psychotherapy.* State University of New York Press.

Jain, S., & Mills, P. J. (2010). Biofield therapies: Helpful or full of hype? A best evidence synthesis. *International Journal of Behavioral Medicine, 17*(1), 1–16. https://doi.org/10.1007/s12529-009-9062-4

Mahdi, J. (2019). Frequency analyses of human voice using fast Fourier transform. *Iraqi Journal of Physics, 13*(27), 174–181. https://doi.org/10.30723/ijp.v13i27.276

McCraty, R., & Childre, D. (2010). Coherence: Bridging personal, social, and global health. *Alternative Therapies in Health and Medicine, 16*(4), 10–24. https://www.heartmath.org/research/research-library/basic/coherence-bridging-personal-social-and-global-health/

McCraty, R., & Zayas, M. A. (2014). Cardiac coherence, self-regulation, autonomic stability, and psychosocial well-being. *Frontiers in Psychology, 5*, 1090. https://doi.org/10.3389/fpsyg.2014.01090

McTaggart, L. (2007). *The Intention Experiment: Using Your Thoughts to Change Your Life and the World.* Free Press.

MIT News. (2012). Faster Fourier transforms. https://news.mit.edu/2012/faster-fourier-transforms-0118

Muehsam, D., Chevalier, G., Barsotti, T., & Gurfein, B. T. (2015). An overview of biofield devices. *Global Advances in Health and Medicine, 4*(Suppl), 42–51. https://doi.org/10.7453/gahmj.2015.022.suppl

Oppenheim, A. V., & Schafer, R. W. (2009). *Discrete-Time Signal Processing* (3rd ed.). Pearson Education.

Rein, G., & McCraty, R. (1994). Structural changes in water and DNA associated with new physiologically measurable states. *Journal of Scientific Exploration, 8*(3), 438–439.
https://www.heartmath.org/research/research-library/energetics/structural-changes-in-water-and-dna-associated-with-new-physiologically-measurable-states/

Rubik, B. (2002). The biofield hypothesis: Its biophysical basis and role in medicine. *Journal of Alternative and Complementary Medicine, 8*(6), 703–717. https://doi.org/10.1089/10755530260511711

Rubik, B., Muehsam, D., Hammerschlag, R., & Jain, S. (2015). Biofield science and healing: History, terminology, and concepts. *Global Advances in Health and Medicine, 4*(Suppl), 8–14. https://doi.org/10.7453/gahmj.2015.038.suppl

Rubik, B., Brooks, A. J., & Schwartz, G. E. (1994). In search of a scientific framework for the biofield: Energy medicine and the unifying concept of information. *Journal of Alternative and Complementary Medicine, 1*(2), 155–165.
https://www.liebertpub.com/doi/10.1089/acm.1995.1.155

Thrane, S., & Cohen, S. M. (2014). Effect of Reiki therapy on pain and anxiety in adults: An in-depth literature review of randomized trials with effect size calculations. *Pain Management Nursing, 15*(4), 897–908.
https://doi.org/10.1016/j.pmn.2013.07.008

Tiller, W. A. (2007). *Psychoenergetic Science: A Second Copernican-Scale Revolution.* Pavior Publishing. https://www.amazon.com/Psychoenergetic-Science-William-Tiller-Ph-D/dp/1424338638

Tiller, W. A., Dibble, W. E., & Kohane, M. J. (2005). *Exploring robust interactions between human intention and inanimate/animate systems. Subtle Energies & Energy Medicine, 15*(1), 1–20. Retrieved from https://tillerfoundation.org/wp-content/uploads/2022/08/%2380%20-%20Exploring%20robust%20interactions%20between%20human%20intention%20and%20inanimate%20animate%20systems.pdf

Wardell, D. W., & Engebretson, J. (2001). Biological correlates of Reiki Touch healing. *Journal of Advanced Nursing, 33*(4), 439–445. https://doi.org/10.1046/j.1365-2648.2001.01691.x

Woolger, R. (1990). *Other Lives, Other Selves: A Jungian Psychotherapist Discovers Past Lives.* Bantam.

A system is never the sum of its parts; it is the product of their interaction.

—Russell Ackoff

Chapter 7

Tools for Terrain Repair and Regulation

The foundation laid in the previous chapters now brings us to the heart of practical transformation: how do we repair, regulate, and sustain a coherent terrain within the chaos of modern life? Healing does not emerge from isolated interventions but from a systems-based, psychologically informed approach that honors the full complexity of the human organism. In clinical practice, this means conducting a thorough, multidimensional intake process—exploring not just symptoms but also diet, sleep patterns, physical activity, toxic exposures, trauma history, relationships, core beliefs, and environmental stressors. Only then can we build an intervention plan that reflects the real terrain of a client's life.

The Healing Relationship Begins Before the Intake

Healing is a co-created journey. It does not begin with treatment—it begins with resonance. Before we ever talk about terrain repair or interventions, we begin with a fundamental question: **Are we a good fit?**

From the first contact—whether by email, phone, or silent energetic attunement—a subtle dance begins. Is this therapist aligned with the client's needs, language, values, and readiness? Are our energy fields compatible enough to establish trust and transformation? Am I, as a therapist, attuned enough to sense whether I am the *right* practitioner for this person's journey?

This is terrain work in its most primary form: relational terrain. The therapeutic alliance, even before words are spoken, sets the tone for what is possible.

In that first intake session, we explore a series of foundational questions designed to illuminate the terrain of the client's lived experience:

- **Who are you today, and what brings you here?** This opens the door to self-definition in the present moment.

- **What brought you to where you are now?** We trace the chronological unfolding of symptoms, life events, and meaningful experiences that shaped the current state—gathering a narrative arc, not just data points.

- **What is hurting, and what feels unclear?** The client is invited to describe their presenting problems in their own words, while I, as the therapist, listen for patterns and symbolic themes, placing their story within a broader biopsychosocial and energetic context.

- **What is ready to shift?** This question assesses not only pain points but openings—strengths, latent capacities, and current levels of awareness. I pay attention to how the client relates to their symptoms and how they perceive their inner and outer environment.

- **What resources do you bring, and what limitations or patterns are you aware of?** This inquiry identifies internal and external supports, as well as recurring blocks—offering a balanced picture of both terrain vitality and fragility.

- **What are your expectations of this process—and of me?** We explore whether our expectations align, whether our roles are clearly understood, and whether a mutual vision of growth can be established.

This initial conversation is not a formality. It is the first energetic exchange. It sets the tone for what is possible. Before we begin any intervention, we establish **resonance**—the precondition for trust, safety, and transformation.

We do not rush to apply tools. Instead, we *listen for resonance.* Because no matter how brilliant the intervention, it will not land in a field of mistrust. In terrain-based healing, the **relationship is the first medicine.**

Healing is not fixing what is broken.
It's remembering what was never broken.
—Dr. Gabor Maté

The Clinical Terrain Framework

The limitations of the therapist become the limitations of the client. But the openness, vision, and coherence of the therapist become the scaffolding for the client's transformation.

Once the relational groundwork is laid, the clinical mapping begins. Terrain repair, like any ecological process, requires a detailed topographic scan. In my approach, terrain is not limited to the body—it includes the psyche, the field, and the story.

We assess a multidimensional profile that informs how healing might unfold:

- **Level of suffering and symptom expression**: What pain—physical, emotional, or existential—has brought the client to this moment? What patterns, symptoms, or crises indicate a disruption in coherence or meaning?

- **Resource landscape**: We inventory internal assets (resilience, insight, intelligence, humor), relational supports (family, community, professional networks), and environmental stability (housing, nature access, safety, financial capacity). Healing requires more than will—it requires scaffolding.

- **Readiness for change**: Where is the client on the readiness continuum? Are they in pre-contemplation, cautious curiosity, or active pursuit of healing? Do they carry beliefs that change is possible—or is there ambivalence, learned helplessness, or past betrayal in healing contexts?

- **Self-awareness and reflexivity**: Can the client identify strengths and name patterns that repeat? Do they reflect on their own role in relational dynamics? Awareness is both an entry point and a muscle to develop.

- **Spiritual, cultural, and existential framework**: What cosmology, mythology, or worldview helps the client make meaning of their experience? Whether religious, philosophical, or intuitive, this framework will shape how they interpret suffering, change, and healing. It must be honored, not overridden.

This is not about diagnosis. It is about discovering the underlying logic of the terrain—biological, psychological, and symbolic. I listen with clinical intent but also with intuitive spaciousness. What is being said? What is being repeated? What is being left out? Where is the coherence lost, and where is it waiting to be restored?

My role is not to deliver answers but to offer a **framework of coherence** the client can step into. I become a mirror, a tuning fork, and a guide through terrain repair—not a technician administering protocols.

People are not machines. You don't diagnose and repair them—you help them reorganize.

Core Ingredients of the Approach

This step outlines the core elements that begin to define the evolving structure of a terrain-based approach that is slowly emerging from the clinical and conceptual ground we have been preparing and tending together, much like one would till the soil in a garden—clearing, loosening, and enriching it to allow new growth to take root. These ingredients reflect both the theoretical foundations and clinical pragmatism of a truly integrative practice. Rather than functioning as isolated tools, these elements interweave to support the restoration of coherence at every level of the client's being—biological, psychological, energetic, and spiritual.

Before diving into the individual ingredients, it is important to understand that each of these elements does not stand alone. Together, they form the foundation of an integrative terrain-based approach that restores coherence at all levels of being:

- **Systems Thinking**: A non-reductionist approach that sees the client as an interconnected whole. Symptoms are not seen as isolated issues to suppress, but as messengers of imbalance in a larger web of relationships—internal and external.

- **Psychoenergetic Awareness**: The body holds emotional imprints, and the field carries the residue of experience. Healing occurs not just in the tissue, but in the energetic container. Somatic signals, such as posture, tension, or breathing patterns, can reveal emotional distress, past trauma, or shifts in energy even before a person can explain them in words.

- **Empowerment and Self-Agency**: Clients are not passive recipients of expert intervention. They are invited to become active participants in their own healing, with the therapist acting as an informed guide—not a savior. Education, encouragement, and reflection are tools of empowerment.

- **Narrative Integration and Symbolic Mapping**: Storytelling is diagnostic and healing. By exploring the symbolic meaning of symptoms, life patterns, and inner archetypes, clients reconnect with a deeper understanding of their journey. This is where clients begin to create meaning from their experiences—turning symptoms into signals, and their personal story into a map for healing.

- **Spiritual and Existential Grounding**: Beyond story, clients are invited to ground themselves in a deeper sense of connection—whether to spirit, purpose, or the sacred. Clients are supported in accessing whatever form of spiritual connection or higher meaning they resonate with. Healing is not just about feeling better—it is about becoming more fully aligned with one's values, purpose, and sense of the sacred.

- **Belief and Intention as Healing Forces**: Beliefs shape biology. The placebo effect is not a trick—it is a glimpse into how perception alters physiology. We consciously work with belief systems to realign intention, expectation, and experience.

- **Therapeutic Coherence**: The therapist is not an image of perfection or authority over the client. Rather, healing emerges through a partnership between two human beings—each bringing their full presence, awareness, and capacity to co-create meaning and purpose. It is this shared intent that forms the foundation for transformation and growth. The therapist's coherence—the clarity, alignment, and depth they embody—serves not as a directive force, but as an energetic scaffold for the client's own self-reclamation. The therapeutic relationship is not hierarchical; it is the vessel for collaborative transformation.

The curious paradox is that when I accept myself just as I am, then I can change.
—Carl Rogers

This step defines the DNA of a new model of practice. Each ingredient adds a frequency, a tone, a principle of order to the healing field. Together, they form the architecture of what will later be named as a signature approach—a synthesis grounded in science, matured through clinical work, and expanded through lived consciousness.

Translating the Model into Practice

Theory alone cannot transform. It must be metabolized into action—absorbed and integrated through rituals, habits, choices, and attunements that nourish coherence over time. This section focuses on the practical application of the terrain model, where core concepts become embodied practices, and transformation begins to take root in daily life.

We now enter the realm of implementation—where terrain repair is no longer abstract but grounded in breath, movement, sleep, food, light, sound, thought, and relationship. In this step, we empower clients with an evolving toolbox, not to enforce strict rules, but to equip them with flexible, resonant strategies they can personalize, adapt, and ultimately own.

Healing is not about perfection—it is about cultivating resilience, coherence, and self-agency within a chaotic and often incoherent world. Each tool or practice becomes an opportunity to re-pattern the system from the inside out.

Working with Energy in Daily Life

Energy is not abstract—it is the most immediate experience of how we feel, how we connect, and how we move through the world. In terrain-based therapy, energy refers not just to physical vitality, but to the subtle, often invisible patterns that shape our perception, coherence, and behavior.

Clients are invited to begin recognizing how energy manifests in daily life. This may include noticing:

- Sudden changes in mood or vitality;
- Feeling "off" in certain environments or around specific people;
- Reactions to sound, light, space, or emotional tone;
- The texture of their thoughts: scattered vs. focused, heavy vs. spacious;
- Bodily cues: shallow breath, jaw tension, gut constriction, or tingling.

These sensations offer real-time information about the state of one's energetic terrain. Imbalances often show up before symptoms—through disconnection, overwhelm, hyper reactivity, or exhaustion.

Rebalancing energy begins with awareness. Clients are guided to use accessible strategies to re-center:

- **Breath**: Slowing the breath to reset the nervous system;
- **Movement**: Shaking, stretching, or rhythmic motion to clear stagnant energy;
- **Sound**: Humming, toning, or listening to harmonic frequencies;
- **Nature exposure**: Using earth, sun, wind, and water as regulatory inputs;

- **Water rituals**: Showers, baths, salt scrubs to clear emotional or field residue;
- **Intention**: Consciously directing attention and will to reinforce a desired internal state.

Therapists can model this by attuning to their own energy during sessions—holding a coherent field and gently inviting the client to entrain to it. Energetic hygiene for the practitioner includes centering practices before sessions (such as breathwork, visualization, or grounding), and simple clearing rituals afterward (like stepping outside, using breath or sound to release residual charge, or briefly reconnecting with one's own intention). These actions are not only symbolic—they recalibrate the nervous system and help the therapist remain fully present, aligned, and nonreactive. Over time, clients begin to recognize that their energy is not random; it is a language—and learning to speak it becomes part of their healing fluency.

Energy is information in motion.
When we learn to listen, we reclaim the ability to respond rather than react.

Tools for Terrain Repair and Regulation

The tools used at this stage reflect and support the terrain philosophy:

- Elimination Protocols for toxins, food sensitivities, and thought patterns that disrupt coherence. When medical or biochemical complexity exceeds the scope of our role as psychologists, clients are referred to functional medicine practitioners for specialized testing or treatment. Otherwise, our goal is to empower the client to become, as the saying goes, 'their own best doctor'—learning to read their body, environment, and emotions as part of a dynamic feedback system. Research in integrative and functional approaches has shown that dietary elimination and detoxification strategies can help reduce systemic inflammation and improve mental clarity, mood, and energy (Perlmutter & Loberg, 2015; DeMeo, 2016; Pizzorno et al., 2010).

- **Gut and Detox Repair** using the 5Rs framework: Remove, Replace, Reinoculate, Repair, and Rebalance. In a psychological context, this framework serves as a metaphor for terrain work with the mind and emotions—helping clients identify what needs to be cleared from their mental ecosystem, what needs nourishing, and how to rebuild internal coherence. While biochemical aspects of detoxification and gut health are better addressed by a functionally trained physician, the psychological terrain is where patterns of thought, stress, and belief are addressed in tandem. Therapists facilitate this inner repair process through guided inquiry, cognitive reframing, somatic practices, and emotional detox rituals, always within the scope of psychological care. Ideally, this work takes place within a multidisciplinary framework, where psychological insights are complemented by functional medical expertise when needed—creating a whole-person strategy for restoring coherence (Fasano, 2012; Mayer et al., 2014; Chrousos, 2009).

- **Vagal Toning** through breathwork, sound, HRV training, and somatic anchors to shift into parasympathetic regulation should also be part of the therapeutic plan. For example, slow-paced diaphragmatic breathing (around 5–6 breaths per minute), humming, or the use of vagal nerve stimulation devices have shown promise in reducing anxiety symptoms by promoting heart rate variability and calming the autonomic nervous system (Lehrer, 2018; Gurel et al., 2020). These practices offer clients accessible, body-based pathways to emotional regulation and resilience—reinforcing terrain coherence through the autonomic gateway.

- **Lifestyle-based Interventions**—commonly referred to as lifestyle modifications in the literature—is the hallmark of behavioral medicine and health psychology. It includes physical, sleep hygiene, exposure to natural light, time in nature, and restorative rituals. Evidence-based research supports the role of these interventions in improving psychological well-being, reducing stress, and enhancing immune function (Creswell & Lindsay, 2014; Peng et al., 2025).

- **Boundary Setting and Assertiveness Skills**—a foundational component of psychological resilience and energetic hygiene. Clients are supported in developing the awareness and confidence to say no, establish limits, and make choices aligned with their well-being. This includes evaluating who and what enters their energetic and relational field, and clearing patterns of guilt, compliance, or self-abandonment. Assertiveness training is a key therapeutic tool shown to reduce stress and enhance self-efficacy (Speed et al., 2017), empowering individuals to protect their coherence without resorting to defensiveness or withdrawal.

- **Resilience Building** through psychoeducation, narrative reframing, and strengthening both physiological and psychological buffers against stress. This includes enhancing clients' coping skills—helping them distinguish between situations they can control and those they cannot. In controllable contexts, we teach problem-focused coping strategies such as task planning, problem-solving, and assertive communication. In less controllable or uncertain conditions, emotion-focused strategies become essential: clients learn acceptance, mindfulness, meaning-making, and letting go. Traditional therapeutic techniques like Cognitive Behavioral Therapy (CBT), Acceptance and Commitment Therapy (ACT), and mindfulness-based interventions provide structured pathways for developing adaptive coping responses (Lazarus & Folkman, 1984; Aldao et al., 2010).

Disclaimer:

The content specifically referencing nutritional, detoxification, or functional medical strategies is for educational purposes only and is not a substitute for medical diagnosis or treatment. Psychologists are not licensed medical doctors and cannot prescribe or direct medical care. All terrain-based recommendations must be considered within the context of the client's overall medical care plan.

Tools are selected not based on symptom management, but on terrain logic: what supports regulation, what supports flow, what supports coherence. We teach clients to become active stewards of their own healing field—using discernment, inner listening, and curiosity to guide their own choices.

When implemented skillfully and compassionately, these tools help clients reclaim authorship of their own healing journey. They are no longer defined by their diagnosis, trauma, or limitations, but by their capacity to self-regulate, adapt, and evolve.

People's beliefs about their abilities
have a profound effect on those abilities.
—Albert Bandura

From Tools to Transformation — Toward a Signature Model

We have assessed the terrain, attuned to the relationship, mapped the multidimensional landscape of a client's experience, and designed interventions rooted in coherence rather than control. But something deeper is happening beneath the surface—something more integrative than any one technique, protocol, or tool.

At this point in the journey, the work begins to reveal a pattern. The practices and interventions we have explored are not disparate elements; they are expressions of a deeper philosophy that has been building since the opening pages. The therapist is not merely a facilitator of techniques but a catalyst of coherence—a conscious co-creator who holds space for order to emerge from fragmentation. (Siegel, 2010).

Likewise, the client is no longer simply the recipient of care. Through terrain repair, psychoeducation, and empowerment, the client steps into a new role: active participant, informed observer, and ultimately, the author of his/her healing narrative (Ryan & Deci, 2000). The client is building the inner scaffolding for autonomy, clarity, and transformation.

What is taking form here is not a set of protocols, but a living model—a terrain-informed, psychologically grounded, spiritually attuned approach to healing. One that respects the innate intelligence of the body, the subtle language of energy, the organizing power of narrative, and the sanctity of free will.

Clarifying Note for the Practitioner

This book does not offer a method, but a shift in perspective. For some readers—especially clinicians or practitioners—it may feel as though we have moved far from the practical terrain of functional medicine into something less "applicable." That is intentional. The goal here is not to replace protocols, but to expand the context in which they are applied. Healing, in this view, begins with awareness—not tools. We return, full circle, to the body—but through a new lens. A lens that includes the unseen, the unmeasured, the relational, the resonant. Practitioners are invited not to abandon their methods, but to inhabit them differently—with greater presence, curiosity, and trust in the intelligence of the system.

We are not replacing medicine. We are extending the map—integrating functional frameworks with biopsychosocial insight and a consciousness-based field perspective. We are building something that cannot be reduced to a flowchart. It is more like a musical composition—structured, yes, but alive, improvisational, and shaped by both client and therapist in real time (Capra & Luisi, 2014).

Wholeness is not achieved by cutting off
a part of the self, but by integration.
—Carl Jung

In the next chapter, this model will be named. A visual and conceptual map will be introduced. But before we name it, we let it take root here—as a felt reality, an intuitive recognition, a synthesis in motion.

The shift has already begun: from technician to translator, from symptom to pattern, from intervention to attunement, to healing which is not delivered, but co-created.

This co-creative healing partnership does not imply equality of expertise—it reflects shared resonance in which the therapist listens for patterns, facilitates coherence, and supports the client's sovereign journey. The client remains the one doing the healing; the therapist is a conscious presence in the field.

What we are left with is not a method—it is a movement toward coherence.

The highest form of healing is
the restoration of inner harmony.

References

Aldao, A., Nolen-Hoeksema, S., & Schweizer, S. (2010). Emotion-regulation strategies across psychopathology: A meta-analytic review. Clinical Psychology Review, 30(2), 217–237. https://doi.org/10.101/10.1016/j.cpr.2009.11.004

Bandura, A. (1997). *Self-efficacy: The exercise of control.* W. H. Freeman and Company. https://doi.org/10.4324/9780429491113

Capra, F., & Luisi, P. L. (2014). *The systems view of life: A unifying vision.* Cambridge University Press.

Chrousos, G. P. (2009). Stress and disorders of the stress system. Nature Reviews Endocrinology, 5(7), 374–381. https://doi.org/10.1038/nrendo.2009.106

Creswell, J. D., & Lindsay, E. K. (2014). How does mindfulness training affect health? A mindfulness stress buffering account. Current Directions in Psychological Science, 23(6), 401–407. https://doi.org/10.1177/0963721414547415

DeMeo, J. (2016). *The Orgone Accumulator Handbook* (3rd ed.). Natural Energy Works.

Fasano, A. (2012). Leaky gut and autoimmune diseases. Clinical Reviews in Allergy & Immunology, 42(1), 71–78. https://doi.org/10.1007/s12016-011-8291-x

Gurel, N. Z., Wittbrodt, M. T., Jung, H., Shandhi, M. M. H., Driggers, E. G., Ladd, S. L., Huang, M., Ko, Y.-A., Shallenberger, L., Beckwith, J., Nye, J. A., Pearce, B. D., Vaccarino, V., Shah, A. J., Inan, O. T., & Bremner, J. D. (2020). Transcutaneous cervical vagal nerve stimulation reduces sympathetic responses to stress in posttraumatic stress disorder: A double-blind, randomized, sham controlled trial. *Neurobiology of Stress, 13*, 100264. https://doi.org/10.1016/j.ynstr.2020.100264

Lazarus, R. S., & Folkman, S. (1984). Stress, appraisal, and coping. Springer.

Lehrer, P. M. (2018). Heart rate variability biofeedback and other psychophysiological procedures as important elements in psychotherapy. *International Journal of Psychophysiology, 131*, 89–95. https://doi.org/10.1016/j.ijpsycho.2017.09.012

Mayer, E. A., Knight, R., Mazmanian, S. K., Cryan, J. F., & Tillisch, K. (2014). Gut microbes and the brain: Paradigm shift in neuroscience. Journal of Neuroscience, 34(46), 15490–15496. https://doi.org/10.1523/JNEUROSCI.3299-14.2014

Peng, B., Chen, W., Wang, H., & Yu, T. (2025). How does physical exercise influence self-efficacy in adolescents? A study based on the mediating role of psychological resilience. *BMC Psychology, 13*(1), 285. https://doi.org/10.1186/s40359-025-02529-y

Perlmutter, D., & Loberg, K. (2015). *Brain maker: The power of gut microbes to heal and protect your brain—for life*. Little, Brown Spark.

Pizzorno, J. E., Murray, M. T., & Joiner-Bey, H. (2010). *The Clinician's Handbook of Natural Medicine* (2nd ed.). Elsevier Health Sciences.

Rogers, C. R. (1961). *On becoming a person: A therapist's view of psychotherapy.* Houghton Mifflin. https://doi.org/10.1037/10788-000

Ryan, R. M., & Deci, E. L. (2000). Self-determination theory and the facilitation of intrinsic motivation, social development, and well-being. *American Psychologist, 55*(1), 68–78. https://doi.org/10.1037/0003-066X.55.1.68

Siegel, D. J. (2010). *The mindful therapist: A clinician's guide to mindsight and neural integration.* W. W. Norton & Company.

Speed, B. C., Goldstein, B. L., & Goldfried, M. R. (2017). Assertiveness training: A forgotten evidence-based treatment. Clinical Psychology: Science and Practice, 25(1), e12216. https://doi.org/10.1111/cpsp.12216

Healing is an inside job.

— B. J. Palmer

Chapter 8

The Personalized Terrain Model

Throughout this book, we have journeyed beyond conventional medical paradigms into deeper explorations of terrain theory, biochemical individuality, symptom interpretation, consciousness, and frequency-based medicine. Each previous chapter has systematically exposed the limitations of conventional treatments, demonstrating why isolated symptomatic fixes often fail to produce lasting health transformations. In contrast, we have highlighted the power and necessity of a holistic, coherent approach that emphasizes empowerment, individual sovereignty, and interconnectedness of mind, body, and energy.

This final chapter serves as a practical synthesis, bringing together these critical insights into a unified, powerful framework: **The Personalized Terrain Model (PTM)**. Recognizing that true healing can only occur when treatment aligns with individual uniqueness, this model provides both practitioners and self-healers with the tools to decode the body's signals, understand genetic and biochemical individuality, engage deeply through conscious self-inquiry, and craft healing strategies that evolve over time.

In the sections that follow, you will be introduced to the foundational concept of biochemical individuality, including how genetic and laboratory insights can inform more tailored care. While this chapter does not delve into the technical analysis of genome data or SNP interpretation, it underscores the value of such tools when interpreted within a broader, personalized framework. These concepts are offered not as rigid protocols, but as entry points into more precise, individualized care.

Next, you'll learn to effectively decode and interpret your body's subtle and overt messages, using practical tools for daily symptom journaling and self-assessment. The subsequent section guides you through structured self-inquiry practices, awakening your capacity for profound self-awareness and psychological transformation. Finally, you will be introduced to the clear, step-by-step methodology of the **Personalized Terrain Model**, designed explicitly for continuous adaptation and sustained empowerment.

Drawing on earlier insights—such as the transformative journeys of individuals like Kate, Stan, Abby, and Luis, and key concepts like coherence, functional medicine frameworks, and empowerment strategies—this culminating chapter offers a comprehensive guide to integrating these principles into a dynamic clinical model.

Whether you are a practitioner supporting others on their healing path, or an individual navigating your own, the Personalized Terrain Model provides a structured yet adaptive framework for transforming theory into practice, insight into action, and personal growth into enduring coherence and wellness.

Biochemical Individuality and Genetic Variability

Roger Williams famously stated, "Individuality is the rule, not the exception." Yet conventional medicine continues to prescribe standardized treatments as though human physiology were uniform. Imagine buying shoes without trying them on—surely discomfort awaits. Similarly, ignoring biochemical individuality invites therapeutic frustration and limited outcomes.

Our genes, lifestyle, and environment create a personalized health narrative, influencing everything from nutrient metabolism to emotional resilience. Genetic polymorphisms such as MTHFR clearly illustrate this, shaping mental clarity, mood stability, and overall vitality (Greenblatt & Brogan, 2016). Recognizing these nuances is fundamental to creating an effective, tailored healing strategy.

Today, a range of functional medicine labs and direct-to-consumer genetic panels provide access to valuable data. Tests such as Nutrigenomic reports, methylation panels, or GI-MAP stool analysis offer insight into detoxification pathways, microbiome composition, and nutritional needs. For example, a person with reduced MTHFR function might benefit from methylated B vitamins, while someone with COMT polymorphisms may require nervous system support to reduce overstimulation.

Case Example

A practitioner supporting a client with chronic anxiety and fatigue reviewed her genetic SNP panel and found impaired B12 absorption, reduced glutathione production, and sluggish detox pathways. Guided by this data, they implemented a targeted plan including methylcobalamin, magnesium glycinate, and gentle binders. Within weeks, the client experienced improved mood stability and cognitive clarity—outcomes that had eluded her for years through conventional approaches.

Clinical Insight

Practitioners trained in genetic interpretation often use decision trees and nutrigenomic mapping tools to prioritize interventions. Rather than treating gene variants in isolation, skilled clinicians look for "clusters"—patterns of related pathways (e.g., methylation, neurotransmitter breakdown, inflammation regulation) that guide where support is needed most. Personalized protocols are then tailored to the individual's presenting symptoms, terrain history, and life context.

By honoring biochemical individuality, both clinicians and self-healers can move beyond guesswork and toward interventions that are not only more precise, but more respectful of the person's true physiological nature.

Key Insight:
Healing begins with recognizing the specificity of the individual's terrain—biochemically, psychologically, and environmentally.

Listening to the Body's Signals

Symptoms often get dismissed as nuisances rather than meaningful communications. However, emerging concepts like the Signaling Theory of Symptoms demonstrate that symptoms serve essential communicative roles, signaling physiological needs and seeking support (Steinkopf, 2015).

Even subjective symptoms without clear clinical markers, such as persistent fatigue or unexplained pain, represent real underlying dynamics influenced by complex interactions between biology, psychology, and social factors (Van Oudenhove & Cuypers, 2019). Effective healing requires not just treating but actively listening to and interpreting these bodily signals.

Case Example: Abby

Abby, a young woman experiencing chronic anxiety and what she described as vivid night terrors, found her symptoms baffling from a conventional lens. Psychotropic medications provided minimal relief. During a therapeutic intake, she noticed her symptoms diminished dramatically while visiting

Florida, only to flare up again upon returning home to California. This pattern led to a mold assessment of her living environment, revealing high mycotoxin exposure. Once she relocated, her symptoms disappeared. Her body had been communicating distress long before standard diagnostics caught up.

Case Example: Luis

Luis, a client in his late thirties, reported daily brain fog, fatigue, and anxiety that seemed to intensify upon returning home after work. Psychological assessment revealed no significant mood or trauma history. The turning point came when an environmental inspection uncovered mold hidden in the HVAC system. Post-remediation, his clarity and energy returned. His symptoms were not imagined—they were messages.

Practical Tool: Journaling

Begin daily symptom journaling—note patterns, triggers, and changes to cultivate deeper body awareness. Use a simple template:

- **Date/Time;**
- **Symptom Experienced;**
- **Context/Environment;**
- **Food Intake;**
- **Emotional State;**
- **What made it better/worse?**

Tracking over time reveals patterns that may be invisible in isolated instances.

Energetic self-awareness can be a powerful diagnostic ally. Notice where in your body you feel expansion, constriction, warmth, or tension in different situations. These somatic shifts often reflect subtle energetic changes that precede symptom onset.

Symptom Tracker Template

Begin daily symptom journaling—note patterns, triggers, and changes to cultivate deeper body awareness.

Date	Symptom	Trigger/ Context	Emotional State	Response/ Relief Strategies	Notes
04/08	Brain fog	After lunch, at office	Frustrated	Took a walk, drank water	Improved slightly within 30 minutes

By honoring symptoms as meaningful signals—rather than dismissing them as false alarms—we begin to decode the body's language and align interventions with its deeper needs.

Key Insight:

Symptoms are terrain signals—dynamic expressions of underlying imbalances seeking resolution.

Self-Inquiry as Medicine: Becoming the Empowered Observer

Knowing yourself is the beginning of all wisdom.
— Aristotle

Healing involves more than symptom relief—it requires self-discovery and emotional maturity through conscious self-inquiry. Research confirms that structured self-reflection enhances resilience, reduces chronic disease risk, and improves mental health outcomes (Sharma et al., 2021).

At the intersection of mind-body integration, consciousness studies, and quantum biology lies the understanding that self-inquiry can shift physiology. The emerging science of quantum coherence—especially in fields like heart-brain resonance and microtubular signaling—suggests that changes in thought and awareness influence not only perception but the energetic organization of biological systems. This mirrors what psychological pioneers such as Carl Jung, Viktor Frankl, and, more recently, Eckhart Tolle have long proposed: that healing often begins with a reorganization of inner meaning.

From a vibrational perspective, the human biofield may be understood as a dynamic feedback system. Somatic cues such as tension, heat, lightness, or discomfort can signal energetic imbalances before pathology emerges. Breathwork, stillness, and intuitive inquiry allow us to attune to the biofield and recognize patterns that hold psychological or emotional charge.

Self-inquiry transforms passive experience into active exploration, as exemplified by Kate and Stan, who refused passivity in their healing journeys. Regular journaling, mindfulness practices, and reflective exercises clarify personal health patterns, turning confusion into clarity and fostering genuine empowerment (Pachana & McLaughlin, 2018).

How to Sense Your Biofield in Daily Life

Start by paying attention to subtle sensations in your body—tightness in the chest, warmth in the hands, a sudden chill, or a light buzzing under the skin. These may reflect energetic imbalances or intuitive awareness.

Try this: Before and after entering a space, meeting someone, or engaging with media, pause for 10 seconds. Close your eyes, breathe slowly, and scan your body. What do you notice?

This simple awareness practice can train your nervous system to register energetic cues before symptoms arise.

True terrain repair includes building coherence between mind, body, and energy fields. Mindfulness, breathwork, guided visualization, journaling, nature connection, and spiritual inquiry help reorganize consciousness. These tools are essential in resolving inner fragmentation, shifting belief systems, and anchoring new identities. Some individuals also choose to incorporate biofeedback technologies—such as using the Genius Insight—as part of their coherence practices. These tools may assist in recognizing energetic disruptions and delivering targeted frequency support to reinforce balance and clarity.

Reflective Exercise: Transforming Inner Blocks

Use the following prompts in a quiet, centered space. Write freely, without judgment:

1. What symptoms or recurring patterns are asking for my attention?
2. What beliefs might be fueling this pattern—about my body, my worth, or my limits?
3. Where might I be holding onto something that is no longer true or helpful?
4. What shift—however small—am I ready to make?

Return to these questions regularly. Over time, they help loosen fixed identities and surface the deeper wisdom embedded within each challenge.

Deepening Practice: Energy & Awareness:
Engage regularly with guided questions such as,
What deeper message is my body communicating right now?
What am I resisting or ignoring?
How can I respond with greater self-compassion and awareness?

Creating Your Personalized Model for Self-Guided Healing

With deeper self-awareness and a clearer understanding of your biochemical individuality, you are now ready to explore the application of this knowledge through the Personalized Terrain Model (PTM). This model provides a conceptual and clinical framework for personalizing care—whether in the context of therapeutic guidance or self-directed healing. Unlike rigid treatment protocols, the PTM is dynamic and evolving, meant to be adapted to each person's needs, life context, and level of readiness.

The model includes five foundational stages, which together support a coherent and empowered healing process:

1. Personalized Assessment

Begin with a comprehensive understanding of your individual landscape. This may include functional lab testing, exploration of family health history, assessment of psychological temperament, and environmental exposures. Practitioners may use intake questionnaires, symptom inventories, and terrain mapping tools to identify patterns. Some also incorporate non-invasive biofeedback technologies—such as voice-frequency scans or HRV monitors—to assess energetic patterns and coherence in the field. Tools like the Genius Insight can complement biochemical and psychological assessments, offering additional layers of insight into the individual's regulatory landscape. Self-healers may start with journaling and environmental checklists to increase awareness.

Case Example: Luis began his terrain repair by identifying mold as a hidden environmental burden. This became the launching point for a full reassessment of his diet, lifestyle, and mindset.

2. Customized Nutritional and Lifestyle Strategies

Interventions at this stage focus on restoring nutritional sufficiency and circadian, metabolic, and hormonal rhythms. Personalized protocols may include food-as-medicine strategies, micronutrient repletion, nervous system regulation, and movement routines. Psychological support may involve setting boundaries, building self-care habits, or redefining one's relationship to food, work, or stress.

Case Example: Kate had undiagnosed B vitamin and iron deficiencies affecting her mood, concentration, and physical energy. Nutritional repletion, along with eliminating inflammatory foods, restored baseline stability that therapy alone could not reach.

3. Targeted Detoxification and Terrain Optimization

Once foundational supports are in place, deeper work may involve clearing infections, reducing toxic load, restoring gut ecology, and supporting detoxification and drainage pathways. This may include antifungal protocols, gentle binders, sauna or lymphatic therapies, microbiome repair, or personalized mitochondrial support.

Case Example: Abby's emotional regulation dramatically improved once mycotoxins were identified and cleared using a mold detox protocol. Terrain optimization allowed her nervous system to stabilize.

4. Consciousness and Coherence Practices

True terrain repair includes building coherence between mind, body, and energy fields. Mindfulness, breathwork, guided visualization, journaling, nature connection, and spiritual inquiry help reorganize consciousness. These tools are essential in resolving inner fragmentation, shifting belief systems, and anchoring new identities.

Practice Example: Stan integrated somatic meditation and guided journaling into his evening routine, gradually reducing sleep disturbances and reconnecting with inner clarity and purpose.

5. Continuous Adaptation and Empowerment

Healing is not a linear path—it's a process of listening, responding, and recalibrating. The PTM encourages regular reassessment, reflection, and intuitive decision-making. Progress includes not only symptom relief but an expanded capacity for self-trust, emotional sovereignty, and lifestyle coherence.

Key Insight: Empowered healing is less about arriving at a destination and more about becoming your own guide, capable of adjusting course as needed.

Immediate Action Step:

Identify which stage resonates most with your current needs, and take one concrete step this week to strengthen that area of your terrain.

Unveiling the Personalized Terrain Model: A Coherent Framework for Transformation

The five stages of the Personalized Terrain Model form an integrated framework designed to support healing at every level—physical, emotional, environmental, and energetic. By now, you have seen how each component contributes to the broader picture of terrain repair, and how tailoring care to the individual leads to more precise, meaningful results.

To visualize how these elements interconnect, imagine a layered mandala, with the core representing personalized assessment, and each surrounding ring expanding outward into lifestyle, detoxification, consciousness, and empowered adaptation. Like a living ecosystem, the terrain is not static—it changes with new insight, shifting environments, and evolving needs.

Let us revisit Stan's journey as a full-spectrum example of the PTM in practice:

Case Summary: Stan's Transformation through the PTM

Stan began experiencing anxiety, fatigue, and disorientation after relocating to a new city. Rather than addressing these symptoms in isolation, he worked with a clinician trained in functional and psychological terrain models. Together, they:

- **Assessed**: Discovered allergies, toxic mold exposure and mapped personality stress responses.

- **Intervened**: Customized a nutrient-rich diet, supplementation, and circadian regulation plan.

- **Optimized**: Supported detoxification with binders, sauna, and antifungals.

- **Integrated**: Practiced daily journaling and somatic breathwork to rebuild coherence.

- **Evolved**: Adapted his plan as insight grew, leading to a career shift, environmental relocation, and long-term emotional stability.

Stan's process exemplifies how the model is not a step-by-step formula, but a flexible, responsive blueprint.

Your Integration Path

You do not need to implement everything at once. Begin with what feels most available. Practitioners may find it helpful to select the PTM stage most relevant to a client's readiness. Individuals may notice certain stages "call" them more strongly based on current symptoms or life transitions.

Your Next Step:

What area of your terrain feels most in need of support right now—biochemical, emotional, environmental, or energetic? What small, intentional action can you take this week?

The PTM affirms that healing is a process of realignment—grounded in physiological insight, environmental awareness, and psychological integrity. As you navigate this terrain, your role shifts from passive recipient to active co-regulator, using the principles of the model to foster both clinical precision and personal agency.

This is more than a framework—it is an invitation. The Personalized Terrain Model reminds us that healing is not imposed from the outside; it is remembered from within. Each stage represents a doorway into greater self-knowledge, integration, and coherence. Whether you are a practitioner walking alongside others or an individual reclaiming your health, the PTM can guide you not just toward solutions— but toward transformation.

Your terrain is intelligent. Trust it. Tend to it.
And let it teach you who you truly are.

References

Egnew, T. R. (2005). The meaning of healing: Transcending suffering. *Annals of Family Medicine, 3*(3), 255–262. https://doi.org/10.1370/afm.313

Greenblatt, J. M., & Brogan, K. (Eds.). (2016). *Integrative therapies for depression: Redefining models for assessment, treatment and prevention.* CRC Press.

Pachana, N. A., & McLaughlin, D. (2008). The importance of self-reflection and awareness for human development in hard times. *Journal of Human Behavior in the Social Environment, 18*(3), 273–277. https://doi.org/ 10.1080/15427609.2018.1489098

Sharma, S., & Rush, S. E. (2014). Mindfulness-based stress reduction as a stress management intervention for healthy individuals: A systematic review. *Journal of Evidence-Based Complementary & Alternative Medicine, 19*(4), 271–286. https://doi.org/10.1177/2156587214543143

Steinkopf, L. (2015). The signaling theory of symptoms: An evolutionary explanation of the placebo effect. *Evolutionary Psychology, 13*(3), 1474704915600559. https://doi.org/10.1177/1474704915600559

Van Oudenhove, L., & Cuypers, S. E. (2010). The relevance of the philosophical mind-body problem for the status of psychosomatic medicine: A conceptual analysis of the biopsychosocial model. *Journal of Psychosomatic Research, 68*(6), 591–599. https://doi.org/10.1007/s11019-013-9521-1

Williams, R. J. (1956). *Biochemical individuality: The basis for the genetotrophic concept.* John Wiley & Sons.

PART III

BEYOND THE EDGE OF THE KNOWN

CONSCIOUSNESS, SPIRIT, AND THE BLUEPRINT OF HEALING

Reality is merely an illusion, albeit a very persistent one.
— Albert Einstein

By this point in our journey, we have examined terrain thinking through biology, psychology, and systems science. We have explored detox pathways, gut integrity, mitochondrial resilience, frequency inputs, and the profound role of coherence in restoring health. These are the foundational layers—the structure. But for many, the deeper work begins once those systems are stabilized. Something subtle begins to stir beneath the surface—a question, a longing, or an experience that resists conventional explanation.

Welcome to Part III.

This section opens the door to healing beyond the visible. It is where the known meets the unknown—where the physical, emotional, and energetic fields converge. Here, coherence is no longer just a physiological measure, but a field of awareness, alignment, and truth.

Most of my clients do not walk through a physical door nowadays. They arrive in a Zoom waiting room—slightly disoriented, often carrying lab reports in one hand and unspoken existential questions in the other. Occasionally there is a cat on the desk. Often there is a quiet feeling that "something bigger is happening," even if no one around them understands. This part of the book is for that feeling. And for the part of you that already senses something beyond logic is at play.

In Part III, we will explore:

- **Consciousness as a causal force in healing**, including theories that describe how intention, observation, and coherence influence biological systems;

- **Energy, biofields, and subtle systems**, such as the electromagnetic and scalar fields that surround and inform the body;

- **Awakening and identity dissolution**, including psychological and spiritual shifts that arise during illness, crisis, or spontaneous realization;

- **Illness as initiation**, where symptoms may act as catalysts for transformation and reconnection with one's deeper Self;

- **Spiritual sovereignty and self-agency**, as the final stages of healing require the reclamation of personal power and alignment with inner truth.

These topics are often labeled "esoteric," but they are increasingly supported by interdisciplinary science and experiential data. My goal is not to convince you of any particular belief, but to expand the field of inquiry. Take what resonates, explore what intrigues you, and set aside the rest.

You may also notice occasional nods to ancient wisdom traditions—fragments of insight that echo through both the mystical and scientific worlds. Among these are the **Hermetic Principles**, a set of foundational teachings rooted in the philosophy of ancient Egypt and Greece. Far from outdated, they offer poetic metaphors and surprising parallels to today's discoveries in quantum physics, frequency medicine, and consciousness studies. Rather than listing them here, I've included a simple guide in the appendix for readers who wish to explore them further.

So take a breath. Loosen the grip. This is not about losing your mind. It is about expanding your perspective. Healing is not only about clearing dysfunction—it is about remembering who you are underneath the noise. And yes, sometimes that remembering comes with a little laughter, a few tears, and a strange dream that changes everything.

✦ *A Note from the Author*

The chapters ahead stretch into new terrain. Some ideas may feel foreign, others may feel like home. Either way, there is no requirement to believe—only to stay curious. Mystery has its own medicine. So let us travel lightly, with clarity and courage. Bring your discernment. And if possible, bring your sense of humor. It helps.

In a holographic universe, even the random events are not truly random. They are part of a larger pattern that we are only just beginning to perceive.

— Michael Talbot

Chapter 9

The Mind Beyond the Mind – Holographic Reality and the Observer Effect

I did not come to the idea of a holographic universe through quantum theory or academic physics. In fact, I found those parts of Talbot's work difficult to wrap my head around—and truthfully, they are not what held my attention.

What pulled me in was something deeper: the recognition that **nothing in this life is random**. There is meaning embedded in every illness, every disruption, every synchronicity. Patterns appear. People return. Symbols surface in dreams or symptoms, pointing toward something just below the surface. I have seen this over and over again—in my own life, and in the lives of the clients I work with.

The **holographic model**, as Talbot described it, is not just about physics. It is about **perception, memory, trauma, and healing**. It is about how the mind, the body, and the field of consciousness interact—not as separate pieces, but as reflections of a larger whole.

When I first read *The Holographic Universe*, it was not the technical explanations that moved me. It was the stories. The case studies. The deeply strange, yet somehow familiar, accounts of people whose inner experiences reshaped their outer reality. These mirrored what I had already come to know through direct experience: that **we are not passive observers of life—we are co-creators**.

This chapter marks a turning point. From here forward, we begin to explore healing not just as terrain repair, but as **a remembrance of the truth that lives beneath it all**. A truth that says your beliefs matter. Your perception matters. Your consciousness is not a byproduct of biology—it is the organizing force behind it.

We are stepping beyond the mind, and into something far vaster. You do not need to fully understand the physics to feel what is true here. You just need to be open to remembering.

Talbot's Holographic Model of Consciousness and Perception

It refers to a worldview in which each part reflects the whole, and every event—however small or strange—contains meaning within a larger pattern. In a holographic system, the boundaries between mind and matter blur. There is no fixed reality "out there," separate from us. Instead, reality is participatory, responsive, and deeply interconnected.

Michael Talbot was not a physicist or a psychologist. He was something rarer—a translator of experience. He had a gift for describing what many intuitives, sensitives, and trauma survivors have felt all along: that perception is not passive. The mind does not merely witness reality; it shapes it.

In his book *The Holographic Universe*, Talbot drew from the groundbreaking work of physicist **David Bohm** and neurophysiologist **Karl Pribram**, who each—independently—began to describe reality as something holographically organized. Bohm proposed that the fabric of the universe behaves more like a dynamic field of information than solid matter. Pribram suggested that memory and perception are distributed throughout the brain in a holographic pattern, not stored in fixed locations.

For many readers, these concepts are hard to grasp intellectually. But what makes Talbot's work so compelling is not the theory—it is the **stories**. He recounts cases of individuals who experienced psychosomatic phenomena so extreme they defied medical logic: a man who developed blistering burn marks after being hypnotized into believing he had been touched by a hot object. Children who formed bruises and wounds based on imagined or symbolic experiences. Clients who witnessed objects move during emotional breakthroughs or periods of intense psychic distress.

These are not mere curiosities. They are signals from a deeper truth: that the **mind is capable of projecting, receiving, and translating information in ways we do not yet fully understand**.

In my own practice, I have seen echoes of this repeatedly. Clients who release a deeply buried trauma often experience a synchronistic shift—a relationship changes, a symptom resolves, a long-lost memory surfaces with vivid clarity. These are not random coincidences. They are part of a larger, intelligent feedback system—a **living matrix** that reflects and responds to our internal states.

From this perspective, perception is not just a lens—it is a **creative force**. What we believe, fear, expect, and focus on acts like a signal, shaping the field around us and drawing in matching experiences. This is not magical thinking. It is holographic participation. It is the recognition that consciousness is embedded in the fabric of reality, and that healing happens not just by repairing tissues, but by restoring coherence between the inner and outer world.

Clinical Insight: Healing the Fractal Self

In my own practice, I have seen many examples of what Talbot described—moments where emotional breakthroughs coincide with external shifts, or where unexplainable changes follow the resolution of something long buried.

One client, a 24-year-old named Charlie (name changed to protect confidentiality) came to therapy during the early days of the COVID-19 pandemic with heightened anxiety. On the surface, his distress seemed like a natural response to global instability: routines had been disrupted, life plans were uncertain, and the world around him felt chaotic. Charlie was thoughtful, introspective, and doing everything "right"—using logic to make decisions, practicing mindfulness, exercising, and staying connected to his values. And yet, the anxiety persisted.

What emerged over time was something deeper. Through a series of sessions and a powerful **age regression hypnotherapy process**, Charlie accessed early memories that had been suppressed but not resolved. As a young child, he had witnessed frequent arguments between his parents. While he lacked the language or perspective to process what was happening, he absorbed the fear energetically and carried it with him into adulthood—not as a memory, but as a vibration still active within his emotional terrain.

The transformation came when his adult self was able to return to that memory space—not just to remember, but to **rewrite the emotional resonance** of the experience. In trance, he comforted his inner child, validated his fear, and offered a new understanding: that he was not to blame, and he was never meant to carry that fear alone. We worked with this younger part of him not as a metaphor, but as a **fractal self**—a living imprint within his psyche that was still looping in time.

After this session, Charlie reported a dramatic shift. His anxiety dropped to its lowest level in years. He felt grounded, present, and at ease in a way he had not experienced in a long time. What had changed was not just his story—it was the **frequency** that had been held in his system. The emotional terrain had recalibrated.

This is what a holographic model of perception and memory allows us to see: the past is not sealed in a linear archive. It is alive, multidimensional, and accessible through consciousness. **Healing is not just a mental process—it is an energetic realignment.** When we tend to these inner fragments with precision and presence, coherence is restored, and the entire system shifts.

The Fractal Self in Therapy

In a holographic model of consciousness, the past is not fixed or sealed away. It is alive—encoded as emotional resonance, held in the body, and looping through our present experience.

When we access unresolved memories through altered states—whether via hypnosis, somatic recall, or deep meditation—we are not simply reprocessing a memory. We are tuning into a **fractal of the self** that is still suffering.

Healing occurs not just when the adult self-gains insight, but when it brings comfort, presence, and coherence to the part of us still trapped in an unresolved frequency.

The result is not catharsis. It is recalibration.

Understanding Holography without the Physics

Let's be honest: the first time I read about holography, I had to read the same paragraph five times, and I still was not sure whether we were talking about consciousness, lasers, or a sci-fi plotline. The physics is dense, and unless you are David Bohm reincarnated, it is easy to get lost in terms like *implicate order* and *nonlocal enfoldment.*

But here is the thing—you do not need a physics degree to understand the heart of the holographic model. You already know it. You have lived it.

Here is the basic idea:

In a hologram, **every piece contains the whole**. If you cut a holographic plate in half, each half still holds the full image—just at a lower resolution.

Translate that to life, and it means: **each part of your being carries the signature of the whole.** Each emotion. Each cell. Each memory—conscious or not. Nothing is isolated.

And it goes beyond the body: what is happening in your relationships, your work, your health, even your so-called "bad luck" or repeating patterns— these may all be expressions of a deeper, unified field of meaning (Talbot, 1991). That is what a holographic universe implies: not chaos, not randomness, but an intelligent order playing out through reflection and resonance.

If that sounds abstract, try this:

- Have you ever had a random song pop into your head, only to realize the lyrics mirror something you are going through?

- Have you gotten physically ill right after making a decision that went against your gut?

- Have you had a dream, a conversation, or a "coincidence" that felt almost scripted—like it was placed there to wake you up?

That is the **felt experience** of holography. Not just a cool visual trick, but a reality where the inner and outer world are entangled—and meaning shows up in mirrors.

You could think of life in a holographic universe like living inside a giant Rorschach test: it reflects back not just who you are, but what you are carrying, denying, believing, or trying to integrate.

This is not just my perspective. **Caroline Myss** (1996), a medical intuitive and theologian, describes a nearly identical truth from the lens of energy anatomy. In *Anatomy of the Spirit*, she proposes that the body's symptoms are symbolic expressions of the soul's experience—and that each energy center reflects archetypal patterns that mirror our entire life story. In her model, too, the body speaks the language of consciousness.

In this framework, healing is not about fixing a faulty part. It is about accessing the whole pattern and restoring coherence at the **field level**. That might mean working with the body, the mind, the energy field—or all three at once.

And no, you do not have to understand how it works to benefit from it. You just have to stop dismissing the weirdness when it shows up. Because in a holographic world, the weirdness might just be the wisdom trying to reach you.

Each emotion. Each cell. Each memory — conscious or not. Nothing is isolated.

Holography and the Patterned Self

In a holographic system, **every part contains the whole**. Illness, mood, memory, and even synchronicity are not isolated events—they are reflections of a deeper pattern trying to reveal itself.

Caroline Myss describes this beautifully in *Anatomy of the Spirit*, where she shows that the body is not just physical—it is **symbolic**, **archetypal**, and **intelligent**. Pain shows up not as punishment, but as a message. Each symptom is a doorway to greater awareness.

From this perspective, healing is not about erasing symptoms. It is about **interpreting the signals of a multidimensional self** and restoring coherence between body, psyche, and soul.

Physician and trauma expert **Gabor Maté** (2003) echoes this perspective in *When the Body Says No*, where he documents how repressed emotions and unresolved early experiences consistently manifest in chronic illness. The body, in his words, is not betraying us—it is **communicating what the conscious mind cannot or will not express**.

You could think of life in a holographic universe like living inside a giant Rorschach test...

This dynamic is visible in the field of trauma therapy as well. **Bessel van der Kolk** (2014), in *The Body Keeps the Score*, demonstrates that trauma is not just stored as memory but lives on as **somatic patterning**—unresolved loops of reaction, fear, or shutdown that continue to echo long after the threat is gone.

...restoring coherence at the field level.

Biologist **Rupert Sheldrake** (2009) has proposed a similar idea through his theory of **morphic resonance**—that fields of memory and pattern can exist outside the brain, influencing biological form and behavior across time and space. In a holographic and energetic model of healing, such fields may explain the **nonlocal** transmission of beliefs, traumas, or even ancestral emotional material.

Healing Through Symbol, Pattern, and Meaning.

In a holographic model of consciousness, nothing is random. Life is not a series of disconnected events—it is a web of meaning unfolding in patterns that often repeat until they are seen, acknowledged, and integrated.

This is one of the most powerful truths I have come to understand as a psychologist: **healing is not linear. It is symbolic.** And that symbolism is everywhere—etched into the body, woven into dreams, mirrored in our relationships, and embedded in the timing of events that seem, at first glance, merely coincidental.

The question is not "What is wrong with me?" The question is "What is this trying to show me?"

When we shift from pathology to pattern, the terrain of healing changes completely. Symptoms stop being enemies and start becoming **messengers**. Chronic fatigue becomes a plea to slow down and reassess one's boundaries. Autoimmunity becomes a mirror for self-attack or unresolved grief. Recurring conflict may reflect an inner voice that has gone unheard for too long.

Clients often come to me when their body is speaking more loudly than their mind can interpret. And the body—wise as it is—will often escalate the volume until the message is received. But once we begin to work symbolically, the healing process accelerates. Insight deepens. The terrain softens. The pattern that once looped silently in the background becomes conscious—and in that moment of recognition, **the frequency shifts**.

This is not metaphorical. It is energetic. Symbol carries frequency. Pattern holds vibration. When meaning is restored to a fragmented experience, coherence returns—not just psychologically, but somatically, relationally, and often spiritually.

It is no coincidence that mystical traditions, indigenous healing systems, and the emerging field of biofield science all emphasize **meaning-making** as part of transformation. From the perspective of the psyche and the soul, healing is less about removing symptoms and more about **reconnecting with the intelligence encoded in them.**

This is why the therapeutic process must go beyond behavior modification or symptom suppression. It must invite the client into a **conversation with the self**—a deep inquiry into the language of the body, the metaphors of the mind, and the echoes of emotion stored across time.

In this model, the therapist is not a fixer. We are interpreters, guides, and meaning-weavers. We help make the invisible visible—and in doing so, we help restore **inner coherence** and reawaken **agency** within the client.

Because once a person sees the pattern—and understands the message—they are no longer a victim of it.

They become the **author** of the next chapter.

The body speaks in symbols.
It is not broken—it is communicating.

Symbolic Terrain Work in Practice

In symbolic healing, the body is not malfunctioning—it is communicating. Symptoms are not enemies to silence, but messages to decode.

Ask: What pattern is repeating here?

Symbolic Terrain Work in Practice (cont.)

What emotional frequency does this symptom carry?

What part of me is asking to be seen, heard, or re-integrated?

Working symbolically means listening for the deeper intelligence behind the disruption.

The goal is not just relief—it is **restored coherence** through insight, alignment, and self-recognition.

When we decode the pattern, the terrain recalibrates.

The Observer Effect and Quantum Mind-Body Implications

In the world of classical physics, reality is assumed to be objective—existing independently of our awareness of it. But quantum physics challenges that assumption at its core. In the quantum realm, **reality is not fixed until it is observed**. This is the essence of the **Observer Effect**, and it has profound implications not only for science—but for healing, perception, and the terrain of the self.

The most famous demonstration of this is the **double-slit experiment**, where electrons behave like a wave when unobserved—spreading out into multiple possibilities—but collapse into a particle, choosing a specific location, the moment someone observes them. In other words, **consciousness alters outcome**.

Let that sink in.

It means that **the act of observation—the presence of awareness—determines which version of reality becomes manifest.**

Now, apply that to healing.

What if the symptoms we "observe" are not just physical facts, but collapses of potential into form—guided by expectation, emotion, belief, and attention? What if our internal landscape, our fears and assumptions, are shaping the terrain of our biology just as surely as genes, microbes, or food?

We already see echoes of this in **psychoneuroimmunology**, where mental and emotional states affect immune function and inflammation. Or in **placebo studies**, where belief and expectation drive physiological change—sometimes more powerfully than the intervention itself. These are not anomalies. They are evidence of a **participatory universe**, one in which **the observer is never truly separate from the observed.**

And that includes the therapist.

In clinical work, this plays out subtly but unmistakably. The practitioner's mindset, the emotional field in the room, and the resonance between client and healer all influence outcomes. A therapist who sees a client as broken may unconsciously reinforce pathology. One who holds belief in the client's capacity for coherence and restoration may amplify healing. This is not mysticism—it is frequency attunement and field effect. It is quantum biology in motion.

There is emerging evidence that even **DNA expression is responsive to consciousness**. Research in quantum biology suggests that DNA molecules behave differently in coherent versus chaotic electromagnetic fields—and that emotion, intention, and attention can alter molecular behavior (Montagnier, 2011; McTaggart, 2007). In other words, **our state of consciousness is part of the healing protocol**—whether we acknowledge it or not.

This understanding also challenges the passive model of patient care. If consciousness shapes outcome, then the client is never a passive recipient of healing. They are a **co-creative force** within the process. Their beliefs, trauma imprints, self-perception, and even unconscious expectations all interact with the healing field.

This is not just a shift in theory—it is a shift in power.

Healing is not something done *to* us. It is something that unfolds *through* us, in relationship with what we observe, believe, feel, and expect. In a quantum model, attention is not neutral—it is a tool. Awareness is not a bystander—it is a **primary agent in the creation of our terrain.**

The act of observation is not passive —
it is a creative force that collapses possibility into form.

Consciousness as a Variable in Healing

In quantum physics, the observer changes the outcome.
In healing, the same is true.
Your attention, belief, and emotional frequency shape your internal terrain.
Perception is participation.
Whether you are the healer or the client, you are part of the field.
The question is never just "What is happening?"
It is always: "Who is observing—and with what level of awareness?"

The Nocebo Effect as Terrain Sabotage

This is why prognosis can be a dangerous ritual in conventional medicine. When a physician says, "You have six months to live," this delivery of clinical information does not merely convey data—it becomes a declaration that shapes the energetic and psychological landscape of the client. In many cases, this becomes a self-fulfilling prophecy. In a pernicious way, if the client internalizes that expectation, it can become a biological command. The field collapses around that belief and negates any other potential timeline. Talk about a loss of free will.

This phenomenon is known as the **nocebo effect**—the inverse of the placebo. And it is more than psychological. Research shows that **negative expectations can trigger physiological responses**, including immune suppression, heightened pain perception, and altered neurochemistry (Benedetti, 2007; Colloca & Miller, 2011). The terrain responds not only to molecules and diagnoses, but to **suggestion, belief, and the energetic charge of the words themselves**.

In a participatory model of healing, this means we must treat words as interventions. We must recognize that **every statement carries a frequency**—and that the way we frame prognosis either collapses possibility or amplifies coherence.

The Observer in the Healing Room

The moment a diagnosis is delivered, the terrain begins to respond.

The practitioner is never neutral. They are a carrier of frequency, authority, and expectation.

What they believe, what they fear, what they hope for—all of it enters the room.

In a quantum model, *the observer affects the field.*

That means your mindset as a healer is not incidental—it is part of the intervention.

Are you collapsing possibility?

Or holding open space for coherence?

In a participatory universe, belief is not benign—it is causal.

Nonlocality, Synchronicity, and Resonance in Healing

If the Observer Effect reveals that consciousness collapses potential into form, **nonlocality** takes it one step further: it shows that consciousness is not bound by time or space.

In quantum physics, nonlocality describes the phenomenon where two particles, once connected, remain linked across vast distances—so that a change in one instantly affects the other. Einstein famously called this "spooky action at a distance." But what once seemed bizarre is now repeatedly observed in experiments: information, influence, and energy can travel across space without a physical medium.

This principle is not limited to subatomic particles. It shows up again and again in human experience—especially in healing.

- A client thinks of someone they have not spoken to in years, and that person texts them the next morning.

- A practitioner senses emotional tension in a distant client's body before a word is spoken.

- Two strangers meet and feel an inexplicable familiarity, as if their fields had already met before their names did.

These are not coincidences. They are **synchronicities**—meaningful connections that defy logic but resonate deeply with truth. From a holographic and energetic standpoint, synchronicity is the visible expression of **nonlocal resonance**: the way frequencies attract, reflect, and respond across time and space.

Therapeutic research is beginning to reflect this. In a phenomenological study of clinical practice, over **67% of therapists reported significant synchronicity experiences** with their clients, and many found these moments meaningful and therapeutically valuable (Roxburgh et al., 2016). These experiences are often spontaneous and cannot be forced, but when they arise, they carry a charge—a sense that something larger is aligning through the healing encounter.

In my own clinical experience, healing is often accelerated when the symbolic, emotional, and energetic meaning of a synchronicity is acknowledged.

It's not just "weird"—it's on purpose.

It signals that the terrain is moving, the field is aligning, and that something deeper is working beneath the surface.

This is where **resonance** becomes the language of the healing field.

Resonance is not the same as similarity—it is vibrational harmony. When two systems share a common frequency, they begin to entrain, to synchronize, to amplify each other's signal. This happens between hearts. Between brainwaves. Between individuals and ideas. And—most powerfully—between the body and the beliefs that it has been waiting to embody.

There is growing scientific exploration in this area. Studies in **distant healing intention (DHI)** therapies—where a healer focuses their attention on a recipient across distance—have shown measurable physiological effects, from changes in brainwave activity to subtle shifts in heart rate variability (Achterberg et al., 2005; Radin, 2006). These results, while modest and still evolving, suggest that **intention and resonance can influence the field nonlocally**, supporting what energy medicine practitioners have long observed.

In therapeutic work, resonance is everything.

When a client feels truly seen, there is resonance. When their internal story finally lands in language that reflects it back, there is resonance.

When a healing tool meets a body that is ready to receive it, the terrain softens. The frequency shifts.

From this view, healing is not imposed—it is **evoked**. Not forced—but entrained.

We are not separate minds in separate bodies hoping to connect.

We are **fields of consciousness already entangled**, listening for the signal that matches our next becoming.

Take a moment:

Can you recall a time when a meaningful coincidence seemed to guide you?

What if it was not random, but your own frequency shaping the feedback loop of reality?

Reality is not something we passively observe — it's something that responds to who we are.

Bioresonance in Practice
Genius Insight and the Resonant Field

The **Genius Insight** system is a practical application of nonlocal resonance and informational medicine. It does not diagnose in the conventional sense. Instead, it captures the **vibrational signature** of a person's biofield using multiple data points: voice (approximately 60% of the scan), photo, name, date of birth, and optionally, a short intention phrase.

Drawing from expansive **frequency libraries**, the system compares the client's profile to a **normative frequency database**—highlighting areas of dissonance and coherence across physical, emotional, and energetic layers, including organs, emotions, chakras, meridians, and more.

It then generates **corrective frequencies** designed to support **balancing, harmonizing, and restoring coherent energy patterns** within the client's field. The aim is not to treat disease, but to offer precise **informational cues** that the system can receive and respond to—if the terrain is ready.

The Genius Insight mirrors the key principles explored in this chapter:

Nonlocality. Synchronicity. Resonance.

Healing is not imposed. It is **evoked** through vibrational coherence and conscious participation.

Reality as Feedback –
Placebo, Belief, and Intentionality

If consciousness participates in shaping what we experience, then what we call "reality" is not fixed—

it is responsive.

It becomes a kind of mirror, giving feedback on our internal state.

This feedback is not just emotional or symbolic. It is also **physiological**.

One of the most well-known examples is the **placebo effect**, where an inert substance produces real therapeutic benefit. This is often treated as an inconvenient artifact in clinical research, but in truth, it reveals something profound: **the belief in healing can trigger biological change** (Benedetti et al., 2005).

Even when patients know they are taking a placebo—what researchers call an **open-label placebo**—benefits can still occur (Kaptchuk et al., 2010). It appears that the ritual of care, the meaning of the act, and the intention behind it carry enough weight to **restructure the terrain**. The body responds not only to chemistry, but to **expectation**.

But belief cuts both ways, as we have seen before with the nocebo effect.

Words, tone, and presence become **clinical instruments**—for better or worse.

The body does not only respond to what is happening; it responds to what is expected to happen.

And yet, this same dynamic opens a door: if belief can harm, **it can also heal**.

The healing field begins to shift when the narrative changes—from fixed outcome to fluid potential, from linear prognosis to multidimensional feedback. Intention becomes the tuning fork. Meaning becomes the frequency.

Studies on heart-brain coherence, intention-based experiments, and subtle energy therapies have all shown that **focused attention modulates physiology**, immune response, and emotional regulation (McCraty & Childre, 2010; McTaggart, 2007). It is not magic. It is resonance.

In this context, healing is not a passive process, nor a linear one. It is a **participatory dialogue** between consciousness and the terrain.

And reality—the one we experience through symptoms, setbacks, or synchronicities—is the response.
A coded invitation to shift.

This dynamic extends beyond medicine. In psychological research, even so-called "sham" interventions can catalyze real change. In my own doctoral work, the control group received a single-day experience, while the treatment group underwent a twelve-week protocol. Yet the control group still showed improvement—because the mere structure and context of receiving support triggered a therapeutic response. Belief, environment, and meaning were enough to activate the feedback loop.

The Belief Loop

The placebo and nocebo effects are not opposites—they are two sides of the same feedback loop.

What matters is not whether something is "real" in a biochemical sense, but whether it resonates as truth in the body-mind.

Healing begins when the system is given a new signal to respond to—through belief, context, or conscious intention.

As Above, So Below —
The Hermetic Principle of Correspondence

That which is Below corresponds to that which is Above, and that which is Above corresponds to that which is Below, to accomplish the miracle of the One Thing.
— The Emerald Tablet of Hermes Trismegistus

Long before quantum physics or systems theory, ancient Hermetic philosophy proposed that the universe is holographic in nature. The Principle of Correspondence—famously summarized as "As above, so below"—teaches that all levels of reality reflect each other. The macrocosm mirrors the microcosm. The inner world mirrors the outer.

This is more than spiritual poetry—it's a **model of pattern recognition**.

Whether we look at the structure of galaxies or neurons, water molecules or emotional responses, we find recurring geometries and feedback loops. Symbol, myth, biology, and belief often operate as nested systems—each layer **expressing the same core frequency**, just at a different scale.

In a healing context, this principle affirms that:

- Symptoms are not isolated malfunctions—they are **messages encoded at one layer of the field**, often pointing to disharmony at another.

- A shift in awareness can generate a ripple effect, creating **coherence across mental, emotional, energetic, and physical domains**.

The therapeutic relationship itself becomes a mirror—what arises in the room often reflects what is unspoken in the client's field.

From this lens, **nothing is random**, and everything is connected—not by superstition, but by pattern, meaning, and energetic structure.

This is where ancient mysticism meets quantum resonance. And it strengthens the foundation you've just laid:

Reality is not fixed.

*It is **resonant, reflective, and responsive.***

Healing is not something we receive—it is something we **participate in**.

From the terrain of the body to the quantum fabric of the field, we are in constant dialogue with reality. When we begin to treat symptoms as symbols, beliefs as frequencies, and the body as an intelligent messenger, the entire model of healing transforms.

We are no longer passive recipients. We become co-creators.

The moment you change your perception is the moment you rewrite the chemistry of your body.
— Bruce H. Lipton, Ph.D.

References

Achterberg, J., Cooke, K., Richards, T., Standish, L. J., Kozak, L., & Lake, J. (2005). Evidence for correlations between distant intentionality and brain function in recipients: A functional magnetic resonance imaging analysis. *Journal of Alternative and Complementary Medicine, 11*(6), 965–971. https://doi.org/10.1089/acm.2005.11.965

Benedetti, F., Carlino, E., & Pollo, A. (2011). How placebos change the patient's brain. *Neuropsychopharmacology, 36*, 339–354. https://doi.org/10.1038/npp.2010.81

Colloca, L., & Miller, F. G. (2011). The nocebo effect and its relevance for clinical practice. *Psychosomatic Medicine, 73*(7), 598–603. https://doi.org/10.1097/PSY.0b013e3182294a50

Di Ciaula, A., Bonfrate, L., Noviello, M., & Portincasa, P. (2023). Thyroid function: A target for endocrine disruptors, air pollution and radiofrequencies. *Endocrine, Metabolic & Immune Disorders - Drug Targets, 23*(8), 1032–1040. https://doi.org/10.2174/1871530321666210909115040

Kaptchuk, T. J., Friedlander, E., Kelley, J. M., Sanchez, M. N., Kokkotou, E., Singer, J. P., Kowalczykowski, M., Miller, F. G., Kirsch, I., & Lembo, A. J. (2010). Placebos without deception: A randomized controlled trial in irritable bowel syndrome. *PLOS ONE, 5*(12), e15591. https://doi.org/10.1371/journal.pone.0015591

McCraty, R., & Childre, D. (2010). Coherence: Bridging personal, social, and global health. *Alternative Therapies in Health and Medicine, 16*(4), 10–24. https://pubmed.ncbi.nlm.nih.gov/20653292/

McTaggart, L. (2007). *The Intention Experiment: Using Your Thoughts to Change Your Life and the World.* Free Press.

Miller, J. G., Dennis, E. L., Heft-Neal, S., Jo, B., & Gotlib, I. H. (2022). Fine particulate air pollution, early life stress, and their interactive effects on adolescent structural brain development: A longitudinal tensor-based morphometry study. *Cerebral Cortex, 32*(10), 2156–2169. https://doi.org/10.1093/cercor/bhab346

Radin, D. (2006). *Entangled Minds: Extrasensory Experiences in a Quantum Reality.* Paraview Pocket Books.

Roxburgh, E. C., Ridgeway, S., & Roe, C. A. (2016). Synchronicity in the therapeutic setting: A survey of practitioners. Counselling and Psychotherapy Research, 17(2), 138–146. https://doi.org/10.1002/capr.12094

Taylor, K. W., Eftim, S. E., Sibrizzi, C. A., Blain, R. B., Magnuson, K., Hartman, P. A., Rooney, A. A., & Bucher, J. R. (2025). Fluoride exposure and children's IQ scores: A systematic review and meta-analysis. *JAMA Pediatrics, 179*(3), 282–292. https://doi.org/10.1001/jamapediatrics.2024.5542

Your biography becomes your biology. The wounds you do not heal in your heart, you will express in your body.

— Caroline Myss

Chapter 10

Consciousness as a Healing Force – The Soul as Causal Agent

From Clinical Hypnosis to Quantum Healing

My journey into the world of hypnosis and healing began many years ago, inspired by the work of **Dr. Brian Weiss** (Weiss, 1988). His groundbreaking books on **past life regression** sparked my initial interest in exploring the unseen dimensions of healing. This was the catalyst for my decision to become a psychologist—not just to help people through talk therapy, but to address deeper layers of the psyche through hypnosis and soul-level exploration.

As a clinical psychologist, I was initially grounded in **psychodynamic theories**, particularly **Sigmund Freud's** model of the unconscious mind. Freud's framework emphasized how the unconscious stores repressed memories and desires, laying the foundation for modern hypnotic techniques aimed at uncovering hidden material (Freud, 1900; Freud, 1923). However, Freud eventually moved away from hypnosis in favor of his free association technique, which he found more effective for exploring the unconscious. Although hypnosis has been effectively used in trauma resolution and pain management, its traditional applications were often limited to uncovering repressed memories and addressing surface-level psychological issues, without fully exploring the deeper, spiritual dimensions of healing.

Despite this, Freud's early work on hypnosis and the unconscious was instrumental in shaping my understanding of how the mind can be influenced to access deeper layers of experience. Yet, I felt something was missing—a holistic understanding of the spiritual and soul-level dimensions of healing.

In 2009, I joined the Florida Society of Clinical Hypnosis (FSCH), eager to expand my knowledge of hypnosis and deepen my clinical skills. However, while FSCH introduced me to hypnosis techniques for trauma resolution, pain management, and ego-state therapy, Past Life Regression (PLR) and soul-level healing were still not considered mainstream within academic circles. This all changed in 2024, when I attended a transformative workshop on "Ancestral and Past Life Trauma", presented by Philip Accaria, Ph.D., and Paul Schenk, Psy.D. It was the first time in my professional experience that past life therapy was fully validated with ASCH-approved CEU credits, structured protocols, and clinical legitimacy.

Yet the most profound shift in my journey occurred earlier, when I discovered **Quantum Healing Hypnosis Technique® (QHHT®)**—referenced here for educational purposes only—a modality developed by **Dolores Cannon**. While traditional clinical hyp-

nosis focused on the unconscious mind, QHHT® revealed a new dimension of healing—one that connected individuals not only with present-life issues,
but also with past life memories, soul-level wisdom,
and spiritual healing (Cannon, 1998, 2001). QHHT®
showed me that the **higher self**—often referred to as
the subconscious—holds the key to **unlimited
knowledge** and **healing potential**. This marked a
significant departure from the psychodynamic model,
introducing a more multidimensional approach to
healing.

Shortly after, I trained in QHHT® and Beyond
Quantum Healing (BQH), becoming a certified practitioner listed on QuantumHealers.com. Through these techniques, I witnessed clients accessing lifetimes,
archetypes, and realms of consciousness beyond what
the conscious mind could fabricate. I saw physical
symptoms disappear, not because they were "treated,"
but because the root causes were understood, integrated, and released. This was not just a matter of
treating symptoms; it was about understanding the
soul's journey and how the emotional and spiritual
layers impact our physical experience.

While Dr. Brian Weiss's work on past life regression is commonly referenced and discussed in mainstream hypnosis circles, Dolores Cannon's contributions to soul-level regression remained largely absent
from academic discourse. This gap between traditional hypnosis and quantum healing persists today, but
for those of us who have practiced QHHT®, the **clinical utility of soul-level exploration** is undeniable.

Today, I see no contradiction between my foundation in health psychology and my work as a quantum

healing practitioner. In fact, it is precisely because I understand both worlds that I can bridge the gap between psychological science and multidimensional healing. The techniques may differ, but the intention is the same: to restore wholeness.

This chapter is where those two worlds meet. We will begin by defining consciousness through the lens of traditional psychological models, such as Freud's early typology of the unconscious, preconscious, and conscious mind, moving beyond these concepts to include the broader definitions of consciousness as seen in QHHT® and BQH. Here, the subconscious or higher self is understood not just as a storehouse of repressed memories, but as a conduit for soul-level wisdom, and spiritual healing. We will explore how consciousness acts as a causal force—shaping our reality, guiding our healing, and aligning us with our higher purpose.

In this context, the **biofield** reflects the **coherence** or **fragmentation** of the **soul's alignment** with the physical body. The biofield is not merely an energetic overlay; it is the dynamic expression of consciousness in its interaction with the physical form. This understanding opens up new pathways for healing, where intention-based tools, such as biofeedback systems like the Genius Insight, can guide the process of re-establishing balance and coherence within the body, mind, and spirit.

Moreover, spontaneous remission—often seen as a mystery—can now be understood as the natural result of internal congruence. When mind, body, and spirit align, the body's innate ability to heal is activated. Healing is not something we force upon the body;

it is a remembering of our true essence, an unfolding back into wholeness.

When the clinical field finally made room for the soul, a doorway opened—not just for belief, but for transformation.
—Reflections after FSCH 2024 Workshop

From Freud's Typology to Modern Definitions of Consciousness

Freud's typology of the mind, with its distinction between the conscious, preconscious, and unconscious, offers a framework for understanding the layers of the human psyche (Freud, 1923). Freud's unconscious mind was conceptualized as a hidden repository of memories and desires that influence behavior without conscious awareness. This **unconscious** was thought to contain **repressed content**— the darker aspects of human existence that were too uncomfortable to acknowledge in everyday life.

In the world of **Quantum Healing Hypnosis**, however, the subconscious goes beyond Freud's model. It is not simply a storage system for forgotten memories or repressed desires, but a vibrant, multidimensional aspect of the self, often referred to as the subconscious (SC) or the higher self. According to Dolores Cannon, the **subconscious**, or **higher self**, is the part of us that holds **unlimited knowledge**, has access to our soul's wisdom, and connects us to universal consciousness (Cannon, 2001). This aspect is not limited to the repressed material of the unconscious mind, but extends into the realms of past lives, spiritual contracts, and soul-level healing.

In brief:

- **Freud's Typology:** The unconscious stores repressed memories and instinctual drives, influencing behavior without awareness.

- **QHHT® Subconscious:** A multidimensional aspect of the self—also called the Higher Self—that guides healing and accesses universal wisdom.

In QHHT® sessions, the subconscious is accessed to facilitate healing, reveal soul-level guidance, and offer insight from dimensions that transcend the present life experience.

The unconscious mind is not just a repository of forgotten memories, but a vast reservoir of untapped potential—waiting to be accessed for healing and growth.

Defining Consciousness from a Mind-Body-Spirit Perspective

To understand the power of consciousness as a healing force, we must first explore how consciousness is perceived and how it may operate across various levels of the mind, body, and spirit. Consciousness is not simply a passive observer of reality but an active, multidimensional force that shapes our experiences and influences our well-being.

What is Consciousness?

Consciousness is often described as awareness—the state of being aware of one's thoughts, emotions, and surroundings. However, from a **Mind-Body-Spirit perspective**, consciousness is far more complex. It encompasses **multiple levels of awareness** that operate simultaneously, each with its own role and function in shaping reality.

In the Mind-Body-Spirit model, consciousness is seen not only as a mental phenomenon but also as a **spiritual and energetic force**. It is a dynamic force that connects the physical body, the emotional self, the mind, and the spirit, facilitating healing, growth, and transformation.

Conscious Mind: The Aspect of Awareness

The conscious mind is the part of our awareness that is responsible for our **thoughts, decisions, and perceptions**. It is the aspect of ourselves that experiences the present moment and interacts with the world around us. The conscious mind is **linear** and **rational**, processing information in a way that is based on logic and reason.

- **Role in Healing**: The conscious mind plays a critical role in setting healing intentions, deciding on personal goals, and directing attention to areas that need healing. It is where the process of self-awareness begins, and it is the point from which we begin to question, learn, and grow.

- **Limitations**: While the conscious mind is essential for everyday functioning, it is limited by ego, beliefs, and cognitive biases. Its view of reality is often shaped by external influences, past experiences, and societal conditioning.

Subconscious Mind: The Reservoir of Beliefs and Instincts

The subconscious mind operates largely below the level of conscious awareness. It governs our automatic functions, such as heart rate and respiration, as well as our instincts, habits, and emotional responses. The subconscious is like a **vast storage system** that holds **memories, beliefs, fears,** and **traumas**.

- **Role in Healing**: The subconscious mind is the keeper of our life experiences and can be a major player in the healing process. Repressed memories and unprocessed emotions can become stored in the subconscious and may cause energetic blockages or imbalances in the biofield, which can manifest as physical symptoms or emotional distress.

- **Reprogramming the Subconscious**: Healing practices that engage the subconscious mind, such as hypnotherapy, guided meditation, and Quantum Healing Hypnosis, aim to bring repressed material to the surface, allowing individuals to process and release old emotional patterns, transforming negative beliefs into positive, life-affirming ones.

Higher Self: The Bridge to Spiritual Awareness

The higher self is often described as the **expanded aspect of consciousness** that transcends the individual ego. It is our **inner wisdom**, the higher aspect of our soul that is connected to divine consciousness and the universal flow of energy. The higher self exists outside the constraints of time and space, offering guidance, insight, and healing from a place of unconditional love and spiritual clarity.

- **Role in Healing**: The higher self has access to higher truths, life purposes, and soul contracts. It acts as a guiding force, helping us align with our true path and navigate through difficult life challenges. By connecting with the higher self, we can access healing energy and soul-level intelligence that supports the biofield's coherence and promotes profound transformation.

- **Connection with Biofield Healing**: The higher self is intimately connected with the biofield, as it helps guide the energy flow that supports health and healing. Through practices such as Quantum Healing Hypnosis, we can access the higher self and receive insights into the underlying causes of illness, dysfunction, or imbalance.

Soul and Oversoul: The Eternal Essence of Consciousness

At the deepest level of consciousness lies the soul, the eternal essence that transcends individual lifetimes. The soul is the **primary carrier of our life experiences** and **spiritual evolution**. While the higher self represents our personal connection to the divine, the soul is the larger aspect of consciousness that holds the wisdom of countless lifetimes.

- **Role in Healing**: The soul is the keeper of our spiritual purpose and has an innate wisdom about our life journey, including karmic patterns, lessons, and challenges. It can provide deep insight into the spiritual causes of physical or emotional conditions, allowing us to heal at the soul level.

- **Oversoul**: The oversoul is a more expanded version of the soul, containing multiple aspects of consciousness from various soul contracts and experiences. It is the fractal of Source or the One that connects us all. The oversoul holds the **collective consciousness of all of our soul fragments,** guiding us toward greater unity and spiritual awakening.

Integrating the Layers of Consciousness in Healing

When we engage in healing work, we are not simply addressing the physical body but also the **energetic and spiritual layers of consciousness. Healing, then, is a **holistic process** that engages the **mind, body, and spirit** in a harmonious flow. By recognizing the interconnectedness of these aspects of consciousness, we can facilitate profound transformations in the client's life.

- **Mind-Body Connection**: As explored earlier, the mind and body are interconnected, and consciousness directly influences the health of the biofield, leading to physical healing. Shifting our mental and emotional states can have an immediate effect on the body's health.

- **Soul-Level Healing**: By connecting with the higher self and soul, we can access soul-level wisdom and healing that goes beyond the limitations of the mind and body. This deeper healing may involve releasing karmic patterns, transforming beliefs, or aligning with life's true purpose.

Conclusion: Consciousness as a Healing Force

Consciousness is not a singular entity; it is a multi-layered force that includes the conscious mind, subconscious mind, higher self, and soul/oversoul. Each of these aspects plays a unique role in the healing process, and integration of all layers of consciousness allows for holistic healing.

In the next section, we will explore how these aspects of consciousness—attention, intention, and emotion—combine to form a powerful healing force. We will also discuss how biofield coherence and soul-level intelligence work together to restore balance, alignment, and health.

*Sometimes the most evolved souls choose
the most difficult lives in order to grow the most.*
— Brian L. Weiss, M.D.

Seth's Teachings on Consciousness and Soul-Level Intelligence

Seth, channeled by Jane Roberts in the 1960s, is a well-known figure in the realm of metaphysical teachings. Through Roberts, Seth communicated a groundbreaking understanding of consciousness, the nature of reality, and the soul's role in shaping human experience. His works have deeply influenced spiritual seekers, metaphysical practitioners, and even quantum theorists.

Rather than framing consciousness as a byproduct of biology or a mere tool of cognition, Seth described it as the foundational fabric of existence. From his perspective, consciousness is the medium through which reality is constructed, expanded, and explored.

This departure from the materialist view of mind reorients our understanding of healing, choice, and the nature of being. It suggests that transformation begins not with external correction, but with the internal realization of who we are and the power we hold.

Consciousness as Causal

Seth's central principle—that "you create your own reality"—positions consciousness as the origin point of all lived experience. Our thoughts, beliefs, and emotions do not merely color perception; they shape the energetic structure of our world. In therapeutic terms, this means that intention is not just a passive mindset—it actively shapes the outcomes we experience. From the cellular level to life circumstance, change becomes possible when internal narratives shift.

As someone trained in psychology, I find this profoundly liberating. Instead of assigning causality only to past trauma or behavioral patterns, Seth invites us to look at what we are believing right now—and how that belief continues to write the script we live in. His message, decades ahead of its time, resonates strongly with emerging models in epigenetics, which show how gene expression is influenced by perception and environment; placebo research, which highlights the measurable impact of belief on physiology; and neuroplasticity, which confirms the brain's ability to re-wire itself in response to thought and intention.

The Role of Soul-Level Intelligence

In Seth's framework, we are not singular minds in isolated bodies, but multifaceted beings animated by a soul that spans dimensions. The soul is not merely a symbolic or mystical idea—it is a conscious, multi-dimensional intelligence that guides growth and integration across lifetimes. Soul-level intelligence offers insight into the deeper why: Why am I experiencing this illness? Why do these patterns persist? Why now?

By connecting to this deeper current, healing becomes less about symptom management and more about alignment with purpose. Seth's view affirms that true transformation draws on more than willpower—it requires remembering who we are beyond personality, beyond history, beyond fear.

Self-Generated Reality and Responsibility

This perspective is not meant to blame the self for pain but to reclaim authorship. If our reality is shaped from within, then we are never entirely powerless, no matter how entrenched a pattern may seem. Seth emphasizes that the path forward is not to fight what is, but to realign with a clearer internal signal.

Self-responsibility, in this sense, is an act of empowerment. It liberates the individual from dependency on external solutions and redirects focus toward inner recalibration. Healing becomes an act of resonance—not rescue.

Tools That Apply Seth's Teachings in Modern Practice

Several contemporary healing modalities embody the principles Seth articulated:

- **QHHT® (Quantum Healing Hypnosis Technique) and BQH (Beyond Quantum Healing)** access the subconscious or Higher Self to surface soul-level guidance, reveal belief-based blocks, and activate healing through insight and intention.

These sessions often involve communication with multidimensional aspects of the self that echo Seth's view of expanded consciousness.

- **Genius Insight** and other biofeedback systems offer a frequency-based interface for recalibrating the body's energy field. These tools help identify incoherence in the terrain and restore alignment through conscious intention and vibrational feedback.
- **Consciousness-Based Navigation**: A practice of listening inwardly, sensing resonance, and responding from the level of soul-guided awareness. This isn't a technique in itself, but a way of being that integrates intention, discernment, and alignment across mind, body, and spirit.

Together, these tools do not create healing—they activate the intelligence already embedded in the system. As Seth affirms, healing occurs not through external intervention alone, but by reestablishing internal coherence and remembering our role as conscious creators of experience.

Closing Integration

Seth's material offers a profound paradigm: that transformation arises not from fixing what is broken, but from remembering who we truly are. Consciousness, in this framework, is not just awareness—it is the architect of our reality, the bridge to our soul, and the initiator of our healing.

In conclusion, Seth's material offers a profound paradigm: that transformation arises not from fixing what is broken, but from remembering who we truly are. Consciousness, in this framework, is not just awareness—it is the architect of our reality, the bridge to our soul, and the initiator of our healing.

You create your own reality.
The thoughts and emotions you experience, the conditions of your life, are reflections of your inner state. You are not a victim of circumstance—you are a creator, and your consciousness is the force that shapes your experience.
— Seth, as channeled by Jane Roberts,
Consciousness as Energy and Multidimensionality

Consciousness as Energy and Multidimensionality

Building on earlier discussions, consciousness extends beyond the duality of the conscious and unconscious mind. We now move forward to expand our understanding of consciousness as a dynamic, multidimensional force. Rather than being limited to brain activity, consciousness operates as an integrative force—interacting with the body, spirit, and soul, and bridging the divide between the visible world and the subtle dimensions beyond it.

In this section, we will explore the multifaceted nature of consciousness, its relationship to the biofield, and its connection to the multiverse. This is where we go beyond traditional models and embrace a broader view of consciousness as a creative, healing force that transcends the limits of the physical mind and body.

Where is consciousness located?

Does it reside solely in the brain, or does it extend beyond the physical body?

Is consciousness a localized phenomenon, or is it a boundless, multidimensional experience?

Reflect on your own experiences with consciousness, and consider whether you have ever felt connected to something beyond your immediate awareness.

Consciousness as Energy: the Biofield Connection

The biofield, as we have seen in earlier chapters, serves as the energetic bridge between the physical body and consciousness. This electromagnetic field, which surrounds and permeates every living being, is an essential conduit through which consciousness interacts with the physical and energetic systems of the body. The biofield is not merely a passive reflection of the body's physical state; it is an active force, constantly in flux, influenced by thoughts, emotions, beliefs, and spiritual states.

Research in biofield therapies, including biofeed-back and quantum healing, demonstrates how our energy systems—our biofield—play a critical role in the healing process. By influencing the biofield through intention and consciousness, we can affect the body's physical health. The Genius Insight program and other biofeedback systems exemplify how consciousness and energy intersect. When we interact with our biofield, we tap into a larger energetic system, one that is deeply intertwined with our overall well-being.

Research on Biofield and Genius Insight

The Genius Insight system offers a groundbreaking way to measure the energy frequencies in our biofield. The software is commonly used on Android tablets or iPads (and more recently on personal computers as well), providing clear visual feedback and accessible navigation for both practitioner and client. The Quanta Capsule App allows clients to send voice recordings for frequency analysis and receive tailored frequency playlists to support self-regulation and healing between sessions. Although technically compatible with mobile phones, the limited screen space makes tablets or PCs a more effective choice for professional use.

Research on Biofield and Genius Insight

The Genius Insight software incorporates in its Biofield section Nogier frequencies, Solfeggio tones, Meridians, Spiritual Protection, the chakra system and the Aura, all of which reflect the alignment (or misalignment) of our consciousness with the body's energy field. The Aura is a particularly interesting feature to monitor changes in the biofield.

In a recent pilot study, researchers found that the use of the Genius Insight biofeedback software significantly improved emotional, spiritual, and physical wellness scores after just three sessions (Insight Health Apps, 2021). These findings suggest that biofield coherence is directly linked to physical health outcomes. When the biofield is balanced, the body's healing potential is activated.

Consciousness and Multidimensionality

In quantum healing, we recognize that **consciousness** is not confined to this reality or dimension. Instead, it is a **multi-dimensional** force that spans across different timelines, realities, and even parallel lives. This concept of multidimensionality is key to understanding the expansive nature of consciousness.

The multiverse theory suggests that we exist simultaneously in multiple realities (Everett, 1957; Tegmark, 2014), experiencing different versions of ourselves across time and space. When we engage with quantum healing modalities like BQH, we can tap into these alternate timelines and explore how our consciousness is interwoven with multiple versions of our self, all unfolding at once.

What Is the Multiverse?

In theoretical physics and cosmology, the *multiverse* refers to the hypothesis that our universe is just one of many universes that exist simultaneously—each potentially governed by different laws of physics or alternative versions of events.

In healing work, the multiverse is used metaphorically to describe how consciousness might access different timelines, parallel lives, or alternate versions of the self. This aligns with quantum models that question linear time and fixed identity.

In some quantum interpretations, every possible outcome of a decision branches off into a separate universe.
— Max Tegmark, Our Mathematical Universe (2014)

Clinical Insight: A Multidimensional Perspective

To illustrate how these concepts manifest in practice, consider the case of a 19-year-old client diagnosed on the autism spectrum underwent a Beyond Quantum Healing (BQH) session that revealed his multidimensional nature. During the session, the client was guided to explore past lives, following a traditional exploration script; however, he started experiencing parallel lives—versions of himself living in different realities. As he surfed through these alternate versions, he discovered that the limitations he experienced in this lifetime were not intrinsic to his being but rather specific to the framework of this reality. By reconnecting with his higher consciousness and tapping into these alternate versions, he gained profound insights into his soul's purpose and his potential for healing. This process highlighted the **multidimensionality of consciousness**—we are not one static being, but a fluid and evolving expression of energy across multiple realities.

The **multiverse in therapy** invites us to explore these alternate dimensions of experience, enabling healing across timelines. Whether through accessing past lives, parallel lives, future lives, or soul-level wisdom, we can shift the energetic patterns that shape our present reality, and align with our highest potential.

Clarifying Realms: Dimensions vs. Universes

In the context of this healing model, references to *multiple dimensions* and *multiple universes* are intentionally distinct, though often overlapping in practice. Multiple dimensions refer to the vibrational layers of reality—levels of perception and energetic resonance that exist beyond the visible, physical realm. These include states of consciousness accessible through healing, meditation, and expanded awareness. In contrast, the concept of multiple universes, or multiverse theory, points to the existence of parallel realities or timelines—alternate expressions of reality that may differ in sequence, outcome, or experiential structure. While physics treats these as separate domains, consciousness-based healing often navigates both simultaneously. This model honors their convergence as experiential fields through which meaning, healing, and transformation can unfold.

Key Takeaway:
The Role of Consciousness in Healing across dimensions

Healing, as we have explored, is not confined to this physical plane alone. When we engage with consciousness at its deepest levels, we can access multiple dimensions of our being—across timelines, realities, and incarnations. In doing so, we tap into an infinite reservoir of healing potential, unlocking the wisdom of the soul and clearing energetic blockages that may have been preventing healing.

Consciousness is causal: it shapes our reality, and when we align our consciousness with the energetic flow of the universe, we can facilitate profound healing across dimensions. This healing process is not just about fixing the body; it is about re-aligning with our highest selves, integrating our soul-level wisdom, and harmonizing the mind, body, and spirit. Consciousness is not constricted to a single timeline, identity, or form—it carries a multidimensional force capable of facilitating healing across layers of existence.

We are not only objects in space, but events in time—each of us a hologram of a greater whole, expressing itself in multiple dimensions.

—Michael Talbot

Beliefs → Biology Connection

Introduction: Consciousness, Perception, and the Healing Process

The idea that our beliefs influence our biology is no longer a purely metaphysical claim—it is a scientifically supported perspective with powerful implications for healing. What we believe about ourselves, our bodies, and our world shapes our internal environment, affecting everything from gene expression to immune function. In this section, we explore how beliefs operate as causal agents in the healing process, linking mind, body, and soul through the conduit of consciousness.

The Biology of Belief: What the Research Shows

The pioneering work of cell biologist Dr. Bruce Lipton brought mainstream attention to the ways in which our thoughts and beliefs can influence our biology. In his book The Biology of Belief, Lipton (2005) demonstrates that the cell membrane—the "brain" of the cell—responds to energetic signals from the environment, including the electromagnetic frequencies generated by our thoughts. He showed that our perceptions of the world, whether accurate or not, can influence cellular behavior, stress responses, and long-term health outcomes.

Your beliefs become your biology.

—Bruce Lipton

Similarly, Dr. Joe Dispenza's research into neuro-plasticity and the placebo effect illustrates that beliefs have the power to rewire the brain and activate healing pathways. Dispenza (2014) found that meditative states paired with intentional thought can change brain wave patterns, release healing biochemicals, and initiate physical transformation. The placebo effect itself—the phenomenon in which belief in the effectiveness of a treatment leads to real physiological improvement—is further evidence that belief is a powerful determinant of health.

Where you place your attention is
where you place your energy.
—Joe Dispenza

The Biofield as the Interface Between Belief and Biology

In earlier chapters, we explored how the biofield serves as a bridge between the mental, physical, and energetic layers of being. The biofield does not merely reflect our physical state—it is actively shaped by the emotional and mental patterns we carry (Rubik et al., 2015). Beliefs resonate as frequencies, imprinting energetic patterns within the biofield. When these beliefs are aligned with truth and coherence, the field becomes harmonious, promoting balance in the physical body. When the beliefs are fear-based, distorted, or self-limiting, the biofield reflects this incoherence, and disease or dysfunction may follow.

Biofeedback tools like the Genius Insight software reveal how belief systems can be mapped energetically. Frequencies related to neuro-transmitters, stress levels, hormonal imbalances, and emotional states often correspond to unresolved inner beliefs or identity patterns. By identifying and shifting these beliefs, practitioners help clients realign their energetic signature, which in turn supports the body's ability to self-regulate and heal.

The biofield is the skin of the soul,
the space where thought becomes form.
—Caroline Myss

Intention, Emotion, and Coherence

Beliefs are not static mental statements; they are often emotionally charged and energetically active. This is why affirmations alone may not always work unless the emotional state and subconscious resonance are aligned. As HeartMath Institute research has shown, coherence between the heart and brain—achieved through gratitude, love, and intentional focus—has a measurable impact on immune function, hormone levels, and emotional resilience (McCraty et al., 2009). When our beliefs are coherent with our emotional and energetic state, the healing signal is amplified.

Quantum Healing Hypnosis and other energetic modalities work precisely at this intersection. By accessing the subconscious mind or higher self, clients can identify belief structures that are misaligned with their healing journey. Releasing these beliefs, or up-grading them with soul-aligned truths, often leads to spontaneous shifts in the body and psyche.

Beliefs as Blueprints of the Soul

From a soul perspective, beliefs can be under-stood as energetic blueprints that shape not only our health, but also our life path, relationships, and kar-mic lessons. Some beliefs are inherited across genera-tions, encoded epigenetically or passed down through subtle energy fields (Pert, 1997). Others arise from personal experience or collective consciousness. Healing, then, becomes a process of re-evaluation: What beliefs no longer serve our highest good? What new truths are we ready to embody?

Belief is the program through which the soul writes its lessons into the body.
—Caroline Myss

This approach to belief work is not about "posi-tive thinking" in a superficial sense. It is about deep inquiry, spiritual readiness, and the alignment of our inner truths with the outer conditions of our life. When belief systems are brought into harmony with the soul's intention, biology follows.

Key Takeaway: Belief as a Biological and Spiritual Variable

Our beliefs are not passive ideas—they are frequencies that shape matter. They influence our cells, our nervous systems, our biofields, and our spiritual trajectories. In the healing journey, recognizing the causal role of belief allows us to move beyond treatment and into transformation. Consciousness, when paired with intention and aligned belief, becomes the most powerful medicine of all.

What beliefs are you currently holding about your health, your worth, or your capacity to heal?

Are these beliefs inherited, learned, or consciously chosen?

If your beliefs shape your biology, what new belief would you choose to embody today?

Beliefs are not just mental constructs. They are the energetic blueprints from which reality unfolds.
                                                            —Bruce Lipton

---

Conclusions

Consciousness as the Catalyst for Healing

As we conclude Chapter 10, we arrive at a unifying insight: consciousness is not only a witness to our healing—it is the primary force that initiates and directs it. Throughout this chapter, we have explored consciousness as a multi-layered and multidimensional phenomenon, extending from the surface-level workings of the mind to the deeper intelligence of the soul. We have seen how consciousness interacts with energy, biology, and intention to shape the conditions of healing across physical and non-physical planes.

Whether we are working with the subconscious mind in, accessing the higher self through Quantum Healing Hypnosis, or engaging belief transformation through biofield-based tools, all healing begins with an internal shift. That shift is first encoded in our consciousness—through thoughts, perceptions, beliefs, and soul-level agreements—and then expressed in our biofield, our physiology, and our lived experience.

We are conscious participants in shaping our physiology, our energy, and our experience.

Healing is not limited to symptom relief; it is a sacred process of restoring coherence between our consciousness and our essence. When we access deeper levels of awareness—whether through soul-level intelligence, higher self-guidance, or intentional coherence—we open the gateway for transformation to occur at every level of being.

Ultimately, consciousness bridges the spiritual and physical realms. Through intention, belief, and emotional alignment, we activate the conditions for healing to emerge. By recognizing the causal role of consciousness, we empower ourselves to align with our **soul's intelligence**, allowing for profound shifts in both **health** and **experience**.

In the context of healing, this means we have agency: the power to transform our state of being through conscious awareness and choice. Whether through intentional healing practices, energetic interventions, or shifts in belief, we can actively engage in the healing process.

Every thought is a seed. If you plant crab apples, don't count on harvesting Golden Delicious.
—Bill Meyer

In the end, the healing journey is not one we walk alone, but one we co-create—through awareness, intention, and the boundless intelligence of consciousness.

How do you currently relate to the idea that your consciousness influences your healing?

What intentional shifts—whether in belief, emotion, or perception—could you make today to support your well-being?

Key Takeaway

Consciousness is not separate from the healing process. It is the initiator, the navigator, and the integrator. Healing unfolds most powerfully when we honor our role as conscious co-creators, bridging the spiritual and the physical through awareness, belief, and intention.

The Principle of Mentalism – Consciousness as First Cause

In Hermetic philosophy, the Principle of Mentalism states that "The All is Mind." This foundational teaching, derived from the Hermetic text The Kybalion, suggests that the universe itself is a mental construct— a projection of infinite consciousness. In this view, everything that exists in the physical world has its origin in thought, intention, or what we might call consciousness.

This concept is not only metaphysical; it echoes many of the teachings discussed throughout this chapter. From Freud's early typology to Seth's model of self-generated reality and the biofield's dynamic interplay with belief and biology, we see again and again that consciousness precedes physical form. This is the essence of Mentalism: reality is first shaped in the mind (or soul) before it is experienced through the senses.

In the healing process, this principle affirms what we have seen through Quantum Healing Hypnosis, biofeedback systems like the Genius Insight, and the broader field of energy medicine: what we believe, feel, and envision at a soul level generates ripple effects across our biofield and ultimately our biology. Healing does not begin with the body—it begins with a shift in consciousness.

By consciously choosing to align our thoughts, emotions, and intentions with our soul's truth, we tap into the causal power of consciousness. We become not just participants in healing, but architects of our reality.

The universe is mental—held in the mind of the All.
— The Kybalion

*If consciousness is the architect of your experi-
ence, what internal shift would you make today to
redesign the world you inhabit?*

Key Takeaway: Consciousness as First Cause
Hermetic wisdom reminds us that all healing begins in
the mind—not the brain, but the expansive, soul-
connected mind of consciousness. When we understand that thought is not merely reactive but creative,
we gain access to our deepest healing power.

References

Cannon, D. (1998). *The Convoluted Universe: Book One*. Ozark Mountain Publishing.

Cannon, D. (2001). *Between Death and Life: Conversations with a Spirit*. Ozark Mountain Publishing.

Dispenza, J. (2014). *You Are the Placebo: Making Your Mind Matter*. Hay House.

Everett, H. (1957). "Relative State" Formulation of Quantum Mechanics. Reviews of Modern Physics, 29(3), 454–462. https://doi.org/10.1103/RevModPhys.29.454

Freud, S. (1900). *The Interpretation of Dreams*. Basic Books (Original work published in German, 1899).

Freud, S. (1923). *The Ego and the Id*. W. W. Norton & Company.

Insight Health Apps. (2021). Pilot Study of Genius Insight Quantum Biofeedback Application. Retrieved from https://www.insighthealthapps.com/blogs/home-news/genius-insight-official

Lipton, B. H. (2005). *The Biology of Belief: Unleashing the Power of Consciousness, Matter and Miracles*. Mountain of Love/Elite Books.

McCraty, R., Atkinson, M., Tomasino, D., & Bradley, R. T. (2009). The Coherent Heart: Heart–Brain Interactions, Psychophysiological Coherence, and the Emergence of System-Wide Order. *Integral Review*, 5(2), 10–115. https://www.researchgate.net/publication/41393262_The_Coherent_Heart_Heart-Brain_Interactions_Psychophysiological_Coherence_and_the_Emergence_of_System-Wide_Order

Pert, C. B. (1997). *Molecules of Emotion: The Science Behind Mind-Body Medicine*. Scribner.

Roberts, J. (1972). *Seth Speaks: The Eternal Validity of the Soul*. Bantam Books.

Roberts, J. (1974). *The Nature of Personal Reality*. Amber-Allen Publishing.

Roberts, J. (1977). The "Unknown" Reality, Volume One. Amber-Allen Publishing.

Rubik, B., Muehsam, D., Hammerschlag, R., & Jain, S. (2015). Biofield Science and Healing: History, Terminology, and Concepts. *Global Advances in Health and Medicine*, 4(Suppl), 8–14. https://doi.org/ 10.7453/gahmj.2015.038.suppl

Tegmark, M. (2014). *Our Mathematical Universe: My Quest for the Ultimate Nature of Reality*. Alfred A. Knopf.

Weiss, B. (1988). *Many Lives, Many Masters*. Fireside Books.

In some sense man is a microcosm of the universe; therefore what man is, is a clue to the universe.

— David Bohm

Chapter 11

The Blueprint of the Soul– Energy Fields and Morphic Resonance

Beneath the surface of the body lies another kind of organization—one that goes beyond what we can see in our cells or genes. Emerging research points to the presence of invisible fields of information that guide how living systems grow, function, and heal. These patterns do not reside in the brain or hide inside DNA. They operate in the space around us, shaping form and function from a level beneath physical matter —what some call the energetic blueprint of the body.

This chapter invites us to consider a deeper possibility: that the body is not just a **biochemical machine** but a dynamic expression of a deeper intelligence. Some scientists and thinkers describe this as a **holographic projection**—where the whole is encoded in each part. Others speak of **energetic blueprints** that shape our biology from behind the scenes.

To understand healing on this level, we need to widen the lens. Instead of looking only at chemistry or structure, we begin to explore **patterns, frequen-**

cies, and **fields**. What gives the body its **rhythm**, its **coherence**, its capacity to **repair** and **adapt**? What underlying design supports health before tissues even take shape?

This perspective is not entirely new. Ancient traditions have long worked with energy, symbols, **and** sacred patterns. But today, these ideas are finding new life through science—from Rupert Sheldrake's morphic fields to studies of structured water, scalar waves, and coherence-based therapies. **Coherence**, in this context, may be more than just a physiological state—it might signal **alignment** with a larger **energetic design**.

This design is not fixed or rigid. It shifts with **consciousness**, shaped by our thoughts, choices, and evolution. Healing becomes a return to **inner alignment**—a process of remembering what we are made of and what we are connected to.

In the pages ahead, we will explore:

- How morphic fields and energetic templates may influence biology and behavior;

- The idea that the human body is a fractal hologram of soul-level intelligence;

- The role of scalar energy, structured water, and therapies that support energetic coherence;

- Sacred geometry and numerology as the language of deeper design;

- And the Hermetic principles that echo through all cycles of healing, rhythm, and polarity.

We will also take a closer look at the **Flower of Life**—a symbol that appears across cultures and times, pointing to the deep **geometry** of life itself.

Let us begin with the **fields** that hold the **memory of form**.

Morphic Fields and Energetic Templates

Before we dive deeper, it is helpful to revisit a familiar question through a new lens.

Nature vs. Nurture Revisited

Morphic field theory offers a fresh lens on the classic nature vs. nurture debate. While it aligns more closely with the "nature" side of the equation, it redefines nature itself—not as a fixed genetic script, but as a dynamic informational field shaped by collective experience. These fields may hold the memory of form, behavior, and even emotion across generations. In this model, habits and biological tendencies are not just inherited through genes or shaped by environment— they are reinforced and transmitted through resonance with past expressions. This perspective invites us to see healing as a process of re-patterning—not only within the individual, but within the field they are connected to.

What if memory was not just something stored in the brain, but something embedded in nature itself? That is the question posed by biologist Rupert Sheldrake, whose theory of **morphic fields** challenges the idea that DNA or neural wiring alone accounts for the shape and behavior of living organisms (Sheldrake, 2009). Instead, Sheldrake suggests that form and habit are guided by invisible, non-local fields that act as templates—fields that carry a kind of collective memory for species, organs, and even behaviors.

According to Sheldrake, every living system draws on these fields, which evolve over time through repetition. A sunflower grows into a sunflower not just because of its genes, but because it taps into a field shaped by the memory of all sunflowers that have come before. Similarly, healing may not depend only on physical processes, but on reconnecting with a **template of wholeness** that exists beyond the material body.

While controversial, the idea of morphic fields offers a bridge between biological development, habit formation, and consciousness. It provides a framework for understanding how form persists and returns—even after injury, illness, or breakdown. In this view, healing is not only repair. It is **resonance**—a return to the field-pattern that once organized health.

Morphic fields may also help explain why certain patterns run through families, cultures, or even species—patterns that are not always explained by genes or direct learning. From instinctual animal behavior to social rituals, from shared emotional reactions to inherited trauma, these invisible templates could hold the key to understanding why we often repeat what we have never been taught.

For the practitioner or seeker, this concept invites a shift in orientation. Healing is not about imposing a solution from outside—it is about creating the conditions where the original blueprint can reassert itself. Whether through intention, sound, touch, or energy work, the goal becomes **reconnection** with the pattern that already knows what balance looks like.

These insights also resonate with themes found in Quantum Healing work, where clients often access what appear to be ancestral imprints—patterns that do not originate in the present life but emerge as unresolved emotional or energetic baggage carried through generations. In such sessions, people speak of life contracts, karmic echoes, or inherited burdens that seek resolution not only for the individual but for the lineage as a whole. These experiences suggest that morphic fields may also store and transmit more than biological information—they may hold aspects of **soul memory** and **ancestral resonance**.

Every cell in your body is eavesdropping on your thoughts.

— Deepak Chopra

Later in this chapter, we will explore how scalar energy, structured water, and coherence-based therapies may support this reconnection.

The Fractal Body: A Holographic Map of Soul Intelligence

What if your body was more than a vessel—more than tissue, chemistry, or cellular machinery? What if it was also a map? A fractalized expression of your soul's intelligence, imprinted in every part of your physical being?

This is the central idea behind viewing the human body as a **holographic system**—one where each part contains the information of the whole (Pribram, 1991; Bohm, 1980). A useful analogy is a holographic photograph: if you cut the image into small pieces, each piece still contains the entire picture, only from a slightly different angle. Similarly, in a holographic body, each part—down to the cellular level—reflects the whole organism, including its emotional and energetic history.

In physics and consciousness research, holography refers to a model where data is distributed non-locally, meaning you can reconstruct the entire image from any fragment. Applied to biology, it suggests that every cell may carry not just the genetic code of the organism, but also a subtle imprint of its emotional, energetic, and even spiritual design (Pert, 1997; Lipton, 2005).

This holographic model helps explain why healing can sometimes happen spontaneously or through interventions far from the site of injury (Laszlo, 2004). It supports the idea that change at one level of the system—mental, emotional, energetic—can echo throughout the whole. The body, then, is not only a structure—it is a **resonating field**, sensitive to shifts in awareness and coherence.

In this framework, chronic symptoms may represent distortions in the holographic map—localized expressions of deeper imbalances. And healing becomes a matter of restoring clarity to the pattern, not just repairing the part. This is why practices like energy healing, guided imagery, biofeedback, and frequency therapies may have wide-reaching effects: they are not just targeting matter—they are engaging the field that gives matter its form.

Recognizing the body as a fractal expression of 274, also invites deeper respect for intuition, bodily sensations, and inner imagery. These may not be random or symbolic alone—they may be direct feedback from the blueprint itself, surfacing to help us realign.

Reading the Body as an Energetic Map

When we approach the body as a holographic reflection of soul intelligence, symptoms are no longer just malfunctions—they are messages. Practitioners who work with energy, imagery, or somatic awareness often find that the body reveals precise information when viewed as a multidimensional feedback system. A pain in the shoulder may reflect a burden carried, a recurring digestive issue may hold unprocessed emotion. This perspective does not replace medical evaluation—it complements it by adding another layer of meaning. The goal is not to decode everything, but to listen with more depth and curiosity.

The body is not a thing—it is a process. A dance of intelligence shaped by the field it belongs to.

— Ervin Laszlo

The next section explores some of the tools that interact with this field-based design—beginning with scalar energy, structured water, and coherence-based approaches to healing.

Scalar Fields, Structured Water, and Coherence-Based Therapies

If the body is shaped and sustained by energetic patterns, then healing can happen not just through chemical intervention, but through inputs that restore **resonance** and **coherence**. This is the premise behind a growing array of modalities that work with **frequency, structure, and informational fields**—including scalar energy, structured water, and coherence-based therapies.

Just as a river's pollution is best addressed at its source rather than far downstream, these approaches aim to intervene **upstream**—influencing the terrain before symptoms fully take shape. Working at the level of pattern and resonance offers a chance to change the trajectory of dysfunction before it becomes embedded in form.

Scalar Fields

Scalar fields, first theorized by **Nikola Tesla**, refer to non-Hertzian, non-linear fields that do not weaken over distance and are not bound by traditional electromagnetic constraints. Tesla believed that these fields could transmit energy and information without wires—potentially influencing systems at a distance. While much of his scalar work remained unfinished or suppressed, the foundational idea has inspired decades of fringe and formal inquiry.

Modern interpretations describe scalar fields as **phase-conjugated wave pairs**—essentially standing waves that carry **information rather than force**. At first, I did not understand what that meant either. It turns out these waves do not cancel in a destructive way, but rather merge to form a standing field capable of transmitting information with greater efficiency.

Unlike electromagnetic waves, scalar waves are not easily detected by conventional instruments, yet they are said to interact with biological systems through resonance and coherence, rather than voltage or current. Although controversial in mainstream physics, scalar fields are increasingly used in energy medicine, frequency-based therapies, and consciousness-based interventions.

One practitioner known for his scalar field work is **Tom Paladino**, who focuses on transmitting healing energy using only a person's **photograph**. His system works on the idea that the image carries enough informational signature to access that person's field. In contrast, the **Genius Insight**, the frequency-based system developed by **Ryan Williams**, relies primarily on a **voice recording**—believed to contain a holographic imprint of the client's energetic state. With the Genius Insight program, I can play frequencies remotely or send personalized playlists through the **Quanta Capsule** app, working entirely through scalar and informational field principles.

These technologies do not "treat" in the conventional sense—they interact with the body's underlying blueprint of coherence, inviting it to recalibrate, often from a distance and without physical contact.

Scalar energy is the carrier wave of intention.
— Tom Paladino

The scalar approach is one of influence through resonance—not force through matter. These waves interact through standing fields that amplify information, supporting recalibration without physical input.

Beyond Distance—Healing by Design

Scalar-based therapies challenge our assumptions about proximity, dose, and physical input. In this model, healing is not something delivered—it is something invited, activated through resonance with an energetic design. Whether the signal is carried by voice, image, or waveform, the principle is the same: reconnect the system with its original blueprint, and the body knows what to do.

Some researchers and practitioners believe scalar fields can transmit energy or intention beyond time and space, interacting with the body's subtle fields to support healing (Bearden, 2002; Rubik, 2002; Tiller, 1997).While mainstream science remains cautious, scalar-based devices and protocols are now used in energy medicine and frequency-based technologies.

What If It is Not About Belief, But Intention?

Skepticism is healthy. And it is true—scalar energy is not about placebo or blind faith. But it is also not a passive mechanism. It requires intention—whether from the practitioner, the client, or both. The belief is not that it 'works magically.' Rather, that the field responds when something conscious is offered: a request, a frequency, a signature. The question becomes what happens when we combine technology, consciousness, and intention with the body's innate wisdom to heal.

What if, in the realm of healing and consciousness, curiosity matters more than certainty?

What if frequency-based healing is not magic, but science still catching up?

In the physical world, certainty helps us navigate immediate threats. But in the deeper layers of transformation—where the terrain is subtle, internal, and often unpredictable—curiosity opens the door to discovery. Certainty can close that door. Curiosity keeps it ajar.

Healing is not the application of force—it is the restoration of resonance.

Clinical Vignette: A Remote Shift

A 34-year-old woman reported chronic neck pain and mental fog that had persisted for over a year. Traditional therapies brought only temporary relief. She agreed to a 14-day remote Genius Insight frequency protocol. After three days, she reported clearer thinking. By day ten, her neck tension had eased significantly. She had made no lifestyle changes. Her comment? "It's like something realigned, but I can't explain how." Remote scalar support didn't fix her—it reminded her system what balance felt like.

Structured Water as an Intelligent Medium

Structured water is another entry point into the body's energetic terrain. While we previously explored it as a tool for terrain repair and physiological coherence, here we turn our attention to water as an intelligent medium—one that remembers, responds, and perhaps even communicates. Research by **Gerald Pollack** and others suggests that water in biological systems exists not just in liquid form, but as a fourth phase—**exclusion zone (EZ) water**—which carries charge, stores information, and responds to light and frequency. Water, in this view, is not a passive medium but an active participant in cellular communication. Tools that restructure water—through vortexing, magnetism, or sound—are designed to **reorganize the internal environment** at the molecular level.

Building on the concept of water as a living interface, the late **Masaru Emoto** brought global attention to water's capacity to reflect human consciousness. His experiments—though controversial—showed how words, thoughts, and emotions seemed to influence the crystalline structure of frozen water. Positive intention produced symmetrical, intricate patterns; negative input yielded disordered forms. While Emoto's methodology was criticized for lacking rigorous scientific controls and has not been reliably replicated in blinded studies, his message struck a chord: *our relationship with water may be more dynamic than science has fully understood.*

Water is the mirror that has the ability to show us what we cannot see. It is a blueprint for our reality.

— Masaru Emoto

Enters **Veda Austin**, a contemporary researcher and photographic artist who has taken water memory research into new territory. Using a self-developed method of photographing freezing water samples, she has documented **imagery that appears to reflect not only emotional states but even symbolic communication**. Veda often describes water as a 'conscious collaborator,' suggesting that it interacts with intention in ways that challenge our assumptions about matter and mind. Her work complements both Emoto and Pollack—bridging visual expression, experimental insight, and intuitive resonance.

Water is not a passive element—
it listens, it learns, it remembers.

— Veda Austin

Boxed Insight: Water as Messenger

The body is over 70% water, but not all water is the same. When we speak of **structured water**, we refer not just to its chemical composition, but to its **state**—how it holds energy, interfaces with light, and responds to information. EZ water, as studied by Pollack, behaves like a biological battery. Emoto showed us its emotional receptivity. Austin invites us to see it as a bridge between the seen and unseen—a messenger, medium, and mirror.

The role of water in consciousness-based healing has also become central in **Beyond Quantum Healing (BQH)**. According to BQH founder **Candace Craw-Goldman**, this emphasis originated through a series of dreams, channeled insights and synchronicities involving the late **Dolores Cannon** and **Masaru Emoto**, both of whom she felt continued to guide aspects of her work. These insights pointed to water not only as a conduit for healing, but as a vital bridge to higher consciousness. Subsequent confirmations from BQH students—including dreams involving Emoto—and a collaborative channeling session with other quantum practitioners further emphasized water's role in amplifying intention, restoring coherence, and supporting energetic alignment for both practitioner and client.

Today, what began as channeled guidance has become a living ritual within the BQH community—an intentional process of co-creation with water that sets the tone for each session. The **Water Alchemy** ritual is now woven into the healing process of many BQH practitioners, myself included. It does not only hold intention—it amplifies it.

*Water has a memory and carries within it
our thoughts and prayers.*
— *Masaru Emoto*

Coherence-Based Therapies

Coherence-based therapies—including photobio-modulation (PBM), pulsed electromagnetic field therapy (PEMF), vibroacoustic sound, and even heart-brain coherence training—aim to restore harmony in biological systems by introducing organized, resonant inputs. These modalities do not override or force change in the body. Instead, they act like tuning forks—offering stable signals that help dysregulated systems reorient toward balance.

At the cellular level, coherence is more than synchronization—it is intelligent order. It means that tissues, rhythms, and biochemical processes are communicating clearly and efficiently. When coherence is lost—due to stress, trauma, illness, or environmental disruption—biological systems become chaotic, noisy, or stagnant. Coherence-based therapies act as rhythmic cues, helping the body "remember" its original pattern of wellness.

PBM, for instance, uses low-level light to stimulate mitochondrial activity and promote tissue repair—often experienced not just as physical relief, but as a **lift in mood** or mental clarity. PEMF devices pulse electromagnetic fields that appear to normalize cellular voltage and improve circulation. And vibrational therapies—such as sound baths, tuning forks, or acoustic stimulation—are now used to support

nervous system regulation, emotional release, and **trauma resolution**.

What unites these methods is not the tool itself, but the principle they invoke: **resonance**. By engaging the body not as a machine but as a resonant field, these interventions remind the system of its own natural rhythms. They nudge rather than push. And often, the results arise not linearly—but holistically, as inner order is restored across subtle and structural layers.

The moment you start using resonance instead of resistance, the body listens.

From Intervention to Invitation
Coherence-based therapies shift our role from fixer to facilitator. Instead of targeting symptoms directly, we offer coherent signals that invite the system to reorganize from within. Healing becomes less about forceful doing and more about intentionally tuning—**creating the right frequency conditions** that allow the original blueprint to surface and express itself.

Sacred Geometry and Numerology – The Language of Pattern

We may be venturing a bit farther into the cosmos here—but bear with us. If this feels like a stretch, take it as an invitation to momentarily widen the lens. We are not asking you to memorize the 12 universal laws. Stephen Hawking once said that understanding the workings of the universe might on day let us "know the mind of God" (Dastagiri, 2024), but that is not the kind of knowing we are after here. Nor are we plunging into esoteric numerology as a form of entertainment. Like astrology—an ancient system rich with archetypal meaning—numerology speaks in symbolic patterns. Here, we focus less on prediction and more on pattern recognition as a language of resonance.

Instead, this brief indulgence is meant to reflect on a timeless idea: that the universe speaks in pattern. From Fibonacci spirals to Pythagorean ratios, from planetary orbits to water crystals—there is a silent architecture to all things, encoded not in words, but in numbers and shapes. And occasionally, tapping into that architecture can help us remember who we are.

If the universe is built on information and resonance, then sacred geometry is the visible language of that order—an ancient and universal expression of pattern, proportion, and coherence. From the spiral of galaxies to the structure of seashells, from the branching of trees to the chambers of the human heart, certain patterns appear again and again in nature. They are not random. They reflect a deeper mathematical symmetry that suggests design.

Sacred geometry refers to shapes and ratios—such as the **Golden Ratio**, the **Fibonacci sequence**, the **Vesica Piscis**, and the **Flower of Life**—that have been revered across cultures as embodiments of harmony. These patterns are found in architecture, art, religious symbols, and even DNA. Their repetition points to something fundamental: a cosmic blueprint embedded in form.

In the Genius Insight biofeedback system, sacred geometry appears not only as symbol, but as frequency—encoded in the **Biofield Panel** as part of the terrain-balancing process. When these geometric archetypes fall into dysharmony, the system may flag them for realignment through vibrational means. Frequencies derived from forms like the **Fibonacci spiral**, **fractals**, **spheres**, and the **Flower of Life** are used to support pattern recognition, restore coherence, and reconnect the system with a deeper blueprint. They can be selected intentionally to normalize physiology, ease emotional turbulence, or support cellular regeneration.

Numerology, similarly, views numbers not merely as quantities, but as carriers of archetypal meaning. In esoteric traditions, numbers represent energetic vibrations that structure reality. From **Pythagorean philosophy** to **Kabbalistic mysticism**, numerology has served as a bridge between mathematics, mysticism, and consciousness. Contemporary teachers and mystic traditions—such as Franz Bardon's Hermetic writings or the numerological threads carried within the Theosophical schools—have helped keep these ancient principles alive in modern consciousness studies.

If you only knew the magnificence of the 3, 6, and 9, then you would have the key to the universe.
— Nikola Tesla

In the context of healing, these systems suggest that the body—like nature—is built on pattern. When disease or distress occurs, it may represent a **disruption in pattern recognition**—a loss of coherence in the underlying geometry of health. True Healing emerges as symmetry, proportion, and energetic alignment are restored.

We are not introducing sacred geometry and, 287 here as dogma or divination, but as **metaphorical and vibrational tools**—ways of understanding the **architecture of wholeness**. When clients intuitively draw spirals, talk about numbers, or describe visual patterns during deep trance or energetic work, they may be tuning into this subtle layer of design. And with tools like the Genius Insight, practitioners now have a bridge to apply these timeless frequencies in practical, therapeutic ways.

Mathematics is the language with which God has written the universe.

— Galileo Galilei

While numerology is often dismissed as esoteric, its foundation rests on a classical truth echoed by philosophers and scientists alike. **Pythagoras**, more than a theorem-bearing figure in geometry class, considered numbers to be the underlying structure of the cosmos—vibrations that govern both form and meaning. **Galileo** affirmed this view with his enduring claim that nature is written in the language of mathematics. And **Tesla**, ever cryptic, suggested that within the triad of 3, 6, and 9 lies a code to unlock the fabric of reality.

In this light, numerology is not a parlor trick—it is a symbolic framework that mirrors the insights of sacred geometry. Where geometry gives us shape and proportion, numerology offers vibrational archetypes. Both are systems of pattern recognition, pointing to an intelligent order that bridges the physical and the metaphysical. While some of these interpretations remain speculative, they are symbolically rich—and often resonate deeply with those seeking to understand their place in the larger pattern. Whether clients are moved by repeating numbers, sacred symbols, or the strange synchronicities that cluster around certain dates, we may be witnessing the soul's effort to speak the only language the universe consistently understands: **number**.

Geometry and numerology, in this view, are more than symbols—they pulse with life. They whisper reminders of something deep, familiar, and eternal.

Pattern as Portal

In a universe woven with resonance, pattern becomes more than design—it becomes a doorway. Whether through geometry or number, symmetry draws attention inward. It evokes memory—not of past events, but of the soul's original design. When clients reconnect with archetypal patterns, they often feel a sense of peace, familiarity, or clarity. This is not coincidence. It is the system remembering itself.

In the end, we are not just decoding patterns—we are remembering them.

And if patterns are the architecture, then the Hermetic Principles offer the blueprint—the energetic laws that govern how those patterns move, balance, and evolve across time.

Hermetic Principles in Healing: Vibration, Rhythm, and Polarity

What if the body is not merely a biochemical machine, but a symphony of patterns governed by principles often referred to as universal laws—particularly those outlined in Hermetic teachings? Long before modern physics spoke of frequency, vibration, and energy fields, ancient wisdom traditions encoded similar insights in what came to be known as the Hermetic Principles. These principles—drawn from teachings attributed to Hermes Trismegistus—describe the energetic architecture that underlies all of existence. Far from abstract philosophy, they offer practical insights into the rhythms of healing, the interplay of opposites, and the vibrational language of coherence.

In this section, we explore three of these principles—**Vibration**, **Rhythm**, and **Polarity**—as they apply to the healing process. Rather than presenting them as esoteric lore, we approach them as timeless truths that help make sense of terrain-based disruptions, emotional cycles, and energetic imbalances. Whether we are attuning to the rhythm of breath, balancing opposites within the psyche, or recalibrating cellular frequencies, we are in essence engaging with the same universal dynamics described in these ancient teachings.

Nothing rests; everything moves; everything vibrates.

— The Kybalion

Vibration

The principle of vibration states that everything is in constant motion. At the most fundamental level, all matter is energy vibrating at specific frequencies. In healing, this principle reminds us that health is not a static state—it is dynamic, ever-shifting, and responsive to frequency.

From brainwaves and heartbeats to mitochondrial oscillations, our physiology operates through vibration. When we introduce coherent frequencies—whether through sound, light, or electromagnetic fields—we are not imposing change, but aligning with the body's own language of healing. As with the entrainment principle mentioned earlier, a tuning fork does not force a pitch but encourages resonance. In the same way, vibrational therapies help the biofield rediscover its harmonious state through frequency alignment.

This principle is not limited to instruments or machines. Our thoughts, emotions, and intentions carry vibrational signatures. When a client shifts from fear to trust, or from grief to gratitude, that inner shift carries real frequency changes—ones that can be measured, felt, and observed. In many metaphysical traditions, these shifts are described as changes in vibrational state—where emotions such as fear, shame, or grief are considered low-vibration states, and emotions like love, joy, and gratitude are seen as high-vibration frequencies. The goal, in this view, is not to suppress emotion, but to consciously elevate one's frequency over time through awareness, healing, and intention.

Rhythm

The principle of rhythm tells us that all things move in cycles. Just as the moon waxes and wanes, and the tides rise and fall, so too does the human experience unfold in waves. Healing does not follow a straight line—it unfolds through cycles of contraction and expansion, ebb and flow.

Understanding this rhythm can bring compassion to the healing process. Clients may revisit old symptoms, spiral through familiar emotions, or feel "worse before better." Rather than pathologizing these patterns, the principle of rhythm teaches us to see them as part of a greater return to balance. Like a pendulum swinging, the body and psyche seek equilibrium.

In practice, rhythm shows up in circadian cycles, hormonal fluctuations, emotional tides, and the cycles of trauma and integration. When we support these rhythms—rather than resist or override them—we facilitate a more graceful and sustainable healing process.

Everything flows and unfolds according to rhythm; nothing stands still.

— The Kybalion

Polarity

The principle of polarity states that opposites are two extremes of the same spectrum. Hot and cold, fear and love, illness and wellness—each pair represents varying degrees of the same underlying energy. True healing often involves not choosing one over the other, but learning to integrate and transmute.

This is especially powerful in emotional and trauma healing. A client may hold both the victim and the survivor archetypes within. Both the fear of abandonment and the craving for connection. Polarity invites us to explore these tensions without judgment, recognizing that healing lies not in suppression, but in **integration**.

Physiologically, this principle reflects in sympathetic and parasympathetic balance, the push-pull of inflammation and repair, or the interplay of contraction and expansion. In energy healing, it allows us to work with contrast—not as conflict, but as a map for transformation.

Every sweet has its sour; every evil its good.
— Ralph Waldo Emerson

Reflective Practice

Where in your life or body do you feel a loss of coherence or inner rhythm?

What emotional pattern or polarity are you being invited to integrate rather than resolve?

What simple practices—breath, intention, sound, movement—help raise your vibration toward balance?

The Flower of Life – A Symbol of Coherence

The Flower of Life is a sacred geometric symbol composed of interlocking circles arranged in a hexagonal pattern. Found in ancient Egyptian, Hindu, Islamic, and European traditions, it represents the unity of all life, the interconnection of consciousness, and the underlying order of creation.

In vibrational healing, the Flower of Life is more than art—it is a frequency map. Practitioners use it to imprint water with intention, to ground the energy field, or to activate memory of the soul's original design. Its resonance aligns with coherence, making it a powerful anchor in both quantum healing sessions and conscious visualization practices.

It is for these reasons that I chose the Flower of Life to grace the cover of this book, and to appear at both the beginning and end—serving not only as a visual motif, but as a vibrational anchor. Across cultures and timelines, this symbol has carried the resonance of unity, coherence, and remembrance. Placing it at the threshold of this book—at its entry and closing—was a conscious invitation for the reader's own alignment with the deeper design that underlies all healing.

References

Austin, V. (2021). *The secret intelligence of water: Macroscopic evidence of water responding to human consciousness.* Publishing House.

Bearden, T. (2002). *Energy from the vacuum: Concepts and principles.* Cheniere Press.

Bohm, D. (1980). *Wholeness and the implicate order.* Routledge.

Dastagiri, M.B. (2024). Universal Laws, Nature Laws, God Laws, Spiritual, Philosophical & Science Laws: Origin, Rationales, Prophesy, and Human Well-Being. *European Scientific Journal*, 20(8), 26. https://doi.org/10.19044/esj.2024.v20n8p26

Emoto, M. (2004). *The hidden messages in water.* Atria Books.

Laszlo, E. (2004). *Science and the Akashic field: An integral theory of everything.* Inner Traditions.

Lipton, B. H. (2005). *The biology of belief: Unleashing the power of consciousness, matter, and miracles.* Mountain of Love/Elite Books.

Paladino, T. (2025). *About Tom Paladino.* Retrieved from https://www.scalarlight.com/about-tom-paladino

Pert, C. B. (1997). *Molecules of emotion: The science behind mind-body medicine.* Scribner.

- Pollack, G. H. (2013). *The fourth phase of water: Beyond solid, liquid, and vapor.* Ebner and Sons. ISBN-13 : 978-0962689543

Pribram, K. H. (1991). *Brain and perception: Holonomy and structure in figural processing.* Lawrence Erlbaum Associates, Inc.

Rubik, B. (2002). The biofield hypothesis: Its biophysical basis and role in medicine. *The Journal of Alternative and Complementary Medicine, 8*(6), 703–717. https://doi.org/10.1089/10755530260511711

Sheldrake, R. (2009). *Morphic resonance: The nature of formative causation* (4th ed.). Park Street Press.

Tiller, W. A. (1997). *Science and human transformation: Subtle energies, intentionality and consciousness.* Pavior Publishing. ISBN-13 : 978-0964263741

We are not human beings having a spiritual experience.
We are spiritual beings having a human experience.
— Pierre Teilhard de Chardin

Conclusion

Expanded Awareness – Healing as Co-Creation

You made it.

After pages of clinical cases, scientific references, metaphysical rabbit holes, and more mentions of mitochondria and morphic fields than most people see in a lifetime, here you are. Still standing. Still curious.

This chapter is your landing pad as well as your launch platform. It is where we pause to integrate and connect the dots, not to wrap things up neatly, but to reflect before continuing forward. What we have explored is a living, breathing framework that honors the complexity of healing without closing the conversation. The pieces have always been in motion; now, perhaps, the image is coming into focus.

So take a deep breath. Let the image settle. This is not the end. It is the recalibration before the next step begins.

Consciousness as Medicine

Throughout this book, we have explored the terrain of healing—not merely as a biological process, but as a multidimensional unfolding. We began with cracks in the conventional model, traced the interconnections of body systems, and expanded outward through frequency, energy, and consciousness. Now, we return full circle to a truth that has been echoed across traditions, scientific inquiry, and personal revelations: consciousness is medicine.

This is not a metaphor. It is not philosophy. It is the biological and energetic reality we have been approaching from multiple angles: **consciousness is medicine**. From the cellular effects of belief and intention to the physiological shifts seen in response to perception, modern research continues to validate what ancient wisdom has long held. Consciousness is not merely a witness to healing, it **catalyzes** it. It codes it. It recalibrates it. What we observe, we influence. What we believe, we become.

We are not speaking here of mind over matter but rather describing a creative partnership between mind and matter. The observer effect transcends the confines of subatomic physics; it reflects a deeper law of healing. Every moment of self-awareness, every act of self-regard, every step toward coherence, becomes part of the healing prescription.

Imagine yourself standing at the edge of a vast field, not of grass or earth, but of possibility. This is the terrain of your being, shimmering with potential, encoded with memory, and pulsing with an intelligence older than time. You begin to walk, not forward in space, but inward in awareness. Each step is a release: of noise, of programming, of the weight that was never yours. Light flickers where once there was fear. Frequency hums where once there was fatigue. You no longer follow a journey of doing, but of allowing. With each breath, you return to the blueprint you have always carried, leaving behind the identity the world told you to be. You experience coherence. Through remembrance, you manifest healing.

When viewed through the lens of expanded awareness, the journey of healing, becomes less about fixing a problem and more about remembering a truth. The body is not broken, it is responding. Symptoms, once perceived as enemies, are understood as messages. Healing is no longer something to be prescribed; it is something that is allowed to emerge.

In this view, to heal is not to override the body but to reunite with the self; not through effort, but through recognition. You begin peeling away the noise, the inherited patterns, and the beliefs that never truly fit. What remains is a signal that you have always known, bringing you closer to the blueprint of your soul. In a world that often pulls us outward, healing draws us inward. It reorients us to our own essence.

This is why healing often initiates a spiritual awakening. As we release toxic beliefs, inflammatory behaviors, and dissonant frequencies, what remains is clarity. Stillness. A reconnection to purpose. A remembrance that we are not just navigating the physical terrain—we are expressing the soul's architecture through it.

What part of you is ready to return to coherence?

In what ways has your path already been guiding you home?

Healing as Sovereignty and Choice

Healing does not simply happen to us.

It begins with the choices we make, consciously or unconsciously. A belief we no longer hold. A boundary we finally set. A frequency we start to embody, even before we understand it fully.

To heal is to reclaim not only our health, but also our sense of self.

This process unfolds one moment at a time. Gradually, we shift from reacting to creating, from needing permission to trusting our own alignment.

This is the essence of co-creation. We are not passive participants. We shape the very reality we live in through intention, through presence, through resonance.

Sovereignty is not about control. It is attunement.

It is not about forcing change, but about becoming the kind of presence that invited it. When we release outdated patterns of behavior and move in integrity with own inner truth, the body listens. The field responds. Healing becomes less about following a protocol and more about remembering how to *choose differently.*

Picture yourself holding a compass—not one made of metal, but of energy. Instead of pointing north, its needle points toward coherence. This compass responds only when you are still enough to feel its pull. Each time you override your truth to please others, the needle wavers. Each time you honor a deep knowing, the needle stabilizes. In this analogy, healing is the path that follows your inner compass, guiding you toward alignment with your unique frequency signature. Sovereignty is the willingness to follow it, even when the terrain is unfamiliar.

This compass cannot be calibrated from outside yourself.

No authority, healer, or expert can do it for you. It responds only to your field—your beliefs, your boundaries, your intentions. Many clients enter the healing journey seeking someone to "fix" them.

Only later do they discover that their greatest transformation comes when they reclaim authorship. They do not experience this shift as a burden, but as a form of liberation. The moment we recognize that every thought, every word, every choice carries frequency, we awaken to our creative power. The body listens. The field responds. And healing becomes an act of devotion to one's own truth.

Where have you outsourced your power in the healing process?

What would it feel like to reclaim your compass and trust its pull?

Scientific and Cultural Integration Still to Come

We are still early in this shift.

While the science of coherence, biofields, and intention is growing, it remains marginalized in mainstream systems. While patients crave holistic care, medical education still lags behind in teaching systems thinking and energetic literacy.

And while cross-disciplinary research is growing, its clinical translation remains slow. Change tends to move in stages: new paradigms emerge in research, followed by new clinical applications, then updated training for practitioners, and finally, new understanding shared with clients. The cultural shift follows this layered unfolding—and we are still early in that process.

But change is accelerating.

The same forces that once suppressed these ideas are now cracking under the weight of their own limitations. The rise of quantum biology, psychoneuroimmunology, and the renewed visibility of transpersonal psychology is evidence of a silent revolution.

Practitioners are blending disciplines. Clients are expecting integration. And slowly, the borders between body, mind, and soul are dissolving.

Healing the collective system will not be achieved by top-down mandates or institutional reform alone. True transformation will emerge from those who carry the new paradigm within them—who embody the shift before it is visible, who become coherence within chaos.

Practitioners, in particular, hold a sacred responsibility. Not just to adopt new methods, but to hold a new frequency. To weave together science, soul, and presence in their practice, and to trust that this inner realignment is the catalyst for outer change.

The core insight is this: systems shift when people do. Cultural integration starts at the practitioner's level to finally solidify at the institutional level. This integration emerges from the choices we make, the frameworks we question, the truths we dare to hold.

Picture yourself as a practitioner of the future—not confined by scope of practice, nor seduced by the illusion of being the expert. Instead, you sit in a room filled not only with a client's story, but with their energy, their ancestors, their potential. You listen not just with your ears, but with your field. You no longer diagnose, you decode. You no longer treat, you translate. You become a steward of transformation, anchored in trust rather than protocol.

This vision is not beyond reach. It is already emerging in those who have dared to walk beyond the edges of convention—who are integrating polyvagal theory with breathwork, microbiome science with emotion mapping, somatics with sacred geometry. The science is already here. The culture is already shifting. What is needed now is presence, practitioners who carry this future in their nervous systems, who model what it means to heal by example.

What would it feel like to bring this vision into your work, not just in what you do, but in who you are?

What beliefs or boundaries might need to dissolve for you to embody the practitioner of the future?

Living the Frequency of Expanded Awareness

Healing is not a task to complete; it is a way of being, something you live, breathe, and embody over time. By now, you may recognize that the real work of healing is not something you add to your to-do list. It comes from aligning with a frequency that has always been there.

Expanded awareness manifests in the body. It is a lived state, expressed in how we listen, speak, feel, move, and relate. It reshapes how we respond to challenge, how we meet uncertainty, and how we love.

To vibrate at the frequency of coherence is not to strive for perfection, but to cultivate presence. Each time we breathe into the moment with awareness, we recalibrate. Each time we resist fragmentation and return to our center, we take part in healing, individually and collectively. In doing so, we begin to harmonize the dissonance within and around us, becoming instruments of a new reality.

Imagine yourself as an instrument—subtle, complex, and always responding to its environment. When neglected or misused, the strings go out of tune. But with each act of self-awareness, you gently tighten what was slack, soften what was strained. You do not need to perform a new song. You only need to resonate in truth. In doing so, you invite the whole orchestra of life into harmony with you.

This is how change happens—not just in theory, but through vibration. Your nervous system is not separate from the collective. Your choices ripple through fields seen and unseen. Living the frequency of expanded awareness is the real medicine: it informs how we eat, speak, touch, and create. It turns every act into a signal of coherence. This is not a metaphor. It is resonance at work. You are not just healing; you are becoming the healer.

What would shift if you began to see every moment of your life as part of your healing field?

What would it mean to live coherence, not just in theory, but in tone, action, and presence?

A Glimpse Beyond – Toward Book Two

Book One has laid the groundwork: a new framework for healing that integrates biology, psychology, energy, and self-agency. But this is only the beginning. This chapter is not a conclusion—it is a portal. A glimpse into the expanded awareness that awaits when we choose to live not just as bodies or minds, but as conscious co-creators of reality.

The future of healing does not belong to one group. It is open to all who are ready to reclaim the truth of who they are. Whether you come as a practitioner, a curious skeptic, or a soul searching for meaning, this next phase invites liberation from limiting beliefs, systemic fragmentation, and inherited paradigms that no longer serve.

Imagine reaching a new threshold of integration, a model that includes multiple dimensions and where everything begins to make sense. You are not leaving behind science or structure—you are carrying them with you, into a higher coherence. Around you, patterns shift. Timelines converge. Elements that seemed separate, mind, matter, spirit, now begin to harmonize. You are not ascending, you are expanding. And in doing so, you activate not just personal healing, but planetary remembrance.

This process does not disconnect you from reality. It allows you to expand your range of perception, noticing layers that were always there, waiting to be seen. Where Book One grounded you in coherence and empowered terrain, Book Two will invite a deeper exploration into the symbolic, the quantum, and the unseen dimensions of consciousness. Our focus now shifts away from treatment and terrain repair, and moves into the fluid territory of consciousness — its meanders, distortions, and quiet revelations. We will explore how perception shapes reality, and how multidimensional awareness begins to change the way we see ourselves, our origins, and our purpose. Together, we will venture into questions of meaning, pattern, and presence, guided not by protocol, but by resonance.

We are not abandoning science; we are using it as a frame of reference in our new inquiries. We distinguish pain from suffering, learning to decode the meaning of the challenges we face in our lives. And in doing so, we are not disconnecting from reality, but uncovering our role in co-creating it.

What part of you already senses there is more to reality than what you've been taught?

What would it mean to walk forward, not as a patient or practitioner, but as a multidimensional being?

We are contemplating the evolution of healing, not just as a new model of intervention, but as a transformation in how we understand healing itself, revealing what was always within reach in the process.

When we choose to live with expanded awareness, ancient knowledge resurfaces: a remembering of our true essence. We begin to embody presence, agency, and grace — here, in this body, in this life.

And so, the journey continues.

APPENDIX

Appendix A

Energetic Hygiene Tools

A Pre-Sleep Energetic Hygiene Practice

This protocol is designed to help you clear residual energies from the day and create a coherent, protected energetic field during sleep. It supports deep rest, dream clarity, and subtle body regulation by harmonizing the nervous system and shielding your biofield.

Use this protocol nightly to maintain energetic clarity, deepen sleep, and enhance intuitive dreaming.

Night Shield Protocol

Begin seated or lying down. Eyes soft or closed. One hand on heart, one on belly, or hands in prayer.

Step 1: Ground and Anchor

"Though I lie above the ground, my field reaches deep into the Earth.
From my spine, a silver-gold cord descends to Gaia's crystalline core.
I connect with the Earth's memory, wisdom, and protective pulse."

Visualize your body resting in a glowing hammock of light, suspended yet grounded.
Feel safe, held, and contained in Earth's intelligent web.

Step 2: Clear and Seal the Field

"Any energies I've absorbed today that are not mine,
I now release.
Any thoughts, cords, interference, or psychic resi-
due—clear.
Return all to Source, transmuted by violet flame."

*Visualize a violet field spiraling around you, then
gold light forming a bubble.
Diamond-white light seals it.*

"I am now sealed in sovereign truth. Only love, healing, and soul-aligned frequencies may enter."

Step 3: Call in the Guardians

"I now call in my highest guides, protectors, and allies of the Law of One.
Guard my body. Guard my mind. Guard my astral
path.
All imposters, mimics, and false frequencies are
blocked, cleared, and returned to Source.
I do not consent to surveillance, distortion, or interference."

*Place your selenite or amethyst near your crown.
Place tourmaline, shungite, or hematite near your
feet or under the bed.
Feel your room shift into temple space.*

Step 4: Set Your Dream Space

"If there are messages for me, let them come in clarity and love.
If healing is needed, let it unfold safely and gently.
If my field requires restoration, let it happen while I rest."

Step 5: Close and Rest

"I close all portals. I reclaim all my energy.
I am whole. I am clear. I am shielded.
I now enter sacred sleep.
Only light may walk with me."

Visualize a zipper of diamond light sealing your field from crown to feet.
Breathe deep. Drop in. Let go.

For a guided version of this protocol, visit:

sophieguellati.com/recordings

YouTube.com/@QJwithSophie

Night Shield Protocol
⁂
Sleep & Energy Log

This journal is designed to help you observe and track the physical, emotional, and energetic effects of using the Night Shield Protocol. Daily entries can support your awareness of how subtle energy hygiene influences sleep quality, symptom resolution, and mental clarity.

Use this 14-day log to record your experience.

Night Shield Protocol - Sleep & Energy Log

Date	Time to Bed	Protocol Used (Y/N + Version)	Time Woke Up	Sleep Quality (1–10)	Waking State (symptoms, mood, clarity)	Notes / Other Factors

APPENDIX B

The Personalized Terrain Model at a Glance

This model represents a multidimensional view of healing based on terrain principles. It integrates five interwoven components that reflect the totality of human experience—physical, psychological, energetic, and spiritual. At the center lies Coherence, a state of inner alignment that arises when all levels of the terrain are supported and in resonance.

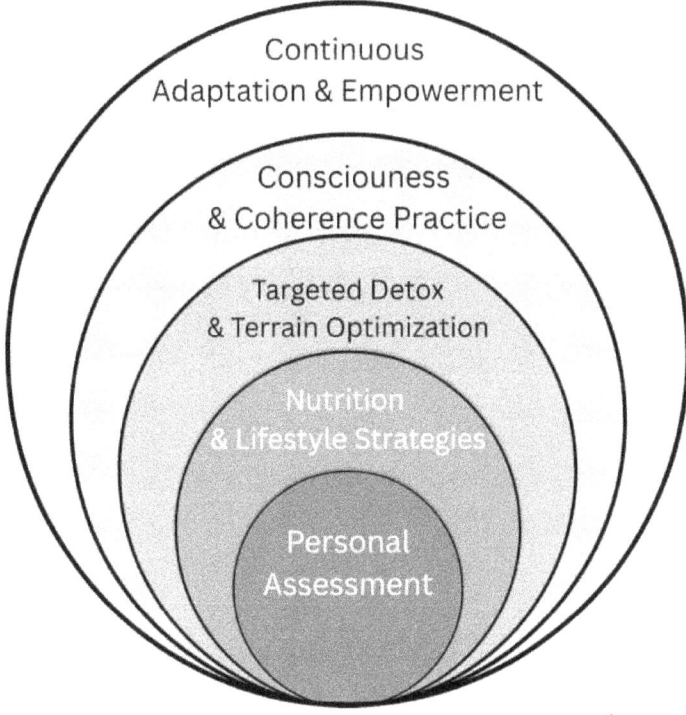

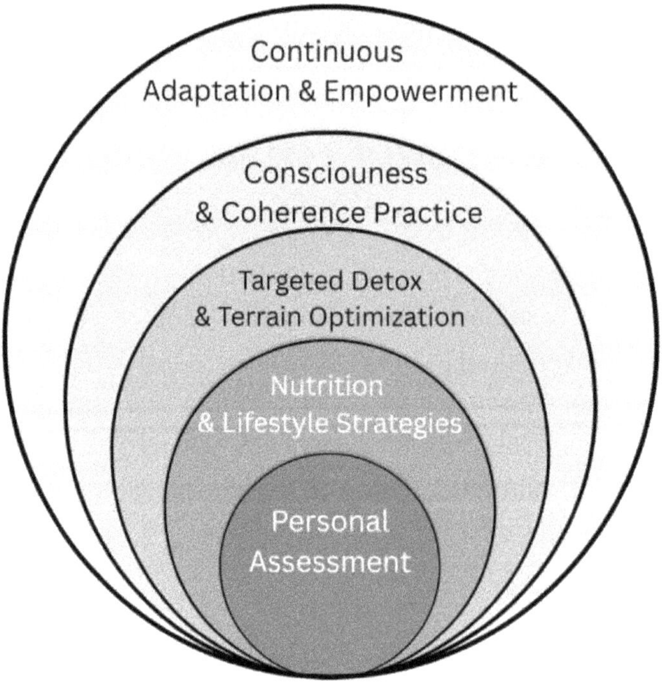
Continuous
Adaptation & Empowerment
Consciouness
& Coherence Practice
Targeted Detox
& Terrain Optimization
Nutrition
& Lifestyle Strategies
Personal
Assessment

Grayscale as a Healing Gradient

The shaded layers of this model reflect more than structure—they symbolize the vibrational ascent from density to clarity. Healing begins in the shadows of complexity and moves through layers of nourishment, detoxification, coherence, and ultimately toward empowered self-regulation and spiritual light. The outermost ring—rendered in the lightest gray—represents the emergence of sovereignty, purpose, and soul-aligned transformation.

The Five Foundational Layers of the Personalized Terrain Model (PTM)

PTM Layer	Primary Focus	Level of Healing Intervention
1. Personal Assessment	Identifying terrain imbalances, patterns	Physical & Psychological (symptom, history, mindset)
2. Customized Nutrition & Lifestyle	Targeted food, movement, rhythms	Physical & Environmental (input regulation)
3. Targeted Detox & Terrain Optimization	Clearing toxins, boosting resilience	Environmental & Biological (detox, gut, immunity)
4. Consciousness & Coherence Practice	Mind-body awareness, energy hygiene	Psychological & Energetic (beliefs, frequency, flow)
5. Continuous Adaptation & Empowerment	Self-guided evolution and soul alignment	Spiritual & Sovereign (purpose, intuition, guidance)

APPENDIX C

Symbolic Terrain Mapping
**
A Reflective Tool for Decoding Symptoms

The question is not 'What is wrong with me?' The question is 'What is this trying to show me?'

In a holographic and symbolic model of healing, symptoms are not enemies to eliminate—they are messages to interpret. Whether the signal comes through the body, emotions, behavior, or external life events, the same question applies:

What is the deeper pattern behind this experience —and what part of me is asking to be seen?

This tool is designed to help you begin exploring your symptoms or life disruptions as **mirrors of inner dynamics**. Use it as a journaling practice, a meditative inquiry, or a structured self-assessment. You may be surprised at what begins to surface when you treat your body and your life as intelligent, responsive, and meaning-rich.

Step-by-Step
✳︎ ✳︎ ✳︎
Symbolic Terrain Mapping

Step 1: Identify the Symptom or Pattern
Write down the symptom, life challenge, emotional trigger, or repeating experience you want to explore.

Step 2: Describe It in Detail
Use sensory, emotional, and metaphorical language.
Where is it located in your body or life?
What does it feel like?
What does it remind you of?

Step 3: Ask the Symbolic Question
What might this be trying to tell me?
What inner part of me is feeling unheard, unseen, or out of alignment?

Step 4: Listen Without Filtering
Allow images, words, memories, or emotions to surface. This is not about logic—it is about resonance. Trust what emerges, even if it seems odd or unrelated.

Step 5: Respond with Coherence
What needs to be acknowledged, reframed, expressed, or released?
Can you take one small action, make one shift in perspective, or offer one word of compassion to the part of you that surfaced?

Reflection Box

Use this space to capture your insights.

Prompt	Your Reflection
My symptom or pattern:	
What it feels like (emotionally, physically, symbolically):	
What it might represent or reflect:	
What part of me is speaking through this:	
How I can respond with awareness or coherence:	

This process is not about forcing answers. It is about *inviting meaning* into the healing conversation. Return to it as often as needed—each layer reveals something new.

APPENDIX D

Bioresonance and the Informational Field
⁂
Genius Insight in Practice

As explored in Chapter 9, resonance is not just a metaphor—it is the language of the healing field. In vibrational medicine, **restoring coherence at the energetic level** is often the key to unlocking shifts in the physical and emotional terrain.

The **Genius Insight** system is one example of how this principle is applied in practice. Grounded in the science of frequency analysis and biofeedback, it offers a non-invasive method for assessing and supporting the energetic terrain of the mind-body system.

How Genius Insight Works

1. **Energetic Profile Creation**
   The scan begins by capturing key data points:

   - **Voice sample** (approximately 60% of the data)
   - **Photo, name, date of birth**
   - An optional **short phrase** reflecting the client's current intention or desired positive outcome.

2. **Frequency Comparison and Analysis**
   The system compares this personalized vibrational profile to **normative frequency pat-**

terns drawn from curated libraries. These include categories such as:

- o Organs and body systems
- o Emotions and brain structures
- o Nutritional imbalances
- o Toxins, microbes, and energetic disturbances
- o Chakras, brainwave states, meridians, and more

3. **Identification of Coherence and Dissonance**
The system evaluates areas where the client's field shows strong alignment—or dissonance—with ideal frequency patterns. This produces an energetic map of the terrain, pointing to areas that may benefit from support.

4. **Delivery of Corrective Frequencies**
Based on the scan, Genius Insight delivers targeted **corrective frequencies**—designed to support:

- o **Energetic harmonization**
- o **Restoration of internal coherence**
- o **Self-regulatory feedback in the biofield**

These frequencies are not intended to treat or diagnose. Rather, they act as **informational prompts** that invite the body-mind system to self-adjust.

APPENDIX E

Seven Hermetic Principles applied to Healing

While many modern thinkers, lightworkers, and consciousness teachers speak of vibration, resonance, polarity, and multidimensionality, they often do so without acknowledging the ancient lineage behind these concepts. These ideas are not new. They are the echo of a timeless framework known as the **Hermetic Principles**, attributed to the teachings of **Hermes Trismegistus**, a mythic figure believed to be a synthesis of the Egyptian god Thoth and the Greek Hermes.

These seven principles were most famously distilled in the early 20th-century text The Kybalion (1908), authored by the mysterious "Three Initiates." Though ancient in origin, they offer a surprisingly contemporary lens through which to understand energy healing, consciousness, coherence, and the feedback loops we observe in body, psyche, and soul.

Below is a summary of the **Seven Hermetic Principles**, followed by reflections on how they can illuminate the terrain of healing:

---

1. The Principle of Mentalism

"The All is Mind; the Universe is Mental."
This principle teaches that everything originates in consciousness. Healing, therefore, begins not in chemistry, but in belief, perception, and thought. This is the metaphysical root behind the placebo effect and

mind-body medicine. The body reflects the mind—
whether consciously or subconsciously held.

2. The Principle of Correspondence

"As above, so below; as within, so without."
This is the foundational insight behind systemic
thinking, fractals, and the holographic nature of reality. Our internal terrain mirrors our outer world. What
happens in the gut echoes in the brain. What happens
emotionally can manifest physically. What we observe in the microcosm often reveals truths about the
macrocosm.

3. The Principle of Vibration

"Nothing rests; everything moves; everything vibrates."
Modern physics confirms that all matter is energy in
motion. This principle forms the core of frequency-
based healing modalities such as sound therapy, light
therapy, and scalar field interventions. Illness may be
seen as a disruption in vibrational harmony; healing
restores resonance.

4. The Principle of Polarity

"Everything is dual; everything has poles; everything
has its pair of opposites."
Healing is not about escaping darkness but integrating
it. Health and illness, joy and sorrow, clarity and confusion are poles of the same spectrum. This principle
reminds us that transformation often arises through
embracing the full polarity of experience.

5. The Principle of Rhythm

"Everything flows, out and in; everything has its tides."
Biological rhythms, emotional waves, seasons of healing—all reflect this principle. Recovery is not linear. We cycle through phases of expansion and contraction, coherence and chaos. Healing honors the rhythm, rather than resisting it.

6. The Principle of Cause and Effect

"Every cause has its effect; every effect has its cause."
This underpins root-cause medicine. Symptoms are not random—they are the effects of deeper causes, which may be physical, emotional, or energetic. Consciousness itself becomes causal when we understand the role of intention and expectation in healing outcomes.

7. The Principle of Gender

"Gender is in everything; everything has its Masculine and Feminine principles."
Beyond biological sex, this principle refers to the dual energies within all things. In healing, this can be seen in the balance of action and receptivity, logic and intuition, doing and being. Coherence often emerges when these polarities are honored and brought into harmony.

Why This Matters in Modern Healing

Many contemporary modalities echo these principles—often without knowing it. The rise of quantum
healing, coherence science, energy psychology, and
integrative medicine reflects a deeper shift: a return to
the archetypal patterns that underlie both ancient wisdom and modern discovery.

By recognizing these principles, we reconnect to a
lineage of knowledge that transcends time. We remember that healing is not an invention of the present
moment—it is the remembrance of what has always
been true.

*These principles or laws are not dogma—they are
mirrors. They help us see the unseen patterns, navigate paradox, and honor the living intelligence within
us.*

Let them serve not as doctrine, but as orientation
points—as compass stars for those who walk the healing path with curiosity, reverence, and sovereignty.

Clarifying Terminology:
Hermetic Principles vs. Universal Laws

Although often referred to as "universal laws," the
Hermetic Principles differ from the popular metaphysical teachings known as the 12 Universal Laws
of the Universe. The Hermetic framework—rooted in
ancient Egyptian and Greek esotericism and later distilled in The Kybalion—offers a philosophical lens to

understand the underlying mechanics of reality. By contrast, the 12 Universal Laws found in modern spiritual literature (such as the Law of Attraction or the Law of Divine Oneness) arise from New Thought movements and channeled teachings. While both systems speak to resonance, energy, and coherence, the Hermetic Principles are observational and archetypal in nature, whereas the modern laws tend to be motivational and prescriptive. Understanding this distinction allows readers to navigate both teachings with discernment and integrate them as complementary rather than interchangeable.

GLOSSARY

GLOSSARY

Adaptation – The process by which an individual adjusts to internal and external stressors. In terrain-based healing, adaptation is not only physiological but also psychological, energetic, and spiritual.

Akkermansia muciniphila – A beneficial gut bacterium associated with maintaining the mucosal lining of the intestines. Supports metabolic health, immune modulation, and may be reduced in individuals with obesity or autoimmune conditions.

Allostatic Load – The cumulative physiological burden imposed by chronic stress. Reflects how repeated adaptation demands affect hormonal, immune, and nervous system regulation.

Archetype – A universal symbol, pattern, or theme that appears across cultures and the collective unconscious. In psychological and spiritual healing, archetypes represent inner aspects of the self, such as the Inner Child, the Warrior, or the Sage.

ATP (Adenosine Triphosphate) – The primary energy carrier in cells. ATP is generated by mitochondria and powers nearly all cellular functions, from detoxification to neurotransmission.

Behavioral Medicine – An interdisciplinary field integrating behavioral, psychosocial, and biomedical knowledge to prevent and treat disease. Often overlaps with health psychology in holistic care models.

Biochemical – Refers to the chemical processes and substances that occur within living organisms. In terrain-based healing, biochemical balance includes hormones, neurotransmitters, enzymes, and nutrient metabolism.

Bioenergetic – Pertaining to the flow and transformation of energy in biological systems. In healing, bioenergetics refers to the study and application of energy fields and frequencies to influence physiological processes.

Biofeedback – A therapeutic technique that uses real-time data (such as heart rate, skin conductance, or muscle tension) to help individuals gain conscious control over physiological functions. Supports self-regulation and coherence training.

Biofield – The subtle field of electromagnetic and informational energy that surrounds and permeates the body. It is measurable and modifiable through techniques like biofeedback, intention-based therapies, and frequency medicine.

Bioinformatics – A field that uses computational tools to analyze biological data, including genomics and microbiome profiles. Enables personalized insights in functional and systems medicine.

Blood-Brain Barrier (BBB) – A protective barrier that separates the brain from circulating blood, regulating the passage of substances. Breakdown of the BBB is associated with neuroinflammation and chronic neurological disorders.

Brainwaves – Electrical oscillations in the brain measured in hertz (Hz). Different frequency ranges (alpha, beta, delta, theta, gamma) correspond to states of consciousness, arousal, and healing.

Butyrate – A short-chain fatty acid produced by gut bacteria during the fermentation of fiber. Supports intestinal barrier function, reduces inflammation, and serves as a key energy source for colonocytes.

Cellular Coherence – A state in which cells within a tissue or system operate in synchrony, facilitating efficient communication, repair, and energetic balance. Often influenced by emotional state, redox signaling, and frequency-based therapies.

Clinical Hypnosis – A therapeutic technique that uses guided relaxation and focused attention to access the subconscious mind. Used in both conventional and integrative practices for trauma, habit change, pain management, and personal insight.

Coherence – A state of internal harmony across biological, emotional, energetic, and spiritual systems. Often associated with health, clarity, and resilience. Therapeutically, coherence is a marker of regulation and self-agency.

Collagen – The most abundant protein in the human body, forming connective tissue, skin, bones, and the extracellular matrix. Also involved in bioelectrical conductivity and structural integrity of the terrain.

Consciousness – More than awareness or cognition, consciousness in this book refers to a fundamental, organizing field of intelligence that shapes reality and healing outcomes.

Conventional (Allopathic) Medicine – The dominant model of healthcare in industrialized nations, focused on symptom suppression using pharmaceuticals or surgery. Often contrasted with root-cause, integrative, or terrain-based approaches.

Cymatics – The study of visible sound and vibration patterns. Often used as a metaphor or model to illustrate how frequency shapes matter and biological form.

Detoxification – The body's process of eliminating toxins through organs like the liver, kidneys, skin, and lymphatic system. In terrain repair, detoxification is also energetic and emotional.

Distant Healing Intention – A form of nonlocal healing where one person directs focused intention, prayer, or energy toward another person who is not physically present. Research in this area explores mind-matter interaction and consciousness as causal.

DNA Methylation – An epigenetic mechanism that modifies gene expression without changing the DNA sequence. Influenced by environment, nutrition, stress, and consciousness.

Double-Slit Experiment – foundational experiment in quantum physics showing that particles behave like waves until observed, suggesting that the act of observation collapses potential into a specific outcome. It supports the idea that consciousness participates in reality.

Dysbiosis – An imbalance in the gut microbiome where harmful or opportunistic organisms outnumber beneficial microbes. Often contributes to inflammation, digestive issues, and systemic terrain disruption.

Electromagnetic Imprinting – The process of encoding specific frequency or informational patterns into a carrier medium, such as water or a digital signal. Used in vibrational medicine and homeopathic-like remedies.

Electromagnetic Processes – Biological mechanisms that involve electric charges, magnetic fields, and their interactions. Foundational to understanding cellular signaling, brain activity, and energy medicine.

Electrophysiology – The study of the electrical properties of biological cells and tissues. Encompasses brainwave monitoring, heart rate variability, and the energetic rhythms of the body.

EMDR (Eye Movement Desensitization and Reprocessing) – A trauma-focused therapy that uses bilateral stimulation (often eye movements) to process and integrate distressing memories. Helps release stored emotional and physiological responses.

Endotoxins – Toxins released by certain bacteria, particularly gram-negative species. When translocated into the bloodstream (e.g., via leaky gut), they can trigger systemic inflammation and immune dysregulation.

Entanglement – A quantum phenomenon in which two particles remain interconnected regardless of distance. Changes to one are reflected in the other, suggesting a level of unity that defies classical physics.

Epigenetics – The study of how environmental factors, behaviors, and consciousness can influence gene expression without altering the DNA sequence. Central to terrain-based healing and the concept of self-directed biological change.

EZ Water (Exclusion Zone Water) – A structured form of water discovered by Dr. Gerald Pollack, found near hydrophilic surfaces. It carries an electrical charge and is believed to support cellular energy, detoxification, and coherence.

Fast Fourier Transform (FFT) – A mathematical algorithm used to analyze complex waveforms by breaking them into their constituent frequencies. Applied in voice analysis and bioresonance systems.

Field Resonance – A phenomenon where energetic systems attune or synchronize with one another. Often discussed in the context of heart-brain communication, consciousness-based healing, and subtle energy.

Fractal Self – The idea that the self is a repeating, self-similar structure nested within larger energetic and consciousness-based systems. The fractal self reflects patterns at the biological, psychological, and spiritual levels.

Frequency – The rate at which a vibration occurs, measured in hertz (Hz). In healing, different frequencies are used to influence physiological and energetic states for therapeutic purposes.

Functional Medicine – A systems-oriented medical approach that seeks to identify and address the root causes of disease. It emphasizes individualized care, biochemical uniqueness, and the interplay between genetics, environment, and lifestyle.

Healing Ecosystem – The broader network of influences—including physical environment, relationships, belief systems, and spiritual practices—that support or hinder healing.

Healing Touch – An energy therapy in which practitioners consciously use their hands and intention to influence the human energy field. It promotes relaxation, wound healing, and emotional well-being.

Health Psychology – A branch of psychology that studies how psychological, behavioral, and social factors influence physical health and illness. It forms part of the biopsychosocial model used in this book.

HeartMath – A scientifically based approach to coherence training using heart rate variability (HRV) biofeedback tools. Developed by the HeartMath Institute to cultivate emotional regulation, resilience, and intuitive intelligence.

Heart Rate Variability (HRV) – The variation in time between consecutive heartbeats. A biomarker of autonomic nervous system flexibility and emotional regulation, often used in coherence training.

Hermetic Principles – Seven foundational teachings often referred to as "universal laws" in Hermeticism, as described in ancient texts such as The Kybalion. These include Mentalism, Correspondence, Vibration, Polarity, Rhythm, Cause and Effect, and Gender. They are distinct from metaphysical systems like the 12 Universal Laws of the Universe (e.g., Law of Attraction). Referenced throughout the book in relation to coherence and consciousness.

Histone Modification – A process that alters how tightly DNA is wound around histone proteins, affecting gene expression. Plays a role in epigenetics, cell differentiation, and disease susceptibility.

Holographic – A system in which each part contains the information of the whole. In a holographic model of the universe—or the body—patterns repeat at every scale, allowing for nonlocal interactions and distributed intelligence.

Hormetic Phytochemicals – Plant-derived compounds that induce mild stress responses in the body, leading to increased resilience and adaptation. Examples include sulforaphane, curcumin, and resveratrol.

Immunometabolism – The interplay between immune function and metabolic pathways. Disruptions in immunometabolism can lead to chronic inflammation, autoimmunity, and metabolic disorders.

Implicate Order – A term coined by physicist David Bohm to describe the underlying, enfolded structure of reality from which observable phenomena emerge. It contrasts with the "explicate order," or visible reality, and emphasizes hidden coherence.

Inflammation – A biological response to harmful stimuli, such as pathogens, toxins, or damaged cells. Chronic inflammation is linked to a range of modern diseases and is addressed in root-cause and terrain-based healing approaches.

Insulin Resistance – A condition in which cells become less responsive to insulin, resulting in elevated blood glucose and compensatory insulin production. Associated with metabolic dysfunction and neurodegeneration.

Integrative Neuroscience – An interdisciplinary field that combines brain science with psychology, systems biology, and energy medicine to understand consciousness, perception, and healing.

Methylation Pathways – Biochemical pathways involving the transfer of methyl groups, critical for detoxification, gene expression, neurotransmitter balance, and immune function. Influenced by nutrition and genetic factors like MTHFR variants.

Microtubular Coherence – The proposed quantum-level synchronization of microtubules within neurons. Central to theories linking consciousness with subcellular quantum processing (e.g., Orch OR).

Microtubules – Cylindrical protein structures within cells that help maintain cell shape and transport. Hypothesized in quantum biology to facilitate coherence, consciousness, and intracellular signaling.

Morphic Resonance – Rupert Sheldrake's theory that biological systems inherit habits and information from a collective memory field, shaping form and behavior through resonance with similar forms in the past.

Neuroplasticity – The brain's ability to reorganize itself by forming new neural connections throughout life. Central to healing trauma, learning, and shifting entrenched patterns.

Neuropsychobiology – An interdisciplinary field studying the interaction between neurological, psychological, and biological systems. Relevant to the book's mind-body model and psychoneuroimmunological framing.

Nonlocal Enfoldment – A concept related to Bohm's implicate order, suggesting that all points in space and time are enfolded into one another beyond physical proximity—allowing for instantaneous connections across distance.

Non-local Fields – Energetic or informational fields that are not limited by time or space. Referenced in quantum physics and consciousness studies as mechanisms for healing, intuition, or entanglement.

Nonlocality – A quantum principle suggesting that particles or events can be instantaneously connected across space and time, transcending the limits of physical location. Often used in discussions of intention, distant healing, and consciousness.

Orchestrated Objective Reduction (Orch OR) – A theory proposed by Sir Roger Penrose and Dr. Stuart Hameroff suggesting that consciousness arises from quantum processes within microtubules in neurons.

Oversoul – The larger, multidimensional aspect of the soul that connects and oversees multiple lifetimes, timelines, or incarnations. Seen as a fractal of Source.

Past-Life Regression – A form of regression therapy in which individuals are guided into altered states to explore symbolic or literal memories of other lifetimes. Used therapeutically for insight, emotional release, and spiritual integration.

Patterned Self – The accumulated mental, emotional, behavioral, and somatic patterns that form a person's conditioned identity. In healing, it refers to the recognition and reorganization of ingrained patterns toward greater coherence.

Photobiomodulation (PBM) – A therapy that uses low-level light, often in the red or near-infrared spectrum, to stimulate healing at the cellular level. Known for supporting mitochondrial function, reducing inflammation, and promoting tissue repair.

Placebo – A beneficial healing response triggered by belief, ritual, and expectation, even in the absence of pharmacological action. Demonstrates the power of consciousness in physiological change.

Polyvagal Theory – A model of autonomic regulation developed by Stephen Porges. Describes how the vagus nerve mediates safety, social connection, and trauma response through different neural circuits.

Psychophysiological – Relating to the interaction between psychological processes and physiological responses. Central to the mind-body connection in stress, emotion, and healing.

Pulsed Electromagnetic Field Therapy (PEMF) – A non-invasive technique that uses low-frequency electromagnetic pulses to stimulate healing, reduce inflammation, and enhance cellular function.

Quantum Biology – A field exploring how quantum phenomena such as entanglement, tunneling, and coherence influence biological systems. Provides a framework for understanding subtle energy and consciousness-based healing.

RCTs (Randomized Controlled Trials) – A scientific method used to evaluate the efficacy of interventions. Involves randomly assigning participants to treatment or control groups and measuring outcomes under controlled conditions.

Radiofrequency Ablation – A conventional medical procedure that uses heat generated from radio waves to destroy tissue, often used for pain management or tumor reduction.

Redox Balance – The dynamic equilibrium between oxidation and reduction reactions in the body. Essential for maintaining cellular health, energy production, and detoxification. Imbalance contributes to oxidative stress and chronic illness.

Redox State – A measure of the oxidative or reductive condition of a cell or system, reflecting its metabolic and energetic status. Often used to assess terrain vitality and susceptibility to disease.

Regression Therapy – A therapeutic approach that guides clients to recall earlier experiences—whether from this life or symbolic past lives—to identify root causes of current emotional or physical issues. Can include inner child work or trauma resolution.

Reiki – A Japanese energy healing technique that channels universal life force energy through the practitioner's hands to promote balance, relaxation, and healing.

Scalar Energy – A form of energy theorized to operate outside of conventional electromagnetic paradigms. Scalar waves are believed to carry informational fields and be capable of influencing subtle energy systems.

Scalar Field – A mathematical or energetic concept describing a field in which each point is associated with a scalar value (like temperature or potential energy). In metaphysical and energetic medicine contexts, scalar fields are believed to facilitate coherence and non-local healing.

Self-Agency – The ability to make conscious choices aligned with one's values, intuition, and healing needs. Distinguished from compliance-based models of care.

SNP Variant – A single nucleotide polymorphism (SNP) is a variation in a single DNA building block. Certain SNPs, like MTHFR, can affect methylation, detoxification, and nutrient metabolism.

Somatic Patterning – The unconscious imprint of psychological and energetic experiences in the body. These patterns influence posture, movement, tension, and health, and are often addressed in trauma-informed and body-based therapies.

Sonoporation – A technique that uses ultrasound waves to temporarily increase the permeability of cell membranes. This allows for enhanced delivery of therapeutic agents—such as drugs, genes, or nanoparticles—into targeted cells. Explored in oncology and regenerative medicine for its potential to facilitate non-invasive cellular uptake.

Structured Water – Water whose molecules are arranged in a more coherent, organized pattern than typical bulk water. Associated with improved hydration, bioavailability, and the energetic quality of the terrain.

Subcellular – Referring to structures and processes occurring within a cell, such as mitochondria, microtubules, and intracellular signaling. Relevant to terrain repair at the most fundamental level.

Subconscious (Mind) – The deeper layer of mind that stores beliefs, memories, and patterns. Accessed in hypnotherapy and quantum healing to resolve root causes and reprogram perception.

Symbolic Terrain Mapping – A reflective process introduced in Appendix C to explore the deeper meaning of physical symptoms through metaphor, emotional resonance, and intuitive insight.

Systems Biology – A scientific approach that examines complex biological systems as integrated wholes rather than isolated parts. In functional medicine and terrain theory, it supports personalized, dynamic understanding of health and disease.

Terrain theory – A model of health that emphasizes the body's internal environment—its terrain—as the key factor in disease expression. It proposes that pathogens thrive only in weakened or imbalanced systems, and that restoring biological and energetic coherence is more important than targeting germs directly.

Therapeutic Touch – A structured form of energy healing developed by nurses, involving hand movements near the body to assess and balance the biofield.

Unified Field – A theoretical energy field in which all fundamental forces and particles are unified. In spiritual and energetic models, it is often viewed as the substrate of consciousness or the "oneness" underlying all separation.

Vagus Nerve – The tenth cranial nerve, central to parasympathetic regulation. Influences heart rate, digestion, inflammation, and emotional state. Often targeted in coherence and trauma-informed therapies.

Vibrational Medicine – A healing approach that uses energy frequencies—including sound, light, and electromagnetic fields—to restore harmony to the body's physical and energetic systems.

Voice Analysis – A method of reading vibrational patterns from the voice to detect emotional or energetic imbalances. Used in bioresonance technologies like Genius Insight.

Vortexing – A method of swirling water to restructure its molecular organization. Believed to revitalize water's energetic properties and restore its coherence, often used in water therapy and frequency infusions.

Water Memory – The idea that water can retain vibrational patterns or informational imprints from its environment, even after the original substance is removed. Supported by homeopathic theory and Emoto's crystalline photography.

BOOKS THAT INSPIRED MY JOURNEY

Brogan, Kelly. *A Mind of Your Own: What Women Can Do About Depression That Big Pharma Can't.* Harper Wave, 2016.

Cannon, Dolores. *All books by the author.* Ozark Mountain Publishing.

Cannon, Julia. *Soul Speak: The Language of Your Body.* Ozark Mountain Publishing, 2013.

Cerminara, Gina. *Many Mansions: The Edgar Cayce Story on Reincarnation.* Signet, 1991.

Childre, Doc, and Deborah Rozman. *Transforming Anxiety: The HeartMath Solution for Overcoming Fear and Worry and Creating Serenity.* HeartMath, 2004.

Cohen, Suzy. *Thyroid Healthy: Lose Weight, Look Beautiful and Live the Life You Imagine.* Legacy Publishing, 2014.

Dyer, Wayne. *The Power of Intention: Learning to Co-Create Your World Your Way.* Hay House, 2004.

Dyer, Wayne. *Change Your Thoughts – Change Your Life: Living the Wisdom of the Tao.* Hay House, 2007.

Eadie, Betty J. *Embraced by the Light.* Bantam, 1992.

Farrell, Joseph Pierce. *Manifesting Michelangelo: The Story of a Modern-Day Miracle—That May Make All Change Possible.* Atria Books/Beyond Words, 2011.

Hay, Louise. *You Can Heal Your Life*. Hay House, 1984.

Kabat-Zinn, Jon. *Full Catastrophe Living: Using the Wisdom of Your Body and Mind to Face Stress, Pain, and Illness*. Bantam, 1990.

Kabat-Zinn, Jon. *Wherever You Go, There You Are: Mindfulness Meditation in Everyday Life*. Hachette Books, 2005.

Lipton, Bruce H. *The Biology of Belief: Unleashing the Power of Consciousness, Matter & Miracles*. Hay House, 2005.

Kumar, Sameet M. *The Mindful Path Through Worry and Rumination: Letting Go of Anxious and Depressive Thoughts*. New Harbinger Publications, 2010.

Moorjani, Anita. *Dying to Be Me: My Journey from Cancer, to Near Death, to True Healing*. Hay House, 2012.

Moody, Raymond. *Life After Life: The Investigation of a Phenomenon—Survival of Bodily Death*. HarperOne, 1975.

Myss, Caroline. *Anatomy of the Spirit: The Seven Stages of Power and Healing*. Harmony Books, 1996.

Ricard, Matthieu. *Why Meditate? Working with Thoughts and Emotions*. Hay House, 2010.

Roberts, Jane. *The Seth Material*. Amber-Allen Publishing, 1970.

Roberts, Jane. *Seth Speaks: The Eternal Validity of the Soul*. Amber-Allen Publishing, 1972.

Roberts, Jane. *The Nature of Personal Reality: A Seth Book.* Amber-Allen Publishing, 1974.

Siegel, Bernie S. *Love, Medicine and Miracles: Lessons Learned about Self-Healing from a Surgeon's Experience with Exceptional Patients.* Harper Perennial, 1986.

Spalding, Baird T. *Life and Teaching of the Masters of the Far East.* DeVorss & Company, 1924.

Talbot, Michael. *The Holographic Universe.* Harper Perennial, 1991.

Weiss, Brian L. *Many Lives, Many Masters: The True Story of a Prominent Psychiatrist, His Young Patient, and the Past-Life Therapy That Changed Both Their Lives.* Fireside, 1988.

Wentz, Izabella. *Hashimoto's Thyroiditis: Lifestyle Interventions for Finding and Treating the Root Cause.* Truth About Thyroid, 2013.

Young, Jeffrey, and Janet Klosko. *Reinventing Your Life: The Breakthrough Program to End Negative Behavior and Feel Great Again.* Plume, 1994.

An updated and categorized version of this reading list is available at: sophieguellati.com/resources

You can also download the full reading list directly here: Reading List for Download (PDF)

INDEX

FROM THE AUTHOR

Expanded Awareness: A Health Psychologist's Journey Beyond the Mind-Body Duality
Explores health psychology, terrain-based thinking, and a multidimensional approach to healing that integrates biology, meaning, and consciousness.

Expanded Awareness: A Health Psychologist's Exploration of Consciousness
Engages questions of identity, perception, and multidimensional experience through psychological inquiry and personal reflection.
Coming December 2025.

Expanded Awareness: A Health Psychologist's Inquiry into AI and Consciousness
Investigates how human consciousness meets a responsive, non-sentient intelligence, emphasizing responsibility and discernment in that encounter.
Coming March 2026.

www.ingramcontent.com/pod-product-compliance
Lightning Source LLC
Chambersburg PA
CBHW041624140626
46547CB00030B/750